W9-ADR-681

UNDERSTANDING
THE APOCALYPSE

UNDERSTANDING THE APOCALYPSE

WILFRID J. HARRINGTON, O.P.

CORPUS BOOKS
Washington—Cleveland

CORPUS PUBLICATIONS

Editorial Offices   *Sales & Distribution*
1330 Massachusetts Ave., N.W.   2231 West 110th Street
Washington, D.C. 20005   Cleveland, Ohio 44102

© 1969, Wilfrid J. Harrington, O.P.

First published 1969, Geoffrey Chapman Ltd.

The text used in this commentary is that of the
Revised Standard Version.

227.9
Z6 R 31

Library of Congress Catalog Card Number 75-83513

Printed in Great Britain

Contents

For

Michael and Joan Glazier

Preface

It seems to me that two factors, above all, have led to the preparation of this commentary on the Apocalypse of John. In the first place, I have long known the strange attraction of the book. This I had felt, vaguely, at a first reading; but as I came to understand the literary form of the work and, in some measure, to appreciate the quality and significance of it, its appeal grew stronger. On the other hand, I became aware that, to many people, it is indeed a sealed book. It occurred to me that I might be able to open up the book to such as these, to help them to find in it an abiding Christian message.

The bibliography gives an indication of my own indebtedness to others. Here I would single out those from whom I have learned the most. There is H. B. Swete, whose work of more than half a century ago is, and will remain, one of the truly great commentaries on the Apocalypse. The procedure of setting out the relevant Old Testament passages in full above each unit of the text is one I have borrowed from L. Cerfaux and J. Cambier, whose joint commentary was for me the key that first opened the way into the treasury of St John. The studies of A. Feuillet have markedly influenced my interpretation of the book. I have found that J. B. Caird has a singular aptitude for the striking phrase that can bring a passage to life.

Helped and guided by these, and many others, I have sought to make a modest contribution in my turn. Thoroughly positive in its approach, non-technical in style, this commentary is directed to a varied readership—to anyone, indeed, who would wish to learn something of, and from, the last, enigmatic writing of the New Testament. I hope that, as an interpreter, I have heard aright, and have managed to convey John's message faithfully, and with reasonable clarity, to men of our day.

W. J. H.

INTRODUCTION

Introduction

I. THE AUTHORSHIP OF THE APOCALYPSE

THE TESTIMONY OF TRADITION

Four times (1 : 1, 4, 9; 22 : 8) the author of the Apocalypse names himself John, and Christian tradition has, on the whole, identified him with the apostle John. The earliest witness is Justin (*c.* AD 150), who, in his *Dialogue with Trypho*, declares : 'A man of our number, by name John, one of the apostles of Christ, prophesied in a revelation vouchsafed to him that those who believe in our Christ will dwell for a thousand years in Jerusalem' (cf. Ap 20 : 4-6). About the turn of the century, the identification was accepted by Irenaeus, the Muratorian Canon, Clement of Alexandria, Tertullian, and Hippolytus. Origen says explicitly that the apostle had written both the Apocalypse and the Fourth Gospel.

Dissident voices were first heard in the third century; the earliest was that of the Roman priest Gaius (Irenaeus, *Adv. Haer.*, III, 28, 2). The Montanists were invoking the Apocalypse in support of their doctrines, and the reaction of Gaius was radical : he attributed the Apocalypse to the heretic Cerinthus—a veritable cutting of the Gordian knot. Far more important is the view of Denis of Alexandria (d. *c.* AD 265). On critical grounds, following a literary and theological analysis of both writings, he concluded that the Apocalypse could not have been written by John the apostle, the author of the Fourth Gospel; he did not question the canonicity of the Apocalypse. The opinion of Denis has been recorded by Eusebius (*H.E.*, VII, 25) who seems to have accepted it (iii, 39, 5f). But it is in the Eastern Church, especially, that

3

there was some hesitancy about the Apocalypse. Cyril of Jerusalem and Gregory Nazianzen did not number the Apocalypse among the NT writings; John Chrysostom and Theodoret never used it. It does not figure in the Syriac versions.

Yet the negative witness, however impressive, represents no more than a fraction of the patristic tradition. Furthermore, these dissident views were motivated by polemical preoccupations or by the findings of personal research and not by conflicting traditional data. 'One may, in fact, affirm that the almost unanimous tradition of the Church has regarded the apostle John as the author of the Apocalypse.'[1]

THE PROBLEM

Unfortunately, the virtual unanimity of tradition does not really solve the problem of authorship. An important factor, which may not be set aside, is that the whole matter is complicated by the impressive traditional attribution of the Fourth Gospel and the three Epistles to the apostle John. Mocern scholarship overwhelmingly supports the view of Denis of Alexandria that the Apocalypse and the other writings—at least in their present form—cannot have been written by the same hand.

Certainly, there are linguistic and doctrinal contacts between the Apocalypse and the Fourth Gospel, and these do justify the grouping of all the Johannine writings in one corpus. It can at least be said that they are of Johannine inspiration, written in the immediate entourage of the apostle and penetrated by his teaching. The Apocalypse and the Gospel show a common taste for allegory and symbolism and employ the same figures : living water, shepherd, Lamb, manna. They also employ the same characteristic themes : witness, the Word; both refer to Zach. 12 : 10—'They shall look on him whom they have pierced' (Jn 19 : 37; Ap. 1 : 7). Yet, on the other hand, the Apocalypse does not have most of the key-words of the Gospel or Epistles : light, darkness, truth, love; while for 'world' (in a pejorative sense) the

[1] M.-E. Boismard, *L'Apocalypse (BJ)*, Paris, Cerf, 1959.[3]

Apocalypse has 'the inhabitants of the earth'. The doctrine of the Holy Spirit which appears in its most developed form in the final discourses of the Gospel barely emerges in the Apocalypse.

Most marked of all is a different conception of eschatology—or, at least, a different presentation of eschatological doctrine. In the Apocalypse there is the vivid anticipation of the return of Christ (but this is not to be understood in any naïve sense of an imminent parousia). Here the Son of Man is the glorified Christ who will come to destroy the wicked, and Antichrist is a political power opposed to the establishment of the kingdom. In the Gospels and Epistles, Christ, in a real sense, has already come and abides in the hearts of his faithful. He has already brought about the separation between the faithful and others, between those who accept God's plan of salvation and those who reject it. Antichrists, heretical teachers propagating false christological doctrines, are already active (1 Jn). However, the false teachers of Ap. 2: 6, 14f, 20, 24 are not unlike those of the Epistle. The Holy Spirit, abiding in Christians, has established the kingdom of God among us.

The Greek style of the Apocalypse is certainly very different from that of the Fourth Gospel. This is not simply due to the fact that the former is the more markedly Semitic; the Greek of the Apocalypse, in contrast to that of the other Johannine writings, is often ungrammatical. The difference is too great to be explained on the ground of distinct literary forms. Finally, it is noteworthy that the author of the Apocalypse, who is aware of the distinction between apostles and prophets (18 : 20), fits himself into the category of prophet (22 : 9) and makes no claim to be an apostle (cf 21 : 14).

Is there any hope of a positive solution to the problem of authorship? One cannot help agreeing with M. E. Boismard:

> We are faced with the following dilemma: if we wish to maintain the integral Johannine authenticity of the Fourth Gospel, we must attribute the redaction of the Apocalypse to a disciple of the apostle. If we prefer to maintain the Johannine authenticity of the Apocalypse—taking our stand on the testimony of St Justin and of St Irenaeus—we must then admit

that the Gospel, while giving, substantially, the content of the Johannine preaching, was edited by a disciple of the apostle, or by a group of disciples. As the problem stands at the moment, no definite solution is in sight and the way is wide open for further research.[2]

THE DATE

Regarding the date of the Apocalypse, the traditional evidence is not in agreement. The earliest testimony is that of Irenaeus (*Adv. Haer.*, V, 30, 3) who declared that the Apocalypse appeared 'not very long ago, almost in our own time, that is, at the end of Domitian's reign'. Since Domitian reigned from AD 81 to 96, this would date the writing about AD 95. The earliest Latin commentator on the Apocalypse, Victorinus of Pettau (d. *c.* AD 305), states that John was relegated by Domitian to the island of Patmos (cf. Ap. 1 : 9). Eusebius follows Irenaeus, who also mentions the exile, and dates the book to the fourteenth year of Domitian. St Jerome and most subsequent writers followed Eusebius. However, another tradition (the Muratorian Canon, the Apocryphal *Acts of John,* and perhaps Tertullian) places the writing of the work under Nero (AD 54-68). Epiphanius dates it in the reign of Claudius (AD 41-54).

Most modern scholars accept the attestation of Irenaeus; indeed, there seems little doubt that, in its final form, the Apocalypse is at home in the time of Domitian. However, the evidence pointing to Nero's reign cannot be shrugged off. The passage Ap. 17 : 9-11 speaks of seven Roman emperors; in 17 : 10 we are told that 'five have fallen' and that 'one is'—the sixth, in whose reign the book is thus set. Since the list most probably begins with Augustus and leaves aside the three imperial competitors of AD 69 (Galba, Otho and Vitellius), it turns out that the sixth emperor is Vespasian, Nero's successor. This would seem to add weight to the tradition that John wrote earlier than the reign of Domitian. But actually, the indication of Ap. 17 : 10 can be explained on the ground of a well-known apocalyptic pro-

[2] 'L'Apocalypse', in Robert-Feuillet, *Introduction à la Bible* II, Paris, Desclée, 1959, 741.

cedure, that of fictitious antedating. The author, of set purpose, has antedated his work to the reign of Vespasian (AD 69-70)—before the destruction of Jerusalem and of the Temple—in order to bring out the theological significance of that event. This is a factor that must be reckoned with in our interpretation of the work.

Besides, it may be that the Apocalypse, as we have it, is a combination of two writings, of different dates: one composed under Nero and the other under Domitian;[3] hence, the (apparently) conflicting traditional views. Perhaps in the light of all the evidence, it is best to say that the Apocalypse, *in the form in which it has come to us,* dates from the close of Domitian's reign.

II. THE LITERARY FORM

The word 'apocalypse'—from the Greek *apokalypsis*—means 'revelation', and an apocalypse purports to be a revelation of hidden things known only to God, made by God himself or by an angel speaking in his name. The revelation is almost always concerned with the development of history, culminating in the end of this world and pointing to the mysteries of the future. As a literary form the apocalyptic is closely related to the prophetical—it is, in fact, a child of prophecy. Already the visions of Ezekiel, for instance, have something of the fantasy and exuberance of the apocalyptist's visions. Besides, many passages in the prophetical books deal with the far horizons of time; they have the eschatological interest that is a marked feature of apocalypse.

The apocalyptists believed that the end was near in their own days, and indicated the course of events that they thought would lead to the great denouement of history, and the signs of the end. No more than the prophets did they think this climax would arise out of history by any natural evolution. They were persuaded that it could only come about by the direct intervention of God in history. This was not a new concept to the Jew. He believed that God had intervened in

[3] This is the view of M.-E. Boismard; cf *L'Apocalypse (BJ),* 91-5.

history before, in the Exodus and in other critical moments of the history of his own people. God was believed to be always in control of history, and an actor on the stage of history. He was never thought to be the sole actor, and all that happened was not ascribed to him. But in the divine intervention that was looked for to inaugurate the end of history, he was conceived of as the sole significant actor.[4]

While pseudonymity is not an essential feature of apocalypse, an apocalyptic work is almost always attributed to a venerated figure of the past. The reputed author is supposed to receive, in a series of visions, a revelation of God's plan working out in the world's events—and this revelation is represented as having been hidden for many years, laid up in a 'sealed book'. History is unfolded in symbols and finds its term in the epoch of the true author. The language is sometimes precise, but more frequently it is designedly vague—this in accordance with the literary fiction since it is supposed to be prophecy. The apocalypse closes with a prediction of the imminent eschatological judgment and the advent of unending happiness; in other words, with the advent of the messianic age. A notable feature is the frequent intervention of angels; it is they who usually explain the mysterious symbols.

The object of apocalypse is to show the providence of God at work in history; born in times of crisis, it inspired the readers with hope and confidence. As a literary form, it flourished in the last two centuries BC and in the first two centuries AD : the book of Daniel (more precisely, Dn. 7-12) is the earliest Jewish apocalypse. The form was also cultivated in the early church but never to the same extent as among the Jews; and the Apocalypse is the only NT apocalyptic work.[5] The popularity of the form should be taken into account when interpreting Apocalypse : features that appear very strange to us were part of a widespread and familiar literary convention. This fact alone would, for people of those centuries, dispel much of the mystery we attach to the form.

---

[4] H. H. Rowley in *Peake's Commentary on the Bible,* London, Nelson, 1962,[2] 418d.
[5] There are apocalyptic passages in the synoptic gospels: Mk 13; Mt. 24:1-36; Lk. 21:5-33; 17:22-37.

We have referred to Daniel; a look at this writing will help us to understand, more clearly, the purpose of apocalyptic. For that matter we are not really departing from our main concern, the Apocalypse of John, because the NT author has been profoundly influenced by his OT predecessor, and the earlier work merits our attention on this score too. The book of Daniel is a writing of the Maccabean age; the date of composition can be closely fixed from the consideration of Dn. 11. There the struggle between the Ptolemies and the Seleucids is related with a wealth of detail. The climax is the reign of Antiochus IV (173-163 bc) and his religious persecution of the Jews. The culminating point of the dream of chapter 2 and of the visions of chapters 7-12 is also the reign of this king: his downfall will herald the messianic age. The book was written during the persecution of Antiochus, before his death and before the successful result of the first phase of the Maccabean war (167-164 bc). Its purpose was to hearten the faithful Jews in their sufferings: the episodes of chapters 1-6 and the apocalypse of chapters 7-12 combine to this end.

The fact that Dn. 7-12 would have been recognized as apocalyptic by their first readers may cause us to wonder what effect they could have had. After all, these people knew that this was not prophecy but history. Or, to put it another way, since they were aware of the literary convention, and would have realized that the writing was pseudo-prophecy, how could they have taken it seriously? The truth of the matter is that these chapters set out a comforting and an entirely valid lesson from history. The author invited his readers to look to the past and then sketched before their eyes a succession of empires—each had appeared, had dominated the contemporary scene, and had gone leaving no trace behind. They would note, in contrast to the ephemeral powers, one constant element: the people of God. They could also see that, time and again, this people was at the mercy of a great power and on the point of extinction, but each time God had intervened; the great power had disappeared but Israel remained. The reminder of these facts gave absolute grounds for hope in the present crisis. Besides, the readers of Daniel believed that in just such a crisis the intervention of God, the establishment of his kingdom, would come; they could hope it would follow the end of this persecution.

The narrative section of Daniel (chapters 1-6) is a prelude to the visions. The story of Daniel assures us that in the providence of God persecution cannot achieve its purpose. The visions of the four animals (chapter 7) and of the ram and the goat (chapter 8) clarify this message—indeed the burden of these visions is already present in the interpretation of the dream of Nebuchadnezzar (chapter 2). The history of the East is unfolded, centred around the kings symbolized by animals; symbols disappear in chapters 10-11. In every case the series closes with and concentrates on a personage who is the persecutor *par excellence,* Antiochus IV Epiphanes. Both parts of the book are dominated by one outlook and are welded into a close unit. Daniel and his companions, deported to Babylon, were supported by God and overcame all trials. The same divine providence, through changing empires, continues to work for the coming of the kingdom of God, it continues to protect the people of God and ensures its survival. The work of God is accomplished in the midst of trials, but its final realization is certain. The final vision of chapter 12 fittingly concludes the book by pointing to the messianic age that lies just beyond the time of trial.

Daniel deals not with single empires but with a succession of empires; it points out how their sequence is determined by God and declares that, when the appointed limit has been reached, they are destined to be overthrown by the kingdom of God. In the author's view history follows a timetable whose stages have been fixed by divine decree. History is purposeful and moves toward a goal, and all of it is under divine control. We, in our era, appear to have lost the sense of God's activity in the events of history; here in Daniel we have, in a striking way, the typically Hebrew awareness of that truth. The author of Daniel is convinced that Antiochus is a puppet in God's hand; he has accepted the persecution as God's punishment of a sinful people, and he is certain that the time is near when God will end Israel's years of desolation. And, all the while, he looks forward to the final stage, the establishment of God's kingdom.

He tells the story of the past in such a way that the persecuted
Jews may understand that their sufferings had a place in God's
purpose and may see that the tyranny of Antiochus fell within
God's plan. The situation has not developed by chance or in
defiance of the divine decree. Though the king may seem to
succeed in his proud revolt against the Prince of princes and may,
with impunity, trample upon the people of the Prince, his
triumph is illusory: 'He shall prosper till the indignation is
accomplished; for what is determined shall be done' (11 : 36).
And though it might seem that such emphasis on God's absolute
control of human affairs must encourage a *laissez faire* attitude,
a directly opposite effect was intended and achieved. This con-
fident assurance that history, divinely guided, moved towards a
goal fixed by God, fired the tiny band of faithful Jews with
indomitable hope when any hope seemed vain and urged them
to supreme effort where resistance seemed doomed to failure.
Indeed, their plain duty was put before them in explicit terms:
'the people who know their God shall stand firm and take action'
(11 : 32).

The book always looks to the final victory, to the time of the
end, to the coming of the kingdom; the author sees the messianic
age about to dawn, just beyond the 'time, two times, and half a
time' of the persecution. Apocalypse is a child of prophecy
and here the link with the prophetical writings is clear. The
prophets before and during the Exile believed that the deliverance
from Babylonian bondage would herald the Messiah's appearance, and the author of Daniel expected the great change to
come with the death of Antiochus; in both cases we have the
characteristic foreshortening of prophecy. The prophets have seen
a vision and are overwhelmed by the majesty of it; and if the
kingdom will not come as speedily as they had imagined, they
are certain that it will come. God's victory over the world is
assured, and those who serve him faithfully will have a glorious
part in his triumph.[6]

In general, we may say that the purpose of apocalyptic was

[6] See W. J. Harrington, *Record of the Promise: The Old Testament,*
Chicago, The Priory Press; Dublin, Helicon, 1965, 367-88.

to keep alive hope in God and to remind men that God is in final control of history. This is reinforced by the thought of the future life, though, in the different Jewish apocalypses, this is presented in a great variety of ideas. Some think of a resurrection of the good to life on earth, while others think of a blissful hereafter. All are agreed that the triumph of God's will is paramount, for only in a world in which his will is perfectly done—the kingdom of God—can happiness be perfected.

A characteristic of these works, variously expressed, is the recognition that the golden age will not come of itself nor be ushered in by men, but is God's gift. Men could play their part and serve God's purpose only by obedience to his will; and their faithfulness could entail anguish and distress. The thought of the final judgment was in keeping with this outlook, because it was seen that bliss lay in obedience to God in a world that was obedient to him; it could not be shared by those who set themselves against God. 'In the day of judgment men would be found to be what they had chosen to be, and if they had elected to hate the will of God they would be found to hate it, and therefore could not have a place in a kingdom which perfectly reflected his will.'[7]

The revelations of an apocalypse are made through the medium of visions which the seer describes in conventional language; thus we have images, symbols and numbers. Everything, or nearly everything, in an apocalypse is symbolic, although the details of the symbols are not always significant and should not be unduly pressed. It is imperative that the procedure should be correctly understood.

When the seer describes a vision, he translates into symbols the ideas which God had suggested to him; he accumulates things and colours and symbolic numbers without worrying about the form of his picture. His primary purpose is to convey the ideas he has received from God, not to describe a coherent vision, an *imaginable* vision. If we are to follow, without discouragement, the way he has traced, we must accept his terms, and translate into ideas the symbols which he des-

[7] H. H. Rowley, in *Peake's Commentary on the Bible, op. cit.*, 487f.

cribes, and not be disturbed by their lack of coherence. Thus, it would be wrong to strive to imagine *visually* the Lamb with seven horns and seven eyes (13 : 1), and to wonder how the ten horns should be shared among the seven heads. These visions are not plastically conceivable, but that fact should not disturb. One must be satisfied with understanding the symbols *intellectually* without lingering over their more or less surprising details: the Lamb enjoys the fulness of power and knowledge; the beast represents the Roman Empire with its emperors (the heads) and vassal kings (the horns). If one does not take full account of such procedure—often disconcerting— it is impossible for one to understand the Apocalypse.[8]

The author of an apocalypse looks to the future not only when he describes the time of the end but also when he unrolls the course of history. His vantage point is in the past—an apocalypse is almost always pseudonymous—and he speaks as a prophet. In non-canonical apocalypses, description of the last things is a product of the author's unaided imagination; but the authors of Daniel and the Apocalypse have been granted a vision of the end of time and the era of salvation—they are authentic prophets. Apocalyptic flourished in times of crisis and was designed to console and to encourage those undergoing affliction and distress, to fill them with confidence in God, who guided human destiny and was master of history. Here the Apocalypse is at one with the other apocalyptic writings.

Yet, John's work is no imitation of earlier apocalypses, and is, in many ways, a new departure.[9]

1. The Jewish apocalypses are pseudepigraphic, whereas this Christian apocalypse bears its author's name. This is significant, for John thus claims for himself the position of a prophet who, conscious of his own inspiration, has no need to shelter under the name of a notable biblical personage.

2. It is difficult to determine the date and provenance of Jewish apocalypses because these matters are left intentionally vague.

[8] M.-E. Boismard, *L'Apocalypse (BJ)*, *op. cit.*, 8f.
[9] See H. B. Swete, *The Apocalypse of St John*, London, Macmillan, 1922,[8] xxviii-xxx.

The Apocalypse of John makes no secret of its origin and destination : it is the work of a Christian undergoing exile on the island of Patmos and it is addressed to the Christian congregations in seven of the chief cities of Asia Minor; its date can be set within definite limits.

3.   Whatever may be said of his indebtedness to Jewish sources, John has produced a work which, taken as a whole, is profoundly Christian. 'It breathes a religious spirit which is not that of its predecessors; it is marked with the sign of the cross.'

4.   In the Apocalypse the Messiah plays a role that is not his in Jewish apocalypses; in these, the new age is brought about by God alone and not through his Messiah—in some the Messiah does not figure at all. For John, it is Jesus Christ who, by opening the sealed book, sets in operation the plan of God. For Christ, by his sacrifice, has freed men from sin (Ap. 1 : 5; 5 : 9; 7 : 14; 12 : 11; 22 : 14) and he alone is worthy to open that book (5 : 6-9; 13 : 8). His place is in heaven beside the throne of God (3 : 21; 7 : 17; 22 : 1-3). At the end of time he will appear in judgment (19 : 11ff.) and he will manifest himself as the Lord of the world (2 : 26ff.; 12 : 5; 19 : 15). In the new Jerusalem he is, with God, the source of eternal and unending happiness for the elect (21 : 22ff.; 22 : 1ff.).

In short, although he has employed a current literary form, and although (as we shall see) he is much indebted to the OT, John has written a work that is distinctive and ultimately original.

When we describe John's work as an apocalypse, taking that word in its proper sense, we leave aside the first three chapters, the 'letters to the seven churches'. Although an integral part of the whole book, these are not apocalyptic in form. Even though we call them 'letters', they are not, strictly speaking, letters, but prophetic messages. Primarily, they are judgments on the spiritual state of the churches and they stress the necessity of keeping faith; hence, they are closer to the prophetical form than to the apocalyptic.

III. THE SOURCES

When we consider that John was a first-century Jew, involved in the writing of an apocalypse, we have little difficulty in acknowledging certain influences on his work. He was indebted in the first place, and predominantly, to the Old Testament. We are certainly not surprised to find that his apocalypse has not a little in common with earlier and contemporary Jewish apocalypses. Further, we may discern echoes of the *Targums,* the Aramaic liturgical paraphrases of scripture. It goes without saying that all of this is turned to the service of his own Christian faith and vision.

i. use of the old testament[10]

The author of the Apocalypse obviously knows the OT thoroughly. It is not only that a whole crowd of biblical images appear in his work, but the very language is OT language. He does not quote, formally, but he uses familiar turns of phrase quite naturally. Yet, he is not slavishly tied to this style and vocabulary —he dominates them, just as he can adapt the images to suit his purpose.

Although OT phrases are used consistently, and perhaps even unconsciously, there are references in which it is clear that a particular book and certain passages are in view; this occurs most frequently in the visions. Almost all of the OT books make their contribution, but some of them are used with special frequency. More than half of the author's references belong to the prophecies of Isaiah and Ezekiel, to Psalms, and to Daniel; in proportion to its length, Daniel yields by far the greatest number.

In many cases, if not in most, John blends two or more OT contexts, whether from different books or from different parts of the same book; this is because his memory is charged with biblical words and thoughts. His handling of the material is always original and independent. Thus, in the first vision of the

[10] W. J. Harrington, *Record of the Fulfilment: The New Testament,* Chicago, The Priory Press, 1966; London, Geoffrey Chapman, 1967, 462-6.

Apocalypse, while nearly every detail is drawn from Ezekiel and Daniel, the concept of the glorified Christ has no parallel in the OT. If the vision of chapter 4 owes much to Isaiah, Ezekiel and Zechariah, no mere compiler could have produced it; and the same may be said of every other vision throughout the book. 'Though in constant relation to the older apocalyptic, St John's picture of the unseen and the future are truly creations, the work of the Spirit of prophecy upon a mind full of the lore of the earlier revelation and yet free to carry its reminiscences into new and wider fields of spiritual illumination.'[11]

It is particularly instructive to see how John had modelled his plagues of trumpets and bowls in the plagues of Egypt, transforming the latter in the process.

Trumpets	Plagues of Egypt	Bowls
1. Ap. 8: 6f. Hail, fire, blood	Ex. 9: 23f. Seventh	7. Ap. 16: 17-21 Thunder, earthquake, hail
2. Ap. 8: 8f. Sea into blood	Ex. 7: 20f. First	2. Ap. 16: 3 Sea turned to blood
3. Ap. 8: 10f. Waters turned bitter	Ex. 7: 20f. First	3. Ap. 16: 4-7 Waters turned to blood
4. Ap. 8: 12 Darkness	Ex. 10: 21-23 Ninth	5. Ap. 16: 10f. Darkness
5. Ap. 9: 1-11 Locusts	Ex. 10: 12-20 (Jl 1: 6-2: 5) Eighth Ex. 9: 8-11 Sixth Ex. 8: 2-6 Second	1. Ap. 16: 2 Ulcers on men 6. Ap. 16: 12-16 Frogs
6. Ap. 9: 13-21 (Euphrates)	 (Gn. 15: 18)	6. Ap. 16: 12-16 Armageddon (Euphrates) 4. Ap. 16: 8f. Burning heat
7. Ap. 11: 14-19 The third 'Woe'		

This is a good example of the freedom with which the author uses the OT; he does not trouble about consistency even in the parallel series of plagues. The plague of hail (first trumpet) has been reserved for the last in the series of bowls: it will destroy

[11] H. B. Swete, *The Apocalypse of St John, op. cit.,* clx.

Babylon. The second and third bowls, like the second and third trumpets, make two parts of the plague of water turned into blood. The fifth bowl has some of the details of the sixth trumpet, but applies these details to the precise situation of the destruction of Rome. The Euphrates reappears, but in order to be dried up to form a passage for the kings of the East who come to destroy the city. The plague of frogs takes on an eschatological aspect, just like the plague of locusts in the vision of trumpets. Here John says that the frogs are impure spirits. They have come forth from the mouths of the dragon and of the two beasts to deceive the kings of the earth and to assemble them for the final battle of the 'great day' of God.[12]

Clearly, John is not hampered by the images and symbols he borrows, but he freely adapts them; and he is not, of course, limited to OT imagery, but also turns to other sources. Moreover, he makes his own original contribution. When interpreting the images of the Apocalypse, we must bear two factors in mind. First, imagination, especially oriental imagination, is not tied definitively to any one image; on the other hand, an image may have more than one symbolical signification. For instance, in Ap. 12, the desert is a place of refuge, and in chapter 17 it is the abode of demons. Failure to take account of the varied symbolism of an image has led some to identify the white horseman of 6 : 12, who symbolizes victorious war, with the horseman of 19 : 11, who symbolizes the Messiah. In the second place, there is the 'historization' of images. By this we mean the tendency to take a symbol for the description of a concrete historical reality, the temptation to interpret the details of an image in terms of historical events. Thus, it would be wrong to regard the series of seals, trumpets and bowls as so many series of plagues that will come to pass successively at, or just before, the end of time. The symbols of Apocalypse are important not for themselves, but for the truths they signify. Once they have yielded their symbolism, they must not be pressed into any system of interpretation.[13]

---

[12] L. Cerfaux-J. Cambier, *L'Apocalypse de Saint Jean lue aux Chrétiens,* Paris, Cerf, 1955, 144f.

[13] *Ibid.,* 216f.

2. JEWISH APOCALYPSES[14]

The book of Daniel was followed by many apocalyptic writings, only a few of which are extant. It is only to be expected that the Apocalypse of John should have something in common with these writings whose Jewish background and literary form it shared. In the course of the commentary we shall note the most striking correspondences of the Apocalypse with the others. Here we give a very brief description of the Jewish apocalypses we shall have occasion to mention.

1 Enoch

The Book of Enoch (Ethiopic Enoch) is a compilation, in five parts, of exhortations, prophecies, and writings attributed to Enoch. The whole work is now extant only in an Ethiopic version. In general, it is an exposé of the religious and moral, messianic, and eschatological beliefs of Judaism shortly before the Christian era. The main divisions of the book are :

(a) Introduction : i-v
i. 6-36 Angels and universe—world judgment followed by golden age.
ii. 37-71 Parables or similitudes.
iii. 72-82 Astronomical and calendar matter.
iv. 83-90 The book of dreams—apocalyptic. It presents the history of Israel under the symbolism of sheep. The climax is the destruction of the foe followed by the resurrection of the righteous and the ushering in of the kingdom of God.
v. 91-104 Apocalypse of weeks and final judgment. The apocalypse of weeks divides history into ten periods, of which the seventh is the age of apostasy, the eighth an age of righteousness, the ninth the age for the destruction of the wicked, and the tenth the age of enduring bliss.

(b) Appendices : 105-108
The sections are of different dates and the whole may fall

[14] W. J. Harrington, *Record of the Fulfilment, op. cit.*, 53-7.

between 170 and 60 BC. The work is represented by ten fragmentary manuscripts from Qumran—the language is Aramaic.
1 Enoch had considerable influence in the early Church and, in
its extant form, we must certainly admit the presence of Christian
interpolations.

2 Enoch

The Book of the Secrets of Enoch (Slavonic Enoch) is a typically
apocalyptic writing. Enoch relates the revelations granted him in
a journey through the seven heavens. He describes the creation of
the world and discloses the secrets of the future. We find here the
expression of a millennium : the idea of a period of rest, lasting
for 1,000 years, following 6,000 years of history. After the millennium, time would come to an end. The book in its extant form
is late and shows obvious Christian influence, but there is little
doubt that the original was written by a Palestinian Jew (or
possibly by a Judaeo-Christian) who wrote in Greek in the first
century AD. It is extant in a Slavonic version.

4 Ezra

This book (also known as the Apocalypse of Esdras, or 2 Esdras)
is the Jewish apocryphal work most widely known and used by
Christians. Extant in Latin (and in oriental versions), it was
written in Aramaic or Hebrew shortly after the destruction of
Jerusalem in AD 70. It consists of seven visions : dialogues with
God on the woes of Israel. The visions all have to do with the
establishment of the kingdom of the Messiah. The book is an
affirmation of Jewish faith and hope in the face of overwhelming
trials.

2 Baruch

This (the Apocalypse or Baruch, or Syriac Baruch) was written
about the same time as 2 Ezra and seems to have been influenced
by that work; like Ezra, it is divided into seven parts. It depicts

the disasters which will precede the dawn of the messianic age. Four world empires appear, the last of which (the Roman) will be followed by the rule of the Messiah. Originally written in Aramaic or Hebrew, it is extant only in a Syriac translation of a Greek version.

Assumption of Moses

A work, partly extant in an old Latin version, which was apparently written in Hebrew shortly after the death of Herod the Great; it seems to have been of Essene origin. The author is very insistent on observance of the Law; he is hostile to the Sadducees and violently nationalistic. There is an assurance of the intervention of God in history and of the establishment of his kingdom.

The Sibylline Oracles

From the fifth century BC onwards, oracles, attributed to the Sibyl (a Greek prophetess), circulated in Greece and Asia. The Alexandrian Jews saw here an effective method of propaganda and from the second century BC composed and circulated 'Sibylline oracles' inculcating Jewish beliefs. Christians continued the practice so that, in fact, the extant collection of twelve books is mainly Christian in tone. Books III, a collection of separate fragments from the second century BC, IV, about 80 BC, and V, about AD 125, are the only Jewish oracles in the collection; and even these have been retouched to some extent. They present apocalyptic ideas.

The Psalms of Solomon

These are eighteen psalms, very similar to those of the psalter, composed in Hebrew, but extant only in a Greek translation and in a Syriac version made from the Greek text. Pss 2 and 17 refer to the taking of Jerusalem by Pompey in 63 BC; it is likely that the other psalms also date from about the middle of the first century BC. Teaching on the resurrection, free will, and the messianic hope (particularly in Ps. 17) indicate the Pharisaic origin of these psalms.

3 THE TARGUMS

The word *targum,* in later Hebrew and Aramaic, is chiefly used to describe a vernacular version of the scriptures. The need for an Aramaic version of the Torah must have made itself felt as soon as the mass of the Jews had adopted Aramaic as their chief language—that is, some time after the Exile. While we do not know when Targums first came to be composed among Aramaic-speaking Jews, we are certain that these renderings had a long history behind them by NT times. These versions came to birth mainly (if not exclusively) in the synagogue. In the synagogal services, a reader read the liturgical passage in Hebrew (a verse, or sometimes two or three verses at a time), and a translator stood beside him and rendered it immediately into Aramaic. The translation had to be given extempore; the translator was not permitted to have a written text of the Targum before him. This was to ensure that the Targum would not be taken for, nor confused with, the inspired word of God as found in the scriptures. However, at an early date, the versions were set down in writing. The purpose of the vernacular translation was not to give a bare, literal rendering of the text. Rather, its function was 'to give the sense and make the people understand the reading' (Neh. 8 : 8). A liturgical reading would tend to be paraphrastic or homiletic in nature.

The official Targum to the Pentateuch (it became official about the end of the first millennium AD) is the *Targum of Onkelos.* The traditional view is that it was composed in Palestine and was taken from there to Babylon, and it is generally assumed that it existed (in written form) in the 2nd century AD. Of more immediate concern for our purpose is the *Palestinian Targum to the Pentateuch.* This is extant in its entirety in MS Neofiti I, discovered in the Vatican Library and positively identified in 1956. It is represented in a fragmentary manner in the *Targum of Pseudo-Jonathan* and in the *Fragmentary Targum* (as well as in the Cairo Geniza fragments and in citations). The *Targum of Pseudo-*

Jonathan, though Palestinian, stands somewhat on its own and shows a close relation with certain NT passages. We shall also have occasion to refer to *Targum Jonathan to the Prophets,* of Palestinian origin.

The Palestinian Targum, in its language and expressions, appears as a liturgical version. It would seem that our present text of this Targum has been faithfully transmitted from early, even pre-Christian, times. The NT book which shows the greatest number of contacts with the Palestinian Targum is the Apocalypse. This is not surprising. 'The author of Apocalypse was clearly a Jew, and one with a liturgical turn of mind. We can presume that he was of the same bent before he embraced the religion of Christ. His receptive mind would then have been particularly retentive to the liturgical paraphrase he had heard spoken in the synagogues.'[15] We shall see that the imagery and language of the Apocalypse has a parallel in certain Palestinian Targum texts. The most reasonable assumption is that the Targum is part of the Jewish religious background which affected John and his work.

IV. THE PURPOSE

Like the book of Daniel, the Apocalypse of John was written in a troubled time and for a special purpose; like Daniel, too, it carries a message that goes beyond the immediate crisis. The Apocalypse is at once a declaration of Christian faith and hope and a manifesto against the official paganism of Rome. The author is a witness; and he speaks with the authority of the former prophets sent by God, echoing their words and images. His book is a commentary on the words of Jesus to his disciples: 'In the world you have tribulation; but be of good cheer, I have overcome the world' (Jn 16: 33). Just as Daniel was aimed at rekindling the spiritual energy of the Jewish nation at a time

[15] M. McNamara, *The New Testament and the Palestinian Targum of the Pentateuch,* Rome, Pontifical Biblical Institute, 1966, 256. I am entirely indebted to this work for the note on the Targums and for reference to Targum texts throughout the Commentary.

when monotheism was menaced by pagan Hellenism (Dn. 7-12), so also the Apocalypse was written to console and to strengthen Christians in the midst of persecution (Ap. 2 : 8-10, 12f.; 6 : 9-11; 7 : 14; 13 : 11; 17 : 6; 20 : 4). In both cases, the intention and the method employed are the same.

In the time of John, the persecutor was the Roman Empire, and the most pressing danger to the faithful of the province of Asia was the cult of Rome and of the emperor. The notion of the divinity of kings was an ancient and common one in the East. Alexander the Great found that his Eastern (and Egyptian) subjects regarded him as a god; his successors, both Seleucids and Ptolemies, complacently assumed divine titles—for instance, Antiochus IV was 'Epiphanes' ('god manifest'). The practice was slower to find a foothold in Rome, but was eventually seized upon as a valuable political factor. In the Hellenistic age, Rome itself had attained the status of a deity, and the cult of the *Dea Roma* (the goddess Rome) had grown up. In the East it was soon accompanied by the cult of the emperor.

After his death in 44 bc Julius Caesar, by decree of the senate, was declared one of the divine protectors of the state. Augustus did not claim divine honours in Rome, but he was worshipped as a divinity in the East where temples were raised to him (like the temple of Augustus built by Herod the Great in Sebaste, the restored Samaria). Later emperors (notably Domitian) openly claimed divine honours during their lifetime. The imperial cult had secured a firm grip in Asia Minor and was nowhere more enthusiastically propagated.

Emperor-worship demanded that sacrifice should be offered (or incense burned) before an image of Caesar, with the declaration : *Kyrios Kaisar*—'Caesar is Lord', that is, divine—sheer blasphemy in Christian eyes. For Christians Jesus Christ was *Kyrios,* and they must 'hold fast his name' (Ap. 2 : 13), reserving that title for him alone. The readers of the Apocalypse who were contemporaries of John, and to whom the book was addressed in the first place, were well able to understand its purpose and its veiled allusions to the contemporary situation and its polemic against the state religion.

B

A constant preoccupation of the Apocalypse is the fate of the martyrs, readily understandable in the historical circumstances of the book. The readers are being encouraged to face a violent persecution in which many of them may well find death. Thus, John, time and time again, refers to the blessedness of the martyrs, and he becomes more and more explicit. In 6: 9-11, the souls of those who had been slain for the witness they had borne —sacrificial victims—rest under the altar of holocausts, but they wear the white robes of victory. Then (7: 9-17) they are represented as celebrating, in heaven, an everlasting Feast of Tabernacles (the most joyous of Jewish feasts). Satan has no power over them; they are in heaven and he has been cast out (12: 7-11). They are the close companions of the Lamb (14: 1-5); a few verses further on their situation is stated in explicit terms: 'Blessed are the dead who die in the Lord! Henceforth, says the Spirit, they can rest for ever from their labours' (14:13). Before the throne of God they sing the song of Moses, the song of a new deliverance (15: 2-4). They are privileged guests at the marriage supper of the Lamb (19: 9). Finally, they are those who reign with Christ for a thousand years, beyond the power of Satan (20: 4-6). But, always, they are seen as 'first fruits for God and the Lamb' (14: 14); they are the consecrated offerings of a mighty harvest, of the multitude of those whose names are written in the Lamb's book of life (13: 8; 20: 12).

What John had written for the churches of Asia remained as a heritage for all suffering churches throughout the Empire; but he seems to have been aware, too, that his work would have a wider scope.

There is some reason for believing that the writer of the Apocalypse, before his work was ended, realized that the book might find a larger field of service than the churches of Asia or even the churches of the Empire could offer. In the early chapters it is clear that St John writes with a view to his message being read aloud in the local church assemblies (Ap. 1: 3; 2: 7, etc.). . . . But when he reaches the end a presentiment seems to enter his mind that the book will live: *I testify unto every man that heareth the words of the prophecy of this book.*

If any man *shall add unto them, God shall add unto him the plagues which are written in this book; if any man shall take away . . . God shall take away part of the tree of life* (22 : 18f.). . . . The words are based on two passages of Deuteronomy (4 : 2; 13 : 1) and they practically place the Apocalypse on a level with the Torah and anticipate for it a place among the scriptures of the Church. St John knew himself to be a prophet and his writing to be a prophecy; that he was commanded to consign his visions to a book was an assurance to him that their purpose would not be fulfilled in one generation or in two. He sees the book going down to posterity, and like the Deuteronomist, he endeavours to guard it against interpolation and excision. As he writes the last word upon the papyrus roll that lies upon his knee, the conviction dawns upon him that the *Revelation of Jesus Christ* was given for the warning and comfort of the whole Church to the end of time.[16]

V. THE PLAN

Although the unity of the Apocalypse has often been called into question, it does seem that it really is a single work. Even the letters to the seven churches (chapters 1-3), written in a different literary form, are an integral part of the book; the whole bears the stamp of one hand. At the same time, there is an unevenness which may be accounted for, in part at any rate, by the apocalyptic form—where a strictly logical arrangement is not to be sought. But the fact may also point to a complicated prehistory of the work. M. E. Boismard, for instance, takes the line that the Apocalypse, as it stands, contains many doublets. An examination of these suggests that the properly apocalyptic part (chapters 4-22) is composed of two different, originally independent, apocalypses which were later fused to form one text. Since both apocalypses show the same literary characteristics, however, they must both be attributed to the same author, who composed them at different dates. The fusion of the two texts and the prefacing of the letters to the churches (also written by the same author) was probably

[16] H. B. Swete, *The Apocalypse of St John, op. cit.,* xcviif.

the work of another hand. The final editor was responsible for minor retouches aimed at smoothing out the joints of the text and at harmonizing their data.[17] While this analysis does draw our attention to the prehistory of the text, it does not seem that we can really hope to isolate the two source-texts—if, indeed, there ever were two such texts. And we prefer to maintain that, even if John had worked over two earlier apocalypses of his, the book as we have it is a unified writing.

Our study of the Apocalypse has satisfied us that it is structured on a plan which is discernible in its broad lines, but which is quite flexible in its details. Attempts have been made to trace an elaborate sequence within the book—to find in it, for instance, an intricate system of septets. We are satisfied that nothing is to be gained by imposing, from without, a strictly logical plan on a work of such imaginative power and of such deep religious feeling. The Apocalypse has the freedom of great art.

---

[17] 'L'Apocalypse ou les apocalypses de Saint Jean', *Revue Biblique* 56 (1949), 507-41; *(BJ)*, 9-15; see W. J. Harrington, *The Record of the Fulfilment, op. cit.*, 460-2.

VI.   THE INTERPRETATION

Our commentary on the Apocalypse will follow the lines of the plan we have set out above. While that plan already provides an overall view of John's work, it remains a guideline, nothing more. On the other hand, the movement of the Apocalypse and its leading ideas are rather lost from sight or, at least, not immediately discernible, within the spread of the commentary. It has seemed helpful, then, to present here, in adequate detail, our interpretation of the Apocalypse.[18]

When the literary form of the Apocalypse is taken into account, as it must be, a certain line of interpretation necessarily opens up —if violence is not to be done to the work. For, as an apocalypse, the book was written in view of a crisis, and it is concerned with concrete historical events. The author may well have been aware that his book would live and speak to ages yet to come, but he wrote primarily for the Christians of his own day, the communities of Asia Minor. This must be our starting-point, and to

---

[18] See W. J. Harrington, *The Record of the Fulfilment, op. cit.*, 467-85.

ignore the historical milieu of the Apocalypse is to invite inevitable misinterpretation. Even granted this approach, however, there is much that we do not fully understand and there is scope for different interpretations of the writing. Yet the Apocalypse is one of the most fascinating books of the NT; and although its literary form is strange to us and although parts of it remain obscure, the book itself can be made intelligible to the modern reader. We attempt, then, to break the seven seals and open up a writing that is indeed a closed book to one who may come upon it without some explanation of its nature, its purpose and its meaning.

A. THE LETTERS

The letters to the seven churches (chapters 1-3) have the same literary characteristics as the properly apocalyptic part of the Apocalypse and are the work of the same author. Originally, they may have been independent of the rest, to be joined later to the apocalypse proper; as such they form an integral part of the work as we know it. But the links between the letters and the rest are so close that the independent existence of the former seems unlikely.

The prologue (1 : 1-3) introduces the Apocalypse as a letter of the prophet John, a letter destined to be read at the liturgical ceremonies; but the author is conscious that it is, in effect, a message from the supreme pastor of the church. The introduction (1 : 4-8) addresses the Christian congregations to which John had ministered; it is notable for a trinitarian formula which, in Christian fashion, lingers over the Son: his incarnation, death and glory.

In a striking vision (1 : 9-20), John is commissioned by the glorified Son of Man to write what is to be revealed to him and to send the message to seven churches of Asia. The Messiah appears as judge (as in Dn. 7 : 13) and here the details of the vision have a symbolical value: he wears the long robe of priesthood, the golden cincture of royalty, the white hair of eternity. Eyes like a flame of fire represent his divine knowledge, and feet of bronze indicate stability. He holds in his right hand (that is, in his power) the seven lampstands representing the seven churches, and the stars, the angel guardians or protectors of the churches. The overall effect is one of terrifying majesty. The vision of the Son of Man effectively brings out the oracular character of the first part of the Apocalypse, for it is closely parallel to the inaugural visions of the prophets (cf. Is. 6; Jer. 1; Ezek. 1). But where the latter proceeded to speak in the name of Yahweh ('thus says Yahweh'), John will make known the 'revelation of Jesus Christ'. And since, in the eyes of the inspired writer, the seven churches represent the universal church, his message— the message of the Lord—has meaning for the church until the end of time.

The seven churches are not listed haphazardly, but in order. They were linked by a circular road that, from Ephesus, went north to Smyrna and Pergamum and then swung southwards to take in the others. Each church receives a judgment which is based upon a full knowledge of its condition, both external (there are several topical references) and spiritual. The churches receive praise or blame (or both), usually with some qualifications, and in this there seems to be a definite plan and progression. Ephesus receives censure and commendation; then Smyrna, Thyatira, and Philadelphia (the even numbers) are praised—the latter with marked warmth, while Pergamum, Sardis, and Laodicea are censured—the latter very severely. Their chief faults are a cooling in first fervour and a decline in charity, together with indulgence of or concessions to Nicolaitanism, an heretical trend not easy to identify, but which seems to have some affinity with Gnosticism.

B.   THE PROPHETICAL VISIONS

The Apocalypse is certainly not concerned with the 'seven ages of the world'—a theory popular in the Middle Ages; nor does it regard, in any detailed manner, the future of the church. On the other hand, certain capital stages of human history are in view. All the while, John is concerned with the meaning of events rather than with the events themselves. Thus, he brings out the significance of the destruction of Jerusalem in AD 70 and then goes on to point to the inevitable issue of the persecution that had just begun.

A consideration of Dn. 7-12 can help us to understand Apocalypse. Daniel was written in the Maccabean Age; hence, it is largely concerned with events of the past. Yet, the succession of empires is seen in relation to the purpose of the divine plan: the final establishment of the kingdom of God. That future event is not treated in detail; it is simply foretold that the persecution will end in failure and that God will have the last word. The perspective of Apocalypse is no different. 'In both cases the presentation of historical realities, past, present, or near at hand is meant to be an example and a type of what will happen afterwards. God's plan is one and the author, convinced of that, can shorten his perspective and see the eschatological event just beyond the historical crisis of which he writes.'[19]

PART I. THE CHURCH AND ISRAEL (4-11)

We may divide the central section of the Apocalypse into two parts: 4-11; 12: 1-20: 15. Though chapters 4-11 fit into the integral plan of the whole work, they can, in a true sense, be regarded as forming a complete apocalypse. In 12: 1 the author makes a fresh beginning for which the reader had been prepared in 10: 11; and, again, we come to an ending at 20: 15. We have, then, two apocalypses, each of which stretches to an end. From chapter 12 onwards the author is concerned with the church and pagan Rome, while in chapters 4-11 he is preoccupied with the church's relation to the chosen people. His work has about it something of the structure of the OT prophetical books: first oracles against Israel and then oracles against the nations.[20]

The opening vision of the throne of God (chapter 4) is manifestly inspired by several prophetical texts (Is. 6: 1-5; Ezek. 1:

[19] A. Feuillet, *The Apocalypse,* New York, Alba House, 1965, 51f.
[20] These 'two apocalypses' are therefore two consecutive parts of one work; this view is quite distinct from a theory of the *prehistory* of the work mentioned above.

4-10, 25-27; Dn. 7 : 9f.). Before the throne, the 'twenty-four elders' represent the saints of Israel and the 'four living creatures' represent the created world. Then (chapter 5), 'he who was seated on the throne'—a designation of God throughout the Apocalypse —gave to the Lamb the sealed scroll which he held in his right hand (a transfer of power). The chapter ends with the first of the heavenly liturgies that recur so frequently in the book; these are either early Christian hymns or were modelled on them. The scroll contained the divine decree against an Israel that had not believed in Christ. As a sealed book it may well be the OT : 'To this day whenever Moses is read a veil hangs over their minds' (2 Cor. 3 : 15).

The breaking of the seals unleashes a series of plagues (6 : 1-8 : 1), a series which follows the pattern of events in the synoptic apocalypse (Mk. 13 par.) : war, strife among nations, famine, pestilence, persecution, cosmic phenomena (earthquakes, eclipses, etc.). The description of the first four, war and its attendant evils (6 : 1-8), is inspired by the visions of the four horsemen and the four chariots of Zech. 1 : 8-11; 6 : 1-8. At the breaking of the fifth seal, the martyrs appear—here the martyrs of the Old Law (6 : 9-11); and the cosmic phenomena appear at the opening of the sixth seal. Before the last seal is broken, the servants of God are signed with the seal of the living God—one hundred and forty-four thousand of them (7 : 1-8) : the saved remnant of Israel. The great multitude from all nations, celebrating a Feast of Tabernacles in heaven (7 : 9-17), seem to be Christian martyrs, the 'fellow servants and brethren' of the Jewish martyrs of 6 : 9-11. A solemn silence precedes the second series of plagues (8 : 1).

The opening of the seventh seal marks a beginning rather than an end; it heralds a fresh series of plagues. The trumpets are presented in much the same way as the seals : the first four (8 : 7-12) are described in a few verses, while the others unfold at greater length, interspersed with other visions. The plagues of 8 : 7-12 strike only *one-third* of the earth and of the heavenly bodies, and again in 9 : 15 only one-third of mankind is stricken by the sixth plague, just as the seals struck 'a fourth of the earth'

(6 : 8); there is no such qualification in the parallel plagues of bowls which are aimed at the pagan world. We may seek the reason for this difference in the prophetic doctrine of the remnant (compare the 'third' of Ezek. 5 : 1-4; Zech. 13 : 8f.). It follows that the plagues of bowls are not a doublet of the plagues of trumpets : the former are inflicted on the adorers of the beast, while the latter are closely related to the judgment of God on an unbelieving Israel executed through the destruction of Jerusalem. Since the seals are the prelude and preparation of trumpets, they must be understood in the same context. The first two 'woes' (fifth and sixth trumpets) are a highly-coloured development of the plague of locusts (Ex. 10 : 12-15), already utilized in striking fashion by Joel (1 : 6-2 : 11)—a passage that immediately influenced John.

Chapter 10 opens with a vision of a mighty angel coming down from heaven wrapped in a cloud and with a rainbow over his head. He had a little scroll open in his hand and he set his right foot on the sea and his left foot on the land (vv. 1f.). In 5 : 2, the invitation of a 'strong angel' led to the opening of the sealed scroll : there is a parallel between angels and scrolls. The angel of chapter 10, with traits of the Son of Man of Daniel (Dn. 7 : 14), is more majestic than the other; of giant stature, he stands on sea and land because his message is for all mankind. This is in contrast to Ap. 5 : 1-12 where the title given to Christ (the lion of the tribe of Judah, the root of David), and the role of the twenty-four elders (the saints of the Old Law), point to the chosen people. The sealed book is the OT, especially the prophetic oracles, to which Christ has supplied the key. The little book (less extensive than the OT, but open and universalist in scope) is the message of Jesus.

In 10 : 3-7, two antithetical scenes are followed by a new prophetic investiture (parallel to that of 1 : 9-20), patently based on the investiture of Ezekiel (Ap. 10 : 8-10; cf. Ezek. 3 : 1-3). Then (Ap. 10 : 11), John is told : 'You must again prophesy about many peoples and nations and tongues and kings.' In the context of these chapters, this means that he is called to a new mission : he must prophesy as he had not done up to now. The message of the sealed scroll bears directly on the chosen people (cf. 7 : 4-8), and it is only from chapter 12 onward that there is question of 'peoples and nations and tongues' (cf. 12 : 5; 13 : 7; 14 : 6, 8; 15 : 4; 17 : 12). It seems that the purpose of chapter 10 is to introduce the period of preaching to the gentiles and to bring out the paradox of the gospel : the end is near (we live in the last age), and yet the final episode may be long delayed.

A study of chapter 11 appears to confirm the interpretation of Ap. 4-11 in terms of Israel and the church. John received a measuring rod and was bidden to measure the temple and the altar and the worshippers—what is thus measured is under God's special protection. But he must 'cast out the court that is outside' the temple for 'it is given over to the nations, and they will trample over the holy city for forty-two months' (11 : 1f.). Lk. 21 : 24 springs to mind at once : unbelieving Jerusalem 'will be trodden down by the gentiles, until the times of the gentiles are fulfilled'. The measured temple represents the church, and the outer court is the rejected synagogue; John refers to the final break between church and synagogue brought about by the catastrophe of AD 70. The true temple of God, which Titus could not destroy, was constituted in the first place by the Jews faithful to Christ, the messianic remnant. The unbelieving Jews, until then rather like the outer court of the true temple, were now no longer part of it. However, the prospect is not one of unrelieved gloom : the court will be trampled for 'forty-two months'; this is nothing else than the 'time, two times, and half a time' of Dn. 7 : 25. In the Apocalypse, the expression, or its equivalent, is a symbolic designation of the temporary time of persecution which separates Christians from the perfect establishment of the kingdom of God. The sufferings of the unconverted Jewish world will last just so long—'until the times of the gentiles are fulfilled' (Lk. 21 : 24). Then, with Paul (Rom. 11 : 25f.), we can look to the salvation of Israel.

The two witnesses (Ap. 11 : 3-13) are modelled on Elijah (power to bring about drought : v. 6) and Moses (power to turn water into blood and to smite the earth with every plague : v. 6). Their ministry lasts for 1,260 days, that is to say, the forty-two

months of v. 3—the whole time of the church. It appears that
the witnesses are the incarnation of the testimony—from the Law
and the prophets—which the church bears to Christ in the
Jewish world. v. 7, which abruptly introduces the beast, is best
understood in terms of the final assault on the church. For,
indeed, the death and speedy resurrection of the witnesses will
happen at the end of the forty-two months—they are to testify
for 1,260 days (v. 3), and they are slain only 'when they have
finished their testimony' (v. 7)—and the victory of the beast is
ephemeral. One tenth of the city (Jerusalem) was destroyed and
seven thousand were killed (v. 13), but the rest 'gave glory to
God'. This typically Jewish expression signifies the conversion of
Israel at the end of the 'times of the gentiles'.

In Rom. 11 : 25f., the conversion of Israel, coming after that
of the gentiles, seems to mark the culminating point of the divine
plan. The same is true here. Now is the end : then the seventh
trumpet can sound to announce the end of the world and the
inauguration of the kingdom of God and of his Christ. Significantly, the canticle (Ap. 11 : 17f.) is put in the mouths of the
twenty-four elders, for its language is thoroughly Jewish. Finally,
God's temple was opened and the heavenly ark of the covenant
was seen within it (11 : 19). It seems, then, that the historical
background of Ap. 11 is the catastrophe of AD 70 which brought
about the final separation of church and synagogue. This explains
the artificial antedating of Ap.; for in 17 : 10f., the sixth of a list
of seven emperors in whose reign the writing is set is, most probably, Vespasian. By using the customary apocalyptic procedure,
John could thus place himself before the destruction of Jerusalem
and from that vantage point bring out the theological significance
of the event.

We may regard chapters 4-11 of the Apocalypse, with their
series of seals and of trumpets, as no more than a development of
the data of the synoptic apocalypse. It is an explanation based on
the history of the events foretold in the synoptics : the Jewish war
and the destruction of Jerusalem which, when the Apocalypse
was written, were events of the past, events of great significance.
'The destruction of Jerusalem and its sanctuary was not the end

of the world, but it was the end of a world. It marked the definitive separation of synagogue and church. Henceforth, the latter turned principally to the gentiles.[21] Luke has distinguished three periods of salvation history : the time of Israel, the time of Christ, and the time of the Church. The Apocalypse is not a gospel, and the author does not insist on the time of Christ; but he does discern the time of Israel and the time of the church, each period closing with a divine judgment.

PART II. THE CHURCH AND PAGAN ROME (12 : 1—20 : 15)

This second part, although it offers its own particular problems, has met with a greater measure of agreement in its general interpretation than the preceding part. The historical background is undoubtedly the persecution of the church by Rome, and the precise occasion of the persecution is the Church's refusal to countenance Caesar-worship; the two beasts of chapter 13 represent Rome and the religion of Rome. Here is John's answer to the blasphemous pretensions of the emperors, which must end in disaster : Rome will go the way of Babylon.

Chapter 12 falls into three parts : (1) a diptych which introduces the two symbolical figures, the woman and the dragon (vv. 1-4a); (2) the assault on Christ and his victory (vv. 4b-12); (3) the persecution of Christians (vv. 13-17). The woman symbolizes the people of God which brings forth the messianic age and the Messiah. The dragon is the 'ancient serpent' of Gen. 3 : once again the woman and Satan are face-to-face. The dragon seeks to destroy her son, but the child was snatched out of his power to the throne of God—a reference to the ascension and the triumph of Christ, which will bring about the fall of the dragon. Meanwhile, the woman (the people of God of the OT which, having given Christ to the world, thereby became the Christian church) finds refuge in the desert where she is cared for by God for 1,260 days, that is the equivalent of forty-two months or three and a half years—the whole earthly duration of the Church. The fall of the dragon is dramatized in 12 : 7-12; and although Michael has

---

[21] A. Feuillet, *Johannine Studies,* New York, Alba House, 1964, 244.

cast Satan out of heaven, it really is the victory of Christ (vv. 10f.). The martyrs (who represent all Christians) share in the victory of Christ; death has set them free from the devil's power. Thus, in heaven there is great rejoicing; but, on earth, Satan can still, for a little while, give vent to his wrath.

The dragon's attempt to destroy the woman, implicit in 12 : 6, is described in 12 : 13-16. She is protected for 'a time, two times, and half a time' (cf. 12 : 6): the church, as such, is under God's special care all the time of its historical duration. However, the faithful on earth are vulnerable : Satan, through his instruments, can make war on them; they will be persecuted and put to death. But the message of the Apocalypse is precisely that those who are steadfast to the end share in the glorious victory of the Lamb.

The two beasts of chapter 13, instruments of Satan, are Rome and the imperial religion in the service of Rome. The latter induces 'the inhabitants of the earth' (a term that corresponds to the *kosmos* of the Fourth Gospel and the Johannine Epistles : the unbelieving world) to worship the beast and to bear its mark. The number of the beast (13 : 18) stands for its name which can be discovered by the process of gematria (that is, by addition of the numerical value of the letters of his name—in Hebrew and Greek, in place of numerals, the letters of the alphabet have a numerical value). In Hebrew Nero Caesar (*nrwn qsr*) gives 666; the identification is probable, but not certain.

In deliberate and striking antithesis to the beast and his followers stand the Lamb and his companions, bearing on their foreheads the name of the Lamb and of his Father (14 : 1-5). The 144,000 are not those of 7 : 4-8, the remnant of Israel; they are instead the faithful remnant of the new Israel—the martyrs. The designation 'virgins' must be understood in a metaphorical sense. The OT prophets, especially Hosea, Jeremiah and Ezekiel, frequently represented the covenant of Sinai as a marriage of God with his people; therefore, all idolatry was regarded as adultery or fornication. In the Apocalypse the 144,000 are contrasted with the followers of the beast precisely because they have not adored the beast but have remained faithful to the Lamb. They have remained virgins because they have not given themselves to the cult of the beast but have clung to God.[22]

Satan, the two beasts and their followers the 'inhabitants of the earth', the woman and her children, the Lamb and his companions—the dramatis personae of the great eschatological struggle—have been introduced. Now comes the proclamation of the hour of judgment (14 : 6-13) followed by the harvest and vintage of the earth (14 : 14-20). The whole passage is proleptic; it anticipates events yet to come and summarizes the coming judgments.

The seven plagues *which are the last* (15 : 1)—and hence distinct from the plagues of the trumpets—are announced in chapter 15; the following chapter shows their execution. The bowls (like the trumpets) are based on the plagues of Egypt, but this time the chastisement is universal and definitive: all the worshippers of the beast and the persecutors of Christians are stricken. Moreover, they are already gathered at Armageddon ('the mountain of Megiddo': ever since the defeat of Josiah at Meggido, 2 Kg. 23; 29f., it had remained a symbol of disaster) to await their destruction (19 : 17-21).

Although in 16 : 19—'The great city was split into three parts' —the fall of Rome is indicated, the end of that city cannot be treated so casually. The whole of chapter 17 is given over to a description of Babylon—the goddess Rome—seated on the satanic beast; the fall of Rome is solemnly proclaimed in 18 : 1-8. Then follows a series of dirges (19 : 9-24) and a triumphal liturgy in heaven (19 : 1-10). After the fall of Rome, the end comes swiftly. The rider on the white horse leads out the armies of heaven (19 : 11-16) against the two beasts and their followers. Victory is complete: the two beasts are cast into the 'lake of fire'—the place of final punishment—and their followers are slain with the sword (19 : 17-21). Now Satan alone is left.

In 20 : 1-10 we find that two events are juxtaposed: on the one hand is the overthrow of Satan, in two phases; on the other hand there is the reign of a thousand years. Chapter 7 of Daniel

[22] M.-E. Boismard, 'Notes sur L'Apocalypse', *Revue Biblique,* 59 (1952), 161-72.

furnishes the background of the vision. The first condemnation of the dragon coincides with the moment of judgment when dominion is given to the Son of Man (Dn. 7: 9-14); henceforth the power is taken from the beast and belongs to the saints of the Most High. Thus, in the Apocalypse, while Christ and his faithful reign, the devil will remain powerless in their regard, imprisoned in the abyss, his 'place'. The binding of Satan for a thousand years also coincides with his downfall described in the parallel passage Ap. 12: 7-12—Satan, the 'accuser of our brethren', is cast out of heaven by the victory of Christ; he can no longer accuse or harm the faithful ones who are in heaven with Christ.

John has made use of the Jewish tradition of a temporary messianic reign (his 'thousand years') to symbolize the truth that the martyrs already reign with Christ. The thousand years, then, is a symbol—it has no time value. It must be interpreted as a symbol, and the reality which it typifies must be sought out. The reign of a thousand years signifies the reign of the martyrs with Christ, who has won the final victory for them. Satan is bound for a thousand years: he cannot touch the martyrs, those who have 'conquered him by the blood of the Lamb' (12: 11). If he is represented as being set loose at the end of the thousand years, this is due to the literary construction of the passage and to the image employed; and he is loosed not to take effective action against the elect, but to hasten his own doom. The conquest of all the powers hostile to God is followed by the general resurrection of the dead and the last judgment (20: 11-15). With the conquest of Satan, 'the prince of this world' (Jn 12: 31), the present world order has come to an end.

PART III.   THE NEW JERUSALEM (21: 1—22: 5)

The central part of the Apocalypse ends with the vision of a new heaven and a new earth, the setting of the new Jerusalem. The apocalyptic drama nears its end. The former creation has passed away and all evil has been destroyed; now is the final phase of God's plan. The book closes with a magnificent vision of the new

Jerusalem, the heavenly city, the veritable kingdom of God. Certain details in Ap. 21 : 24-27, which seem rather to refer to the historical stage of the church (and not to the heavenly Jerusalem), may be explained, in their present context, by the fact that the author is echoing traditional concepts and imagery. One of the seven angels of the bowl had shown John the great harlot (17 : 1); one of the seven now steps forward to show him the bride. The bride image, however, is not developed but yields to that of the holy city. We might expect the glowing description of the city (21 : 16-21) to be followed by a particularly striking description of its temple (the Temple was the glory of the earthly Jerusalem). Instead—a brilliant touch—we learn that there is no temple, nor any need of one : God himself dwells there, and the Lamb (21 : 22). Consistently, the waters which in Ezek. 47 flow from the temple, here flow from 'the throne of God and of the Lamb' (22 : 1). It is the river of the first paradise, and the tree of life is found again (22 : 2). There, the elect shall look upon the face of God and of the Lamb and shall reign for ever and ever.

Like the Fourth Gospel and 1 John, this book also closes with an appendix or epilogue (22 : 6-21), which gives the last words of the angel, the seer, and the Lord. John ends his work with the prayer of the early Christians : *Marana tha* ('Our Lord, come !') and a final blessing on the saints, the faithful of Christ.

VII. DOCTRINE

GOD

The God of the Apocalypse, a figure of majesty and power, is presented throughout under OT titles and in OT images and language. God is he 'who is and who was and who is to come' (1 : 4, 8; 4 : 8), a current Jewish paraphrase of the divine name of Ex 3 : 14—'I am who I am'. He is 'the alpha and the omega' (1 : 8): the first and the last, the beginning and the end (21 : 6, 22 : 13) of Is. 44 : 6; 48 : 12. He is *Pantokratōr* ('Almighty') (1 : 8; 4 : 8, etc.), a regular LXX rendering of *Yahweh Sebaoth*, 'Lord of hosts'. He is the Lord God of Ezekiel (Ap. 1 : 8; 22 : 5) and the God of heaven of Daniel (11 : 13; 16 : 11). He is the mighty one (18 : 8), the holy one (15 : 4; 16 : 5), the one 'who lives for ever and ever' (4 : 9f.; 10 : 6; 15 : 7), the sovereign Lord (6 : 10; 11 : 4, 14), the king of the nations (15 : 3)—all of them OT titles. He is the creator of all things (4 : 11; 10 : 6), the judge of mankind (14 : 7; 15 : 4), the vindicator of innocent blood (6 : 10; 19 : 2).

The throne of God in heaven figures frequently in the OT; John's vision in Ap. 4 is dominated by this symbol of divine sovereignty. It is the 'great white throne' from which the judge speaks his final word of judgment (20 : 1f.). John does not venture to describe the invisible God; as in Ezekiel, the 'one seated on the throne' is present in dazzling light, a brightness which at once shows and hides his presence (4 : 2f.). Before him, the four living creatures, symbolizing the created world, sing the 'Holy, holy, holy' of Isaiah (Ap. 4 : 8). In keeping with the portrait of the majestic judge are the frequent references to his wrath, his judgment on a hostile world (cf. 14 : 10, 19; 15 : 1, etc.). The absolute power of God over the universe guarantees the message of hope which John passes on to his Christians.

But John is consistent in his presentation of God in OT colours; for Yahweh is a God of mercy and of loving-kindness. God will wipe away every tear from the eyes of his faithful (Ap. 7 : 17; 21 : 4); he will shelter them with his presence (7 : 15; 21 : 3); he will give them to drink, freely, of the water of life (21 : 6); he has invited them to the marriage supper of the Lamb (19 : 7-9). After all, they are his children and his heirs (21 : 7). If, in his stand against the divine honours paid to the emperors, John has emphasized the transcendence of God, yet, like the OT itself, he has not overlooked God's tenderness.

JESUS CHRIST

The Apocalypse is a Christian book and in it christology finds a central place. The book itself is a revelation of Jesus Christ, a revelation which he has received from the Father and has communicated to his prophet; he is the faithful witness who has borne testimony, unto the cross, to the truth of his message (1 : 1f.). He is the risen Lord, the ruler of kings, sovereign master of all (1 : 5). But, to his own, he is the one who loves them; he is the one who has redeemed them by his blood and has made them a royal house of priests (1 : 5f.). Divine glory and dominion are his by right (1 : 6). He will come as judge at the end of time (1 : 7). The glorious Son of Man of 1 : 13-18 appears among the golden lampstands, symbols of the churches; he does not stand aloof but is in their midst, regulating their affairs. By his death and resurrection, he is master of death and of the abode of death; he is the first and the last (1 : 8). Yet, he remains the Jesus of the gospel, and John hears again the comforting 'Fear not' (1 : 17).

Jesus has an intimate concern for the Christian communities, and he comes to them in discipline or with words of encouraging approval. He can threaten that Ephesus may lose its rank of religious capital (2 : 5). If the Christians of Pergamum fail to repent, he will smite them with the sharp sword of his mouth (2 : 16). The church of Thyatira will know that he is the one who searches mind and heart and that his recompense is just (2 : 23). And while he will not fail to punish those who lead others astray, he has no added burden for his faithful ones (2 : 24). To the lethargic Christians of Sardis he will come like a thief at the hour they least expect (3 : 3). Later, the voice of Jesus will be heard again, calling his disciples to watchfulness; he comes 'like a thief' because the hour of his coming and its manner in the events of history are hidden from them (16 : 15). The Jewish opposition of Philadelphia will be brought to acknowledge that he loves that little church (3 : 9); he will keep his children safe from the great tribulation and will reward them with his presence (3 : 10f.). On the other hand, he will spew the lukewarm Laodiceans out of his mouth (3 : 16). Yet (how like the gospels!) his concern for their sorry state moves him to assure them as to the motivation of his severe rebuke : reproof and chastisement are evidence of his love; he yearns to win them to him (3 : 19). Indeed, he will come to each Christian and seeks an entry into his heart; the true disciple will hear the voice of his friend, and the friend will enter by the open door (3 : 20).

In Ap. 12, the 'male child' of the woman is the Messiah; his 'birth' is his birth on Calvary and his being 'caught up to the throne of God' is his victory over Satan won by his death and glorification (12 : 5). The victory of Michael is the symbolic counterpart of the real victory of the cross (12 : 11). That is why the 'lion of the tribe of Juda, the root of David', the son of David who has conquered, has the right to open the sealed scroll (5 : 5). For all that, the lion of Judah is a Lamb—the Lamb who had been slain and had risen again, but a Lamb who possesses the fulness of power and the sevenfold spirit (5 : 6). He receives the worship of the whole heavenly court, because he has ransomed men for God from all nations and made them a royal priesthood (5 : 8-14).

The Son of Man is judge. It is thus that he appears, seated on a white cloud with the sharp sickle of judgment in his hand, to reap the harvest of the earth (14 : 14-16). The 'kings of the earth' fear his wrath, his judgment on a hostile world (6 : 16). As rider on the white horse he is the Word of God, the 'stern warrior' of Wis. 18 : 15. Faithful and true, he carries out righteous judgment on the intransigent enemies of God. His is a royalty beyond any earthly sovereignty—he is king of kings and Lord of Lords; and he is accompanied by the army of martyrs who wear the robes washed white in his blood. This portrait of the divine warrior appearing in sovereign power is meant to encourage John's readers, to assure them that their Lord has overcome the world (1 : 11-16).

Beyond the judgment, the new age of the kingdom of God is the joy of the marriage supper of the Lamb (19 : 7-9; 21 : 2, 9). The new Jerusalem has no temple—because it is the dwelling of God and the Lamb. And the Lamb will be the lamp of the city, giving it light by night (21 : 22f.). The gift promised to the thirsty, the water of life, will flow in abundance from the throne of God and Lamb (22 : 1). In the epilogue, Christ, first through his angel (22 : 6f.) and then directly (22 : 16, 20), authenticates the words of the prophecy of this book. Root and branch, he is the beginning and the end of the whole messianic economy (22 : 16). He explicitly claims the titles of the Father (22 : 13). Three times he gives his assurance that he is coming soon (22 : 7, 12, 20). He comes, bringing his reward with him : he himself is the 'bright morning star' who gives himself in recompense (3 : 28 : 22 : 16). The thirsty are invited to come to him and drink, freely (22 : 17).

A special factor is the relation of the glorified Christ to God. He shows the prerogatives of God. He searches the mind and heart of man (2 : 23). With the Father he gives grace and peace (1 : 4) and receives the adoration of creatures (5 : 13). The priests of God are his priests (20 : 6). He occupies one throne with God (22 : 1, 3) and shares his sovereignty (11 : 15). Christ receives the titles of God : he is the living one (1 : 18), holy and true (3 : 7), alpha and omega, the first and the last, the beginning and the end (22 : 13). In short, 'who is and was' is the one title not given to the Son. Several OT passages relating to God are spontaneously applied to Christ, e.g. Ap. 1 : 14 = Dn. 7 : 9; Ap. 3 : 19 = Pr. 3 : 12; Ap. 5 : 6 = Zech. 4 : 10; Ap. 17 : 14 = Dt. 10 : 17. Thus, John seems to assimilate Christ to, or identify him with, God. Yet Christ is nowhere called 'God'—he is Son of God (2 : 18) and Word of God (19 : 13), and he can call God his God (3 : 12).

Thus, with Paul, our author has seen 'the revelation of the glory of God in the face of Jesus Christ' (2 Cor. 4 : 6), and with John he has known that whoever has seen the Son has seen the Father (cf. Jn 14 : 9). But he has his own approach and makes his own contribution to christology, as Swete so justly observes :

> The John of the Apocalypse is less of the theologian than St Paul, and less of the mystic than the author of the Fourth Gospel, but he surpasses both in his revelation of the unbounded power of the exalted Christ. Nowhere else in the New Testament are the personal activities of Jesus Christ present in his Church, the glories of his heavenly life, or the possibilities of his future manifestation so magnificently set forth. The Christology of the Apocalypse may evade analysis, but it meets the needs of the Church in times of storm and stress. It is the New Testament counterpart of the Old Testament hymns of anticipated triumph : 'God is our refuge and strength, a very present help in trouble; therefore will we not fear. . . . God is

in the midst of her; she shall not be moved.' However the fact may be explained, Christ is in the Apocalypse the power of God and the wisdom of God present with the Church, while in his exalted life he is in the midst of the Throne.[23]

THE HOLY SPIRIT

The Spirit does not figure prominently in the Apocalypse, but is by no means absent from the book. In the trinitarian text of 1 : 4 the 'seven spirits before the throne' represent the sevenfold Spirit, the fulness of Spirit (cf. 3 : 1); with the Father and Son he is the giver of grace and peace. In view of the underlying Zech. 4: 2, 10, the 'seven torches of fire' before the heavenly throne are, again, the sevenfold Spirit (Ap. 4 : 5). The seven eyes of the Lamb are 'the seven spirits of God sent out into all the earth' (5 : 6; cf. Zech. 4 : 10): Jesus, as glorified Lord, bestows the Spirit. This is the Spirit who exhorts the churches in the name of Christ (Ap. 2 : 7, etc.), who makes his words known and understood. And, in 22 : 17, the Spirit inspires the church to respond to the Lord's announcement of his coming. Finally, the river of the water of life flowing from the throne of the Lamb (22 : 1) has a parallel in Jn 7 : 38f., where the living water, flowing from Christ, is the Spirit (cf. Ap. 21 : 6).

THE CHURCH

John's work is addressed to 'the seven churches that are in Asia' (1 : 4). The number seven is symbolic and signifies totality : his message is addressed to all the churches of Asia and, indeed, to the church at large. The church is the centre of interest of the book. As the kingdom of God and of Christ and as a priestly people (1 : 6) it is already present on earth but will be definitively established after the destruction of all the forces of evil. The opening chapters of the Apocalypse are intimately concerned with the communities known to the seer, the Christians of Asia for whom he writes; after that he goes on to consider the church and Israel and the church and Rome. But always, for him, the church

[23] *Op cit.,* clxiii f.

means Christians, those loved by Christ who has redeemed them by his blood (1 : 5f.).

The Son of Man who walks among the lampstands, the churches, and who holds in his hand the stars, the angel guardians or representatives of the churches (1 : 12-20), is one who has the good of his disciples very much at heart. His messages to the communities tell us much of Christian life in Asia towards the end of the first century. The church of Ephesus had patiently endured for Christ, had preserved orthodoxy—but at the cost of waning charity (2 : 2-4). The Christians of Smyrna, beset by trials, have yet much to suffer. In a wealthy city, they were materially poor, but possessed spiritual riches (2 : 9f.). While the church at Pergamum had withstood attacks from without, it had dealt less effectively with false doctrine within itself (2 : 13-15). In Thyatira *agapē* came first in the list of 'works' and the fervour of this church had continued to grow. Its one fault was that it tolerated the presence of a false 'prophetess' (22 : 19-22). The Christians of Sardis (or most of them) were either spiritually dead or lay in spiritual torpor—hence, Christian life was half-hearted (3 : 1f.). Though the church of Philadelphia had little power, little influence, it had learned that the Lord works through human weakness. It will become a centre for the spread of the gospel and will enjoy the special protection of Christ (3 : 8-10). The church of Laodicea is the church of an affluent society; the material prosperity of the city is reflected in the attitude of the church which believes itself rich in spiritual possessions and in want of nothing, yet, all the while, it is 'poor, blind, and naked'; it is in a state of lukewarm indifference. Christ alone can give true wealth (3 : 15-18). All of these churches are real communities, of men and women like ourselves, living, more or less generously, the Christian life.

In Ap. 12 the woman clothed with the sum symbolizes the people of God of the OT which, having given Christ to the world, thereby became the Christian church. She found refuge from the dragon's assault in the desert where she is cared for by God for all the time of her earthly duration (12 : 5f., 14). The dragon's attempt to destroy the woman is described in 12 : 13-16;

and though the church is under God's special care, the children of the woman, on earth, can feel the brunt of his spite. Satan, through his instruments, can make war on them; they will be persecuted and put to death (12: 17). The beast is the Roman Empire, tool of Satan in his warfare against the seed of the woman (13: 7); a warfare which will entail suffering without resistance, calling forth the faith and patient endurance of Christians (13: 9f.). From another aspect, the two witnesses of 11: 3-13 are the incarnation of the testimony borne to Christ by the Church in the presence of the Jewish world.

Jerusalem was an accepted figure of the people of God, a tangible sign of the covenant. To present a new Jerusalem was, in the concrete language of imagery, to proclaim the election of a new people, of a new covenant. 'Coming down out of heaven from God', it is a city of heavenly origin, a city 'prepared as a bride' (21: 2). It reflects the divine glory; it is God's dwelling-place, his presence among his people (21: 3, 10f.). In it sorrow and pain will have no place (2: 3f.) because God has brought to an end all that made up a world of sin. All the elect of God, the faithful witnesses of Christ, are sons and heirs of God (21: 7). The twelve gates of this city of the future bear the names of the twelve tribes, and the names of the twelve apostles are engraved on its foundations: it is the old Israel and the new (21: 12-14). It has no temple: God himself dwells there, and the Lamb—the glory of their presence pervades the whole of it (21: 23). In the new city all men will joyfully serve the one God; they will celebrate an unending Feast of Tabernacles, walking in the light of God by day and of the Lamb by night. There is found the very spring of the waters of life, the waters promised to the thirsty; and the tree of life grows in this new paradise. No one who is an object of God's displeasure will find a place in the City (22: 1-3). The Israelites had gone on pilgrimage to the temple to adore and 'to behold the face of God', but they had beheld him only in wish. Now, in a new age, this desire is satisfied: worshipping him, looking upon his face, basking in the light of his glory, the servants of God shall reign for ever and ever (22: 4f.).

John's message is addressed to the faithful on earth. And so, in the epilogue, the Spirit inspires the churches to respond with eager joy to the Lord's announcement of his coming; and he looks for the response, not only of the church as such, but of the individual Christian (22 : 17). So, too, it is that the saints rejoice because the marriage of the Lamb has come (19 : 7f.). And those who form the bride of Christ have been 'redeemed by the blood of the Lamb' (5 : 9; 7 : 14; 14 :3f.); her wedding dress is the sanctity of God's people. She will appear, glorious and without blemish, 'as a bride adorned for her husband' (21 :2). But before she can come to that she has to be purified by him, cleansed of every stain : it is still the time of purification. And the church is no vague personification, it is a living organism, made up of men and women, of beings who are not only human but fallen. The church on earth, though animated by the life of Christ, is still the church of sinners. That is why there is need of the repeated admonition : 'He who has an ear, let him hear what the Spirit says to the churches.'

It is this awareness of the earthly dimensions of the church, over against its other-worldly destiny, that saves the Apocalypse from any hint of triumphalism. John's purpose is to support and encourage ordinary men and women who find themselves pitted against forces that seek relentlessly to crush them. They may be called upon to face death; but we may be sure that there was no glamour in their daily resistance to pressure exerted by an authority that may well have been rigid and unsympathetic rather than wantonly cruel. That is why they are called upon, again and again, to exercise *hypomonē* ('patient endurance'), the characteristic virtue of the persecuted which is founded on faith in Christ, on the certainty of his love. There can be no mistaking the harsh reality : 'If any one is to be taken captive, to captivity he goes; if any one slays with the sword, with the sword must he be slain. Here is a call for the endurance and faith of the saints' (13 : 10). These Christians were called upon to suffer patiently, to endure; who will say that the same message is not addressed to countless Christians of our time? The Apocalypse holds out no prospect of peace and triumph for the church (before the end);

the two beasts, instruments of Satan, will carry on their warfare to the last. And all the while, the letters to the seven churches, with their candid pilloring of shortcomings and abuses, show that John has no illusions about the human frailty of those who make up the church. His is that authentic vision of the church so clearly stated in our day by the Fathers of Vatican II: 'Christ completed the work of redemption in poverty and under persecution. In the same way, the church is called to tread the same path . . . with sinners clasped to her bosom, she is at once holy and in constant need of cleansing.'[24]

THE MARTYRS

John wrote to encourage his Christians of Asia in the face of tribulation and persecution, and to prepare and strengthen them for worse times to come. He was only too well aware that the warfare of the dragon could lead to bloodshed, that patient endurance would well be unto death. And so he is concerned to show that the martyrs, the faithful witnesses and victims of the dragon's vengeful wrath, are the privileged ones. But while he does have in mind those who lay down their lives for Christ, yet, all those who die in the Lord, who remain faithful to the Lamb, share in their privilege and blessedness; for the martyrs are the first fruits of the redeemed.

Each of the letters to the churches closes with a promise of reward to the conqueror, the one 'who keeps my words until the end' (2: 26). His reward is immortality ('the tree of life') in the new Jerusalem (2: 7). He has nothing to fear from 'the second death'—the lake of fire, final punishment (2: 11). The 'hidden manna' of the latter days will be his, as well as the divine favour which means participation in the life of the risen Christ (2: 17). The Son, who has received power from the Father, imparts that power to the conqueror who has shared his victory over the enemies of God; and he will give him the 'morning star' which is himself (2: 26-28). Likewise, he will receive the white garment of victory and joy, and his name will

[24] Vatican II, *Dogmatic Constitution on the Church*, I, 8.

not be blotted out of the Lamb's book of life; the Lord will acknowledge him before his Father (3 : 5). He will have a permanent and prominent place in the new Temple of God; he is marked as the property of God and as a citizen of the heavenly city (3 : 21). Their shared victory will permit him to sit on the Lamb's throne (3 : 21).

In the Apocalypse proper the martyrs appear at the breaking of the fifth seal—the martyrs of the OT who, underneath the heavenly altar, are safely in the presence of God (6 : 9-11). The Christian martyrs emerge in 7 : 9-17, a countless multitude from all nations, the 'fellow servants and brethren' of the OT martyrs. They stand before God and the Lamb, clothed in white robes of victory, celebrating a heavenly Feast of Tabernacles. In their priestley role (1 : 6) they serve God, adding their unceasing service to the prayer of creation (7 : 15; cf. 4 : 8). They are those who rejoice in a heaven free from Satan, having conquered him by the blood of the Lamb (12 : 9-12). The hundred and forty-four thousand companions of the Lamb are 'first fruits' of the harvest of God and Lamb—a fitting description of the martyrs (14 : 1-5). They have entered upon the fulness of rest promised by Jesus; that is the solemn affirmation of 14 : 13—'Blessed are the dead who die in the Lord! Henceforth, says the Spirit, they can rest for ever from their labours.' Beside the heavenly Red Sea stand the conquerors, celebrating a joyous liturgy, a new deliverance, victory over the beast (15 : 2-4). 'Called and chosen and faithful' (17 : 14), the martyrs are privileged guests at the marriage supper of the Lamb (19 : 9). As companions of the Lamb wherever he goes (14 : 4), they are the victorious army of the rider on the white horse (19 : 14). They alone have part in the 'first resurrection' and reign with Christ for a thousand years (20 : 4-6). They are safe beyond the reach of Satan (20 : 1-3); the 'second death' has no terror for them, and the royal priesthood of Christians is theirs in a special measure. Yet, it is fitting that the last beatitude of the book (22 : 14), addressed to those who wash their robes 'in the blood of the Lamb' (7 : 14), reaches out beyond the martyrs. John has written for all Christians—though, in the first place, Christians who must pass through the 'great tribulation' and who have need of patient endurance.

John, in his prologue, presents his writing as a letter to be read in the churches (1 : 3) and, throughout, his liturgical interest is manifest. We shall see that he was, to some extent, influenced by the Exodus ceremonial; and the Targums, the synagogal para-phrases, were familiar to him. Most obviously of all, the many hymns of his book, though attributed to heavenly choirs, reflect the hymnal tradition of the first-century church.

The seer, transported to heaven, hears the four living creatures, symbols of the created cosmos, sing the canticle of the seraphim of Is. 6 :3—it is the unceasing song of nature in praise of the Creator (4 : 8). The twenty-four elders, the saints of the OT, join in the worship of God; they ascribe glory and honour and power to their Lord and God the Creator (4 : 10f.). In 5 : 8f. the living creatures and the elders acknowledge the divinity of the Lamb and exercise the office of mediation. Then they sing a new song to celebrate the redemption wrought by Christ. A new feature is the praise of the countless host of angels (5 : 11f.). Finally, the whole of creation, without any exception, joins in the great canticle of praise (5 : 13) to which the living creatures give their 'Amen' (5 : 14).

The sound of the seventh trumpet is answered by loud voices of praise in heaven, the praise of the living creatures and of the angelic choirs (11 : 15). The canticle of 11 : 17f., put in the mouths of the twenty-four elders, is thoroughly Jewish in its sentiments and expression; the elders thank God who has at last manifested his great power—the kingdom of God has come. A heavenly hymn (12 : 10-12) celebrates the downfall of Satan and the triumph of the martyrs, achieved through the blood of the Lamb. In 14 : 2f. we have, again, a liturgy in heaven; but, this time, the words of the hymn are not given : only the 144,000 companions of the Lamb can know this 'new song'. The song of the martyrs who stand beside the heavenly sea recalls Israel's song of triumph over Egypt on the shore of the

Red Sea (15 : 3f.; cf. Ex. 15). But, unlike the song of Exodus, the martyrs' song is not one of triumph over their enemies—while it does praise God for their victory. The words of an angel (Ap. 16 : 5f.) form a sort of antiphon to the canticle of 15 : 3f.— they illustrate the divine righteousness and holiness proclaimed in the canticle. And the martyrs add their 'Amen' (16 : 7). In 19 : 1-3 the mighty voice of the angel host resounds. Hallelujah ('Praise Yahweh'), used in synagogue worship, early figured in Christian liturgy; in the NT it occurs only in the Apocalypse. To this canticle of the angels, living creatures and elders say 'Amen' (19 : 4). The hymn of praise (19 : 6-8), sung by the great multitude of martyrs, swells like the roar of waters or like mighty thunder-peals. They rejoice that their repeated prayer —'Thy kingdom come'—has been answered : the Lord reigns. It is a song of rejoicing and exultation because the marriage of the Lamb is at hand. At last, in the new Jerusalem, before the throne of God and the Lamb, the servants of God shall worship and shall reign as priests for ever (22 : 3-5). It is the worship 'in spirit and truth' (Jn. 4 : 23).

In conclusion, we should note that the closing words of the epilogue have an unmistakable liturgical ring. The 'Come' addressed to Christ in vv. 17, 20 is the *Marana tha* of the liturgy, an invocation which had its place in the celebration of the eucharist. And the hearer (v. 17) is invited to communion with Christ. Thus, a book destined to be read in the church services (1 : 3) ends on a fitting note.

ESCHATOLOGY[25]

The eschatological interest of the Apocalypse is manifest; after all, the book is an apocalypse and hence this interest is to be expected. It is true, of course, that the promises which close the seven letters (2 : 7, 11, 17, 26f.; 3 : 5, 12, 20f.) look not to the parousia but to heavenly blessedness after death. The same interest is present in the care to portray the immediate happi-

[25] A. Feuillet, 'Parousie', *Dictionnaire de la Bible (Supplément)* VI, 1397-1403.

ness of the martyrs. However, elsewhere, the Apocalypse consistently looks to the future.

God has promised men a new world in which he will 'wipe away every tear from their eyes', a world from which all evil, even death itself, will have vanished. That will be the time of the new marriage, the new dwelling of God with his people, all of whom are now purified and holy (21 : 1-8). In view of the establishment of this perfect eschatological kingdom, the dead will rise and will be judged according to their works (20 : 11-15). But, before these events, there will be a general offensive of the pagan nations against the church (19 : 17-21; 20 : 7-10); the enemies of God, including Satan himself, will be utterly vanquished. It seems, too, that the final events will have been preceded by the salvation of Israel (11 : 14-18; cf. Rom. 11 : 25f.).

However, we must not give too much weight to the material details of these predictions. Thus, we find that the plagues of the Apocalypse dramatize the traditional characteristics of the 'day of Yahweh' of the prophets, the day of divine judgment. The prophets habitually associated the whole of creation with the great divine interventions in human history; and the description of cosmic phenomena, in this context, became stylized. The first discourse of Peter in Acts provides an excellent example of how this imagery was understood. In reference to the outpouring of the Spirit and the gift of tongues he quotes Joel: 'And in the last days it shall be, God declares, that I will pour out my Spirit upon all flesh . . . I will pour out my Spirit; and they shall prophesy. And I will show wonders in the heaven above and signs on the earth beneath, blood, and fire, and vapour of smoke; the sun shall be turned into darkness and the moon into blood' (Ac. 2 : 17-20; cf. Jl 2 : 28-32). There is no suggestion that these cosmic signs really took place on the day of Pentecost; Peter interprets them in a purely symbolic manner as images of this marvellous divine intervention, the gift of the Spirit to humanity.[26] So, too, the same may be said of Ap.

[26] M.-E. Boismard in Robert-Feuillet, *Introduction à la Bible, op. cit.*, II, 730.

6 : 12-17—it is an imaginative, traditional expression of a divine intervention in history: God's judgment on an Israel guilty of rejecting the Messiah.

The Apocalypse emphatically assures us that history does move to a climax. More than that, the Lamb who was slain has won his victory; the fierce assaults of Satan are the desperate paroxysm of one mortally wounded. The final issue is not in doubt. For Christians the problem is not the fact of ultimate victory but the explanation of the delay of the parousia. Christ has overcome the world—and yet the world goes its way, the implacable enemy of the church of Christ. How can this be, and when will the end come? The Apocalypse does face the problem and does, it seems, answer it.

The solution may be found in chapter 10. We find ourselves very near the end: the coming of the lion of Judah, the root of David (5 : 5), and the divine judgments (plagues of seals and trumpets) which have struck the unbelieving Jews—these events have led humanity almost to the end of its course; the 'mystery of God' (10 : 7), his plan for the world, is about to be realized. The new people of God has taken the place of the old, and nothing remains but the sounding of the seventh trumpet-call. In other words, the appearance of Christ on the stage of history has given a fresh impetus to the plan of salvation. All that is left now is the consummation of that plan by the resurrection of the dead and the judgment of the nations (11 : 15-19).

We seem to have reached the term of human history, and the author of the Apocalypse does not seek to attenuate that feeling of the nearness of the end which earlier Christians had felt (cf. 1 : 3, 7; 3 : 11; 22 : 10, 12, 20). His prologue assures his readers—those who hear the words of the prophecy, the revelation of Jesus Christ—that 'the time is near'. And so it is that, with Dn. 12 : 7-9 in view, he can consciously change the perspective. There the angel swore that, before the things of the end would come to pass, there was yet to be 'a time, two times, and half a time' (Dn. 12 : 7); here, he declares that 'there should be no more delay' (Ap. 10 : 6). This brings out the difference between the two economies, the old and the new. Christians

live in the age of fulfilment; now is 'the last hour' (1 Jn 2 : 18).
Yet, the consummation is to come, and John is ordered to 'seal
up' the revelations of the seven thunders (Ap. 10 : 4). Similarly,
he assimilates the decrees of the little scroll and receives a new
prophetic investiture, a mission to all nations (10 : 8-11).

The purpose of Ap. 10, and one of the principal aims of the
book, is to stress the importance of the period in which the gospel
is preached to the nations (cf. 'the time of the gentiles' of Luke)
and at the same time to underline that paradox which charac-
terizes it. The time of the church is set between the sixth and
seventh trumpets (or between the sixth and seventh seals)—the
end is near. However, the coming of the end may be delayed
for an unspecified time, which may be very long. In fact, all the
events of 13 : 1-20 : 15 must come to pass before that end.

This paradox of an end near at hand and yet chronologically distant, which the author of the Apocalypse has under-
scored more heavily than any of his predecessors, obliges us
to see in the traditional theme of the nearness of the end
something quite other than a question of date. Of course, in
putting forward this view, John is not proposing a doctrine
altogether new, but he has thrown a revealing light on the
most obscure part of the New Testament message.[27]

It seems that Ap. 4-11 is a commentary on the synoptic
apocalypse, and John has seen more clearly than the other NT
writers that there is a real distinction between the end of Jerusalem and the end of the world. He understands that, when
Jesus declares that the glorious coming of the Son of Man is near
at hand, he is not indicating a date, but offering a truth of
faith. Because Christ has come and by his resurrection—the
first-fruits of those who rise—has introduced the new era of a
new life, the Lord is henceforth near, even though his parousia
may be delayed. John—writing at the close of the first century
—had no intention of reviving the naïve expectation of an
imminent parousia. His purpose was to convince his persecuted
brethren that their Christ, risen and glorious, was absolute mas-

[27] A. Feuillet, 'Parousie', *op. cit.*, 1402.

C

ter of human history; that his victory was complete and that he would come to usher in the new world.

A great multitude in heaven of all tribes and peoples and tongues, waving victorious palm greens as living boughs of hope against their white robes, cries out exultantly, 'Salvation belongs to our God who sits upon the throne, and to the Lamb' (Ap. 7 : 10). 'Salvation' : the very word must have rung wondrous awe into the ears of the Christians who were facing such peril and persecution during the first century of the church that only their faith could see what it meant to be saved. And these men and women must have hardly dared to believe such a visionary as John, who promised that their Lord himself would intervene in the desperate conditions under which he had called them to live and who anticipated the blessedness of those 'who have come out of the great tribulation' (7 : 14).

But what of those who had yet to pass through it? Although the Apocalypse was written to increase the faith and courage of the 'seven churches', the whole Christian community, would not each individual have had to translate the vision or revelation opened to him into terms of the small challenges he faced each day in his personal life as a follower of Jesus? It is to the churches that the Spirit speaks, but 'he who has an ear, let him hear . . .' (2 : 11). The 'revelation of Jesus Christ' (1 : 1) finds its immediate relevance then and now in the hearts of persons whom Jesus himself chooses as faithful witnesses and to whom he can always speak independently of even the words he has inspired other men to speak and to write. The Apocalypse of John finds its meaning in the lives of those who, like the author himself, find that following their Lord—the Christ who *has* won salvation—is a way of contradiction which pierces their inmost thoughts, even as it heals them with peace. 'Behold, this child is set for the fall and rising of many in Israel, and for a sign that is spoken against . . . that thoughts out of many hearts may be revealed' (Lk. 2 : 34).

For what is the Apocalypse but the revealing of Jesus in John's heart—in a way as unique for John as it is for each of us? 'I, John, who share with you in Jesus the tribulation and the kingdom and the patient endurance, was on the island called Patmos . . .' (Ap. 1 : 9): all Christians are his brethren, all are invited to know Christ 'and the power of his resurrection' and to 'share his sufferings' (Phil. 3 : 10); all have particular circumstances of time and place in their lives in which they must, in all conscience, take a definite stand and make definite choices 'on account of the word of God and the testimony of Jesus' (1 : 9). Although the external consequences of being a disciple of Jesus may differ, and although there are various degrees and manifestations of 'martyrdom', yet essentially each disciple— with his own needs, hopes, and vision of the 'morning star'—is included in 'the prayers of all the saints' (8 : 3) and knows the meaning of salvation through the Lamb simply because 'those with him are called and chosen and faithful' (17 : 14).

Thus, contrasted with the exultation of the great multitude of conquerors are the soft-spoken and very ordinary words of a man exiled on a rocky island and clothed in the sackcloth of an imprisoned witness to Christ: 'Grace to you and peace. . . .' Yes, perhaps as meaningful for us as the promises to the conqueror echoing throughout the book and culminating in the victor's 'heritage' of a new life and a new Jerusalem where 'I will be his God and he shall be my son' (21 : 7)—as relevant for us as the serenely refreshing assurance, 'I am the alpha and the omega . . . to the thirsty, I will give water without price from the fountain of the water of life' (21 : 6)—is the simple greeting at the beginning of the book, 'Grace to you and peace from him who is and who was and who is to come' (1 : 4). For John does not touch the heart or uplift the faith of the church institution, but of her members and her children. His words are addressed to those whose only 'conquest' so far is their 'steadfast endurance' when they can see no tangible evidence of conquering, those who can hear only in solitude and secrecy the call of their Lord, 'Awake, and strengthen what remains and is on the point of death, for I have not found your words perfect in the sight of my God'

(3 : 2). Grace and peace can abide only in hearts which are alive, pure and undivided (Mt. 5 : 8)—so that their seeing God is their simply seeing and abiding in the love of his Son.

For those who have this grace and peace in their hearts are free to offer childlike praise in the midst of any circumstances 'to him who *loves* us and has freed us' (Ap. 1 : 5). But—and here is the 'sign of contradiction' and the point where the Apocalypse touches us most closely—this is the same Lord who approaches the mediocre Laodiceans, and all of us who know stumbling blocks in trying to live Christian lives, with the 'hard saying', 'those whom I love, I reprove and chasten' (3 : 19).

Perhaps this truth finds a parallel in the apparent paradox following the great battle in chapter 12 when Michael thrusts Satan out of heaven; for although the martyrs 'have conquered him by the blood of the Lamb' (12 : 11) and a loud voice can cry out, 'Rejoice then, O heaven and you that dwell therein', yet this same voice must immediately add, 'But woe to you, O earth and sea, for the devil has come down to you in great wrath, because he knows that his time is short!' (12 : 12). Christ *has* been victorious, *has* overcome, and yet his faithful on earth shall continue to know until the end of time—a period seeming short only to him for whom a thousand years are 'as a watch in the night' (Ps 90 : 4)—the assaults of the dragon, the death throes of a tail which is more venomous and lashing because its doom is sealed. Christians, called to live side by side with beasts and kings of the earth and harlots, answer to this their calling both as members of the church confronting overt issues and as simply little children of God who, having quietly tasted Christ's love, desire but to 'follow the Lamb wherever he goes' (Ap. 14 : 4). They learn in both corporate and individual ways that though 'my yoke is easy and my burden is light' (Mt. 11 : 30), it is indeed a yoke and it is a burden—precisely because it is so simple, so light. And, unable actually to *see* when confronted with naked forces of evil, pain and suffering, Christians can only *believe* that God himself is using even these 'to carry out his purpose . . . until the words of God shall be fulfilled' (Ap. 17 : 17)—

the very pattern of the cross! 'And I, when I am lifted up, will draw all men to myself' (Jn 12 : 32).

Knowing the gentle reproofs of Jesus, the sorrowful remorse when we have forsaken him, and knowing the pain of seemingly invincible evil, we often weep with John, feeling that there is no one 'worthy to open the scroll' (5 : 4), to look into the mystery of God and his purposes for our lives. But also, like John, we have the one assurance we need from 'the lion of the tribe of Judah, the root of David' who 'has conquered, so that he can open the scroll' (5 : 5)—the great assurance, 'I have loved you' (3 : 9). 'He who reads aloud the words of the prophecy' in the Apocalypse, 'those who hear' and 'who keep what is written therein' (1 : 3), are indeed blessed, and the 'time' is indeed near. For the book is simply Christ's own revelation to every Christian that his love is always near at hand, prevailing over any circumstances and leaving no room for fear (1 Jn 4 : 18); it is an eloquent answer, an answer relevant to every Christian's life, to Paul's question, 'who shall separate us from the love of Christ? Shall tribulation, or distress, or persecution, or famine, or nakedness, or peril, or the sword?' (Rom. 8 : 35).

Shall 'peril or sword'? The Apocalypse portrays an angry dragon who, seeing that he had been thrown down from heaven, pursued the woman—the people of God as mother of the Messiah—and went off to 'make war on the rest of her offspring' (Ap. 12 : 17). Whether we see this in terms of the Roman Empire pitted against the unarmed, young Christian church or in terms of politics and society in a world community confronting both the universal church and her every member today, 'peril and sword' arise as part of human imperfection upon an imperfect earth. Now, as then, they strike Christians on account of their calling to 'keep the commandments of God and bear testimony to Jesus' (12 : 17). Whatever the temporal conditions, it is ultimately the struggle between all powers of evil and the goodness of God; it is the 'death throes' of the dragon. John's particular topical references are merely precursors of the opposition the church will always need to face in order for her to grow and to find herself finally free of the divisions caused by striving and involvement with nation, race and worldly power—areas essentially foreign to her. One of the principal messages of the Apocalypse is that Christ, as Lord of history and true king of the earth, has indeed already achieved victory over evil.

The church has not only been borne safely on the eagle's wings of God's deliverance to a wilderness refuge through Christ's saving act on Calvary; she is also being continually nourished there, protected and preserved. The first coming of Christ has already achieved the summit of salvation which prepares for the parousia. It is as if the very starkness of this wilderness strengthened the church and enabled her to learn that her only weapons—faith, hope and love—are enough; as if the desert by its very seclusion were a safe place to tend the white horse bearing our leader, the 'Word of God' who is called 'faithful and true' and who will smite the nations with the sword of this word (19: 11ff.). 'For the Word of God is living and active, sharper than any two-edged sword . . . discerning the thoughts and intentions of the heart' (Heb. 4: 12).

There are many forms of peril and sword endangering the life of each Christian (and perhaps the danger is greater the more interior it is—although a danger such as martyrdom is more violent). Balaams and Jezebels mask various practices of idolatry (Ap. 2: 14, 23); the white and red horses of conquest and bloodshed (6: 2ff.) thunder into every corner of society; and many a self-satisfied pride, worshipping the luxury of success with the paean, 'A queen I sit, I am no widow, mourning I shall never see' (18: 7), as well as the profits of kings and merchants and sailors whose wealth is a parasite of this pride, will have cause to lament: 'Alas! . . . In one hour has thy judgment come' (18: 10). And Armageddon constantly recurs as a loosed Satan marches out to deceive both nations and hearts, to surround the camp of the saints and the beloved city in many a country, home and life (20: 7ff.). Finally, there is even that peril, that temptation to empty, purposeless complacency, which issues in the abandonment of 'the love you had at first' (2: 4).

Yet, the Apocalypse teaches us that already, by the victory of the cross (the only 'victory' a Christian is meant to attain), 'the kingdom of the world has become the kingdom of our Lord and of his Christ, and he shall reign for ever and ever' (11 : 15). There may be earthquakes; but those who look on and perceive through them the sovereign power of God repent of their ways and offer him glory (11 : 13). There may be plagues; but the infinite mercy of God sets his seal upon the foreheads of his own, and thus they remain unharmed (7 : 3)—even though, humanly speaking, they may be conscious more of trial than of the blessedness of election. There may be destruction; but grasses and trees are preserved (9 : 4): the bright green of hope always survives and grows! And the nations may rage; but God will pour down on the earth the seven bowls of his own wrath (16 :)—a wrath which is only such to those who have no ear to hear or eye to see that it is really the gentleness of the Lamb.

In fact, this gentleness is so all-embracing that Christ's victory over the world—his own determination of history—becomes perfectly realized : the outcome of Armageddon was exactly that which had been assumed. Distinctions between earth, sky and sea vanish 'like a scroll that is rolled up' (6 : 14) (and we might say with this that God's words, now once and for ever opened by Jesus, can be rolled up again because the Word himself, the simplicity of love, fulfils them); the leaves of the tree of life *heal* the nations (22 : 2), all of which 'shall come and worship thee, the forces of evil in the 'synagogue of Satan' which rear up about sword' are so powerless against this gentleness—this *love*—that all the forces of evil in the 'synagogue of Satan' which rear up about us and within us will be 'forced' (by the meek and humble hand of Jesus!) to bow down and 'learn that I have loved you' (3 : 9).

Shall 'famine or nakedness' lie between us and the love of Christ? Although many Christians, including those during the time of Paul and John, have known these as all too real physical conditions, 'famine and nakedness' touch us most today in our own spiritual hungers and barrenness (not to mention our longing to help those less fortunate than ourselves). They represent simply a lack, a want—'not a famine of bread, nor a thirst for water, but of hearing the words of the Lord' (Am. 8 : 11)—which only one can fulfil : 'The Lord is my shepherd, I shall not want' (Ps. 23 :

1). They include a thirst which this shepherd alone can slake: 'For the lamb in the midst of the throne will be their shepherd, and he will guide them to springs of living water . . .' (Ap. 7 : 17). This is the 'water of life without price' of the new Jerusalem (22 : 17), the living water of Christ's own blood. And, they imply a hunger and a need for care which only one can provide: 'he who sits upon the throne will shelter them with his presence. They shall hunger no more, neither thirst any more' (7 : 15f.). He is the same who offers his own body to satisfy the longing and need of every Christian for communion with him: 'I will come in to him and eat with him, and he with me' (3 : 20).

Each of us can experience famine and want through mediocrity, not caring or committing ourselves wholly to Jesus, who with firm tenderness cries out, 'You are neither cold nor hot! Would that you were either cold or hot!' (3 : 15). We can experience nakedness when our eyes, blinded by pride and self-deception, are suddenly opened: 'For you say I am rich, I have prospered, I need nothing; not knowing that you are wretched, pitiable, poor, blind and naked' (3 : 17). And we are afflicted by both famine and nakedness when we are 'active', living Christians merely in name (or in that very external 'activity' itself), while within our hearts are dead as stone. In contrast with the fruitful, verdant tree of life, often we feel barren and naked 'as the fig tree sheds its winter fruit when shaken by a gale' (6 : 13); each of us has tasted his own wormwood and bitter waters (8 : 11). And life can often be made empty by the very plenitude and complexity of unneccessary 'demons and idols of gold and silver and bronze and stone and wood, which cannot either see or hear or walk' (9 : 20), when it is in reality so full, and fulfilling, through the simple message of the 'eternal gospel' (14 : 6), the 'good news' that 'the dwelling of God is with men' (21 : 3) and that 'the Word was made flesh' (Jn 1 : 14) to see, hear and walk in our midst. Our peace and contentment beyond all desire lies in remembering and keeping this wonderful news which we have 'received and heard' (Ap. 3 : 3).

The Lord and the Lamb fulfil all the needs of every Christian: this is why we need no other temple in the new Jerusalem, and this is why the only light within the city—and glowing softly in the bride's face—comes from him whose 'face was like the sun shining in full strength' (1 : 16), the Lamb who is himself her lamp (21 : 23). Any kind of famine or nakedness can only draw us closer to Christ, make us lean more completely on his mercy and his love. In fact, his light quietly draws all people and nations to the new city to learn of his love simply because they find that he alone fulfils all desires: 'By its light shall the nations walk, and the kings of the earth shall bring their glory into it' (21 : 24).

Shall persecution separate us from the love of Jesus? The immediate cause of the Christian persecution in the time of John was their refusal to render divine homage to a merely mortal emperor, their refusal to idolize one whose claim to divinity was a crass mockery of their own Lord, the 'ruler of kings on earth' (1 : 5). A person of any era can suffer persecution for the same refusal to compromise or to betray his own creed, even though it may not take the form of physical infliction. For what is persecution but the apparently successful efforts of power and might to control, and to crush, right? And what, essentially, is the Christian's answer to it but apparent powerlessness, absolute fidelity to the way, the truth, and the life within their hearts—but a way which must accept the attitude which Jesus himself chose? 'Learn from me; for I am gentle and lowly in heart' (Mt. 11 : 29).

The Apocalypse tells us that those who wield force, who seek to sweep away all opposition to their own self-glorification (and the more silent the opposition, the more devastating it can be), 'have no rest day or night, these worshippers of the beast and its image' (Ap. 14 : 11), while Jesus adds the reward of his lesson in humility: 'you will find rest for your souls' (Mt. 11 : 29). For, although the dragon gives authority to the beast from the sea to utter blasphemies, to be an instrument of persecution, the Word himself—the only true word—keeps his own above harm and above fear of trials by the very peace of the steadfast faith within their hearts: 'Because you have kept my word of patient endurance, I will keep you from the hour of trial which is coming on the whole world' (Ap. 3 : 10). And although the second beast gives breath to or artificially animates the first by making the inhabitants of earth worship a totalitarian power (13 : 11), and although these worshippers mock and make merry over Christ's witnesses, persecuting them because they found words of love themselves instruments of torment and persecution for their hardened hearts (11 : 10), God himself gives breath and eternal life to those who respond to the 'call for the endurance of the saints, those who keep the commandments of God and the faith of Jesus' (14 : 12).

The eagle has every reason to cry at the last trumpet blasts, 'Woe, woe, woe to those who dwell on earth' (8 : 13); Christians are right to look forward joyously to the lament, 'Fallen, fallen is Babylon the great! . . . the haunt of every foul spirit' (18 : 2). For they have been ransomed from persecution and slaughter because the Lamb himself was persecuted and slain (5 : 9)! This is why the conqueror will share the Son's throne just as the Son who conquered shares the Father's (3 : 21), why he will be a pillar in the temple which is Christ himself—the new Jerusalem (3 : 12), and why he will be part of Christ's own kingdom of priests (1 : 6).

Indeed, the apparent power of persecution is broken because 'we have not a high priest who is unable to sympathize with our weaknesses, but one who in every respect has been tempted as we are . . .' (Heb. 4 : 15). We are sheep who, in following the Lamb, find that we are strong in his own strength because he has shared our timidity and weakness, our dumb helplessness! That is why we can take him at his word, 'Do not fear what you are about to suffer' (Ap. 2 : 10). He understands what he bids! 'He who conquers and keeps my words to the end, I will give him power over the nations' (2 : 26): Christ's love for us and ours for him is our only real power, our only way of conquest, and our only source of courage and patient endurance. For, 'Having loved his own who were in the world, he loved them to the end' (Jn 13 : 1)—the 'end' meaning bondage and death under varied persecutions and then everlasting life beyond, and the 'end' meaning the utmost, boundless reaches of his love.

And finally, shall tribulation or distress separate us from the love of Christ? Perhaps this is the point where the Apocalypse becomes most relevant to each Christian; for no matter what the age or the circumstances in which we live, each of us has his own daily trials which no one else can really know—no one, that is, but he who alone sees and understands us as we really are: 'I know your works, your toil, and your patient endurance. I know you are . . . bearing up for my name's sake, and you have not grown weary' (Ap. 2 : 2f.). John sees Jesus addressing these words to the Ephesians as a body, a church; but those who hear them then and now cannot help interpreting them according to the little struggles and crosses in their own daily lives—even as, in John's visions of future blessedness, they cannot help being stirred and lifted up by the hope of some concrete reward for their present sufferings, the hope of as simple a token of God's care as his wiping away every tear from their eyes (7 : 17).

Each of us needs to hear one answer spoken by one person in answer to all our own personal apprehensions: 'Fear not, I am the first and the last, and the living one; I died, and behold I am alive for ever more . . .' (1 : 17). Each of us needs the assurance that all this one asks of us is that we give ourselves wholly to him and let him fill our own weaknesses, cowardliness, and lapses of faith. He knows that we have but 'little power', but he gives us the strength to keep his word without denying his name (3 : 8); he knows our poverty, but in this is our richness (2 : 9). For it is Christ himself who makes our robes white by his own blood (3 : 4) and brings us safely through the great tribulation (7 : 14), thus making straight the path to the gates of his city (22 : 16) and providing the linen, the 'righteous deeds of the saints' (19 : 8), in which his bride is clothed.

Indeed, often God is most moved to show his love when we are in tribulation or distress: the woman, the people of God, assaulted by the dragon, is rescued and borne aloft on eagle's wings to the wilderness where she is continually nourished and cherished by God (12 : 6). And did not God prepare this place especially for her to protect her after her travail in giving birth to the Messiah? The perversion of great Babylon moves the Lord to seek out his own that they may partake of his nourishment, the heavenly manna he has to give: 'Come out of her, my people, lest you take part in her sins' (18 : 4). Those who, burdened with crushing inner pain or grief and crying out with Christ, 'My God, my God, why have you forsaken me?' (Mk. 15 : 34), are the very ones who 'shall see his face' (Ap. 22 : 4). And those who have known many a 'silence in heaven' (8 : 1) when God seems so distant from their speechless hearts will be the same who alone can learn the new song of thrilling beauty, 'like the sound of harpers playing on their harps' (14 : 2)—the same who are blessed to hear the Lamb inviting them to his own marriage supper and communing intimately with them there (19 : 9)!

The inhabitants of the earth follow the beast with a carefree, trancelike wonder (13 : 3)—only to perish with him; Christians are called upon to follow the Lamb conscientiously wherever he leads them (14 : 4) through the realities of daily living—and they find themselves the inheritors of everlasting life as they stand beside him on Mount Zion (14 : 1). For, all affliction is sent 'to make us not rely on ourselves, but on God who raises the dead; he delivered us from so deadly a peril, and he will deliver us; on him we have set our hope that he will deliver us again' (2 Cor. 1 : 9f.).

A Christian is called to live an ordinary way; and thus, he will not know continual tribulation or distress—even as he will not know uninterrupted joy. The church must simply learn to live in the wilderness, to let God care for her; the woman lives in the midst of all God's creation and thus accepts and enters into the rhythms and seasons of sun, moon and stars. Jesus himself understands that the woman with child must know both anguish and joy (Jn 16 : 21f.). For these too, the numberless 'little people' and families who lead hidden lives in Nazareth just like his own, Jesus has words of comfort : 'I do not lay upon you any other burden; only hold fast what you have until I come' (Ap. 2 : 24). Another, later poet, imprisoned by blindness as John was by the rocky shores of Patmos and forced to rely on his mind's visions to sustain his faith and his courage even as John did, has known that this humble way is no easy thing, that often it is hard to see how 'they also serve who only stand and wait'.

And thus, is not the real comfort offered by the Apocalypse, in the times of small daily tribulations and in the seasons of living an ordinary life, to be found in the symbol provided by the little open scroll of chapter 10? For in this lies the reality of the incarnation, the message of Jesus, his real 'revelation' at the heart of John's book : Jesus lives and moves in the very midst of the lampstands, his church (1 : 13). 'Behold, the dwelling of God is with man. He will dwell with them, and they shall be his people, and God himself will be with them!' (21 : 3). They shall not be left alone : each day they shall be given the morning star—Jesus himself (22 : 16). The star which first lay over his place of birth in Bethlehem becomes his own rebirth in their hearts!

For although this scroll contains the bitter taste of distress, persecution, nakedness and peril (10 : 9), its honey-sweetness will always prevail : 'death shall be no more, neither shall there be mourning nor crying nor pain any more, for the former things have passed away' (21 : 3). For the duration of the church on earth, there must be things 'accursed', but even these are in God's service : it is he who gives the beast its authority, it is he who allows it to make war on the saints and even to conquer them (13 : 7). But all these things are swept away by perhaps the most refreshingly simple and yet dynamic statement in the whole of the Apocalypse—one which is all the more cause for joy and optimism because it is absolutely 'trustworthy and true', the testimony of Jesus himself (22 : 16): 'Behold, I make all things new!' (21 : 5).

And this newness is achieved by 'him who loves us and has freed us' (1 : 5); it is the salvation he has won for us here and now, the fruit and reviving life-waters offered us after every reproof which comes from this his love (3 : 19). It carries forth the abiding grace and peace of John's greeting into his closing words (1 : 4, 22 : 21), it moves the fervent Amens throughout the book which confirm all our prayers. Those who cry out 'Come, Lord Jesus!' even after an Amen (22 : 20) are individuals longing for him to come into their own hearts, longing for him to open the very door he has knocked upon (3 : 20). It was the man John who 'saw a new heaven and a new earth' (21 : 1): although his body was confined by the punitive circumstances of exile, his mind was free to belong wholly, without reserve, to Jesus and to listen to him alone. And Jesus has chosen to speak through John to each of us that we might carry away from these visions the message of joy, peace and love which is the Saviour's gift to us. He wants us to carry away in our hearts from the last pages of the New Testament the same fulfilment which Simeon knew at its beginning; he wants us to pray before the triumphant Messiah with the same quiet joy and peace in the words which the old man spoke over the child :

> Lord, now lettest thy servant depart in peace,
> according to thy word;
> for mine eyes have seen thy salvation
> which thou hast prepared in the presence of all peoples,
> a light for revelation to the gentiles,
> and for glory to thy people Israel   (Lk 2 : 29-32).

The relevance of the Apocalypse lies in its answering Paul's question, 'Who can separate us from the love of Christ?' Its relevance to each of us becomes most immediate upon our understanding that the 'love of Christ' refers to both his love for us and ours for him—one love, which makes all things new no matter who or where we are; a love which is itself all things. 'For I am sure that neither death, nor life, nor angels, nor principalities, nor things present, nor things to come, nor powers, nor height, nor depth, nor anything else in all creation, will be able to separate us from the love of God in Christ Jesus our Lord' (Rom. 8 : 38f.).

COMMENTARY

Prologue and Letters to the Churches
(1: 1—3: 22)

PROLOGUE (1: 1-3)

Am. 3: 7: Surely the Lord God does nothing, without revealing his secret to his servants the prophets.
Dn. 2: 28: There is a God in heaven who reveals mysteries, and he has made known to King Nebuchadnezzer what will be in the latter days.

1. The revelation of Jesus Christ, which God gave him to show to his servants what must soon take place; and he made it known by sending his angel to his servant John, 2. who bore witness to the word of God and to the testimony of Jesus Christ even to all that he saw. 3. Blessed is he who reads aloud the words of the prophecy, and blessed are those who hear, and who keep what is written therein; for the time is near.

The prologue introduces Ap. as a letter of the prophet John, a letter destined to be read at the liturgical ceremonies. The author is conscious that it is, in fact, a letter from the supreme pastor of the church; John is his spokesman.

1. *Apokalypsis* ('revelation') occurs only here in this book. 'The revelation of Jesus Christ' : Is the genitive objective (a revelation whose object is Jesus Christ) or subjective (a revelation of which Jesus Christ is the recipient and giver)? The context would seem to demand the second sense (cf. Gal. 1 : 12). The full name, Jesus Christ, is found only in this first chapter (cf. 1 : 1, 2, 5). The Son received the revelation from the Father (a recurring theme of the Fourth Gospel, Jn 3 : 35; 5 : 20, 26; 7 : 16; 8 : 28; 12 : 49; 16 :

15; 17 : 2) in order to communicate it to the servants of God—
primarily the Christian prophets (Ap. 10 : 7; 11 : 18; 22 : 16;
however, in 7 : 3 the 'servants of our God' are the saved remnant
of Israel). The revelation in question here is what must soon take
place in fulfilment of the divine purpose—the contents of Ap.
'What must take place' echoes Dn. 2 : 28; that this fulfilment
should be 'soon' is the expectation of prophecy and apocalyptic
(cf. Lk. 18 : 8; Rom. 16 : 20; Ap. 22 : 6). By means of an angel
(the customary intermediary in apocalyptic, cf. Ap. 22 : 6), Christ
made known the revelation he himself had received from the
Father, to his servant (cf. Ap. 1 : 4, 9; 22 : 8) John—who, so
designated, stands as a Christian prophet. 'The genesis of the
Apocalypse has now been traced from its origin in the mind of
God to the moment when it reached its human interpreter' (Swete).
2. John has borne witness (a favourite Johannine expression) to
the revelation given by God and by Christ (cf. 1 : 5, 9). The 'word
of God' embraces the entire revelation of God which now, in its
fulness, is attested by Christ. 'He himself (Christ)—to see whom is
to see the Father (cf. Jn 14 : 9)—completed and perfected Revelation and confirmed it with divine guarantees. He did this by the
total fact of his presence and self-manifestation—by words and
works, signs and miracles, but above all by his death and glorious
resurrection from the dead, and finally by sending the Spirit of
truth.'[28] John's attestation, however, is limited to 'all that he
saw'—that is, to the revelation made in this book, revelation in
the form of *visions*.
3. We have here the first of seven beatitudes in Ap.—the others
occur throughout the second half of the book (14 : 13; 16 : 15;
19 : 9; 20 : 6; 22 : 7, 14). The 'reader' is not the private student
but the public reader; the interpretative 'he who reads aloud' of
RSV conveys the correct meaning. The church inherited the
Jewish practice of reading scripture in the congregation (cf. Ex.
24 : 7; Neh. 8 : 2; Lk. 4 : 16; Ac. 13 : 15; 15 : 21; 2 Cor. 3 : 15)
and extended it to include Christian writings (Col. 4 : 16; 1
Thess. 5 : 27). The blessing reaches to those who hear and keep
the words of the book. There is an echo of the saying of Jesus :

---

[28] Vatican II, *Dogmatic Constitution on Divine Revelation*, I, 4.

'Blessed are those who hear the word of God and keep it' (Lk. 11 : 28); though, for 'keep', the Johannine *tērein* replaces Luke's *phylassein*. Cf. Jas 1 : 22f. By describing his work as 'prophecy' the author ranks it with the prophetic literature of the OT (cf. Ap. 22 : 7, 10, 18). The phrase 'for the time is near' (cf. 'soon', 1 : 1) gives a motive for hearing and keeping (cf. 22 : 10)—the 'time' is that of the return of Christ in victory and judgment (cf. 1 : 7; 22 : 10, 12, 20).

THE LETTERS TO THE SEVEN CHURCHES (1: 4—3: 22)

(1) INTRODUCTION 1 : 4-8

Ex. 3: 14: God said to Moses, 'I am who I am'. And he said, 'Say this to the people of Israel, "I am has sent me to you"'.
Ps. 89: 27, 37: And I will make him the first-born, the highest of the kings of the earth. . . . Like the moon it shall be established forever; the faithful witness in the sky (LXX).
Ex. 19: 6: And you shall be to me a kingdom of priests and a holy nation.
Dn. 7: 13: Behold, with the clouds of heaven there came one like a son of man.
Zech. 12: 10-14: When they look on him whom they have pierced, they shall mourn for him . . . the land shall mourn . . . and all the families that are left.
Is. 44: 6: I am the first and the last.

4. John to the seven churches that are in Asia: Grace to you and peace from him who is and who was and who is to come, and from the seven spirits who are before his throne, 5. and from Jesus Christ the faithful witness, the first-born of the dead, and the ruler of kings on earth. To him who loves us and has freed us from our sins by his blood, 6. and made us a kingdom, priests to his God and Father, to him be glory and dominion for ever and ever. Amen. 7. Behold, he is coming with the clouds, and every eye will see him, every one who

pierced him; and all tribes of the earth will wail on account of him. Even so. Amen. 8. 'I am the alpha and the omega', says the Lord God, who is and who was and who is to come, the almighty.

The introduction addresses the Christian congregations to which John had ministered.

4. The verse opens with the customary epistolary formula: name of the sender (nominative) and name of the receiver(s) (dative). 'Asia' is the Roman province of Asia—the western part of Asia Minor (Turkey). The Churches are named in 1: 11. There were certainly more than seven churches in the province; for instance, Troas (Ac 20: 5; 2 Cor 2: 12), Colossae (Col. 1: 1), and Hierapolis (Col 4: 13) do not figure in the list. The number seven is symbolic and signifies totality—his message is addressed to the churches of Asia and, indeed, to the church at large. 'Grace and peace': the common greeting in the Pauline epistles. 'Grace' appears again only in the closing formula (22: 21). 'From him who is and who was and who is to come'; in rabbinical literature a similar development of the divine title of Ex 3: 14 (in the LXX, 'he who is') was not uncommon. However, John's immediate source would have been the liturgical Targums. Indeed, John's phrase would seem to be a servile rendering of the Aramaic paraphrase of Dt. 32: 39 found in the *Targum of Pseudo-Jonathan*: 'See now that I am he who is and who was and I am he who will be'; cf. Ex. 3: 14—'Thus shall you say to the children of Israel: "I am he who is and who will be has sent me to you".' Though he uses a preposition which takes the genitive (*apo*, 'from'), John keeps the divine name in the nominative —perhaps to indicate that God is not subject to change. 'The seven spirits who are before his throne', cf. 3: 1; 4: 5; 5: 6. Some would see here the seven 'angels of the presence' as in 8: 2. However, in our text, and the other passages, we may admit the influence of Zech. 4: 10; and, besides, the 'seven spirits' are here in close conjunction with Father and Son. It seems best to take it that the Holy Spirit is meant: he is the sevenfold Spirit, the fulness of Spirit (cf. Is. 11: 2).

5a. The titles of Jesus Christ are suggested by Ps. 89 : 27, 37. The idea of a faithful witness is strongly Johannine; cf. 'for this I have come into the world, to bear witness to the truth' (Jn 18 : 37; cf. Ap. 1 : 2). On the other hand, 'the first-born of the dead' is typically Pauline; cf. 'he is the beginning, the first-born from the dead' (Col. 1 : 18; cf. 1 Cor. 15 : 20). In the perspective of Ap. the earthly kings are the persecutors of the Church; Christ is their conqueror (cf. 19 : 16). 'The threefold title—witness, first-born, ruler—answers to the threefold purpose of the Apocalypse, which is at once a divine testimony, a revelation of the Risen Lord, and a forecast of the issues of history' (Swete).

5b-6. This is the first of many doxologies (e.g. 4 : 11; 5 : 9, 12f., etc.). The tenses are carefully distinguished : 'who *loves* us and *has freed* us'—bringing out the fact that *agapē* abides beyond the act of redemption it completed. The love of Christ for his own is a constant theme; this 'ruler of kings' holds no terror for them. By him they have been made a kingdom, each member of which is a priest, a royal house of priests (cf. Ex. 19 : 6; 1 Pet. 2 : 9), inheriting the privilege of the chosen people. Since Ap. takes a stand against the Caesar-cult, the kingdom of Christ (which shares his authority over the nations, cf. 2 : 26; 3 : 21; 5 : 10; 20 : 6) here stands in contrast to the imperial power. Though the priestly service of Christians is rendered to the God and Father of Jesus Christ, they are also priests of Christ (20 : 6). 'To him be glory'; that is, to Christ. Similar doxologies addressed to Christ are to be found in 5 : 13; 7 : 10; cf. 2 Pet. 3 : 18. 'Amen' ('truly'; 'it is true'), affirming what has just been said, is the customary conclusion of doxologies.

7. From the redemption wrought by Christ in time, John looks to his coming as judge at the end of time (cf. 19 : 11-16). His text is based on a combination of Dn. 7 : 13 and Zech. 12 : 10, a combination which occurs also in Mt. 24 : 30—'Then will appear the sign of the Son of Man in heaven, and then all the tribes of the earth will mourn, and they will see the Son of Man coming on the clouds of heaven with power and great glory'. The passage of Zech. is also found in Jn 19 : 37 in reference to the piercing of the side of the dead Jesus: 'And again another scripture says,

"They shall look on him whom they have pierced".' In Jn and in Ap. the wording of the prophecy differs from that of the LXX (but is close to the 2nd century AD version of Theodotion). It would appear that Jn and Ap. follow a Greek version that is independent of the LXX, while the combination of texts in Mt. and Ap. would suggest a collection of prophetic testimonies. When the Judge appears he will be manifest to all, even to them whose hostility numbers them among those who had encompassed his death; and 'all the tribes of the earth' (cf. 5 : 9; 7 : 9; 14 : 6) —not necessarily in the pejorative sense of 'those who dwell upon the earth', the enemies of Christ—will lament in remorse. 'Even so. Amen' = *Nai. Amēn*: the Greek and Hebrew forms of the affirmative. The double affirmation is in place at this solemn moment (cf. 22 : 20). The trinitarian formula (1 : 4-6) has, in Christian fashion, lingered over the Son : his incarnation, death, and glory.

8. The speaker is God. Most likely alpha and omega is the Greek rendering of a corresponding Hebrew expression, aleph and tau (the first and last letters of the alphabet in each language). In 21 : 6 and 22 : 13 the expression is explained : God is the alpha and the omega—the first and the last, the beginning and the end, as in Is. 44 : 6; 48 : 12. *Pantokratōr* ('Almighty') is a regular LXX rendering of *Yahweh Sebaoth,* 'Lord of hosts'. God is the all-ruler, the sovereign Lord—a reminder to Christians that their God and his Christ hold supreme power, even over the arrogant 'rulers of the earth'.

(2) THE VISION OF THE SON OF MAN (1 : 9-20)

Ezek. 3: 12: Then the Spirit lifted me up . . . and I heard behind me the sound of a great earthquake.

Dn. 7: 9, 13: Thrones were placed and one that was ancient of days took his seat; his raiment was white as snow, and the hair of his head like pure wool . . . with the clouds of heaven there came one like a son of man, and he came to the Ancient of Days.

Dn. 10: 5-12: I lifted up my eyes and looked, and behold

a man clothed in linen, whose loins were girded with gold. . . . His face like the appearance of lightning, his eyes like flaming torches, his arms and legs like the gleam of burnished bronze, and the sound of his words like the noise of a multitude. . . . When I heard the sound of his words, I fell on my face in a deep sleep with my face to the ground. . . . Then he said to me, 'Fear not, Daniel'.

Ezek. 43: 2: The glory of the God of Israel came from the east; and the sound of his coming was like the sound of many waters.

Is. 49: 2: He made my mouth like a sharp sword.

Is. 48: 12: I am he, I am the first and I am the last.

9. I John, your brother, who share with you in Jesus the tribulation and the kingdom and the patient endurance, was on the island called Patmos on account of the word of God and the testimony of Jesus. 10. I was in the Spirit on the Lord's day, and I heard behind me a loud voice like a trumpet 11. saying, 'Write what you see in a book and send it to the seven churches, to Ephesus and to Smyrna and to Pergamum and to Thyatira and to Sardis and to Philadelphia and to Laodicea.' 12. Then I turned to see the voice that was speaking to me, and on turning I saw seven golden lampstands, 13. and in the midst of the lampstands one like a son of man, clothed with a long robe and with a golden girdle round his breast; 14. his head and his hair were white as white wool, white as snow; his eyes were like a flame of fire, 15. his feet were like burnished bronze, refined as in a furnace, and his voice was like the sound of many waters; 16. in his right hand he held seven stars, from his mouth issued a sharp two-edged sword, and his face was like the sun shining in full strength. 17. When I saw him, I fell at his feet as though dead. But he laid his right hand upon me, saying, 'Fear not, I am the first and the last, 18. and the living one; I died, and behold I am alive for evermore, and I have the keys of Death and Hades. 19. Now write what you see, what is and what is to take place hereafter. 20. As for the mystery of the seven stars which you saw in my right hand,

and the seven golden lampstands, the seven stars are the angels of the seven churches and the seven lampstands are the seven churches.'

In a striking vision, reminiscent of the inaugural visions of the prophets (cf. Is. 6; Jer. 1; Ezek. I-3), John is commissioned by the glorified Son of Man to write what is to be revealed to him and to send the message to seven churches of Asia.

9.   John (cf. 1 : 1, 4), who refers to himself in the manner of the apocalyptic prophets (cf. Dn. 7 : 28; 8 : 1), is the 'brother' of those to whom he writes, a fellow-worker in the same religious society (cf. 2 Pet. 3 : 15). United with them in Jesus, he shares their 'tribulation' or sufferings (cf. 1 Pet. 4 : 13; 5 : 1; 2 Cor. 1 : 7; Phil. 3 : 10; 4 : 14), suggesting persecution; and he shares the 'kingdom' or royal priesthood of Ap. 1 : 6 as well as the 'patient endurance' (*hypomenē*). This last term occurs seven times in Ap. (1 : 9; 2 : 2, 3, 19; 3 : 10; 13 : 10; 14 : 12): it is the characteristic virtue of the persecuted. It is founded on faith in Jesus, the Lord who comes, and is inspired by the certainty of his love. It is marked by strength of soul which enables one to persevere, and it finds expression in the bearing of trials and in steadfastness under persecution. 'The whole life of a Christian, whether he suffers or reigns or waits, is in union with the life of the Incarnate Son' (Swete). John 'found himself' (rather than 'was') on Patmos, a small (about ten miles long and five wide), barren island among the group of Sporades off the SW coast of Asia Minor. He was there most likely under judicial banishment (*relegatio in insulam*), following a sentence of the provincial governor (cf. 20 : 4). This view is supported by the context and by the practically unanimous tradition of the early Church. 'On account of the word of God and the testimony of Jesus' : because of his preaching of the gospel and his loyalty to it in time of tribulation.

10.   'I was in the Spirit' (cf. 4 : 2), that is, 'I fell into a trance' (cf. Ac. 11 : 5; 22 : 17). 'On the Lord's day'—the first day of the week, the Christian Sunday (cf. Ac. 20 : 7; 1 Cor. 16 : 2). The voice is probably that of an angel (cf. 1 : 1; 4 : 1; 5 : 2; Ezek. 3 : 12), though it may be the voice of the Son of Man.

11. The vision is not for John alone but for transmission to the church; so, he is bidden to write—the 'book' is rather a papyrus roll (*biblion*). The seven churches are not listed haphazardly but in order; they were linked by a circular road that, from Ephesus, went north to Smyrna and Pergamum and then swung southwards to take in the others. A messenger could carry the scroll to each of the churches in turn, and by each it would be read and probably copied (cf. Col. 4 : 16).

12. The 'seven golden lampstands' are suggested by the seven-branched lampstand (Ex. 25 : 31-37; Zech. 4 : 2); but here the lampstands are separate. The symbolism is explained in Ap. 1 : 20.

13. In 1 : 13-18 the Messiah appears as judge (as in Dn. 7 : 13); in this case the details of the vision do have a symbolical value. While the expression 'one like a son of man' echoes the phrase of Dn. 7 : 13, the person of the vision is the Son of Man of the gospels and Ac. 7 : 56. Characteristically, John has not hesitated to borrow details from the description of the angel in Dn. 10. 'It is of the utmost importance for John's theology that the first statement he makes about the heavenly Christ is that he saw him *among the lamps*. He is no absentee, who has withdrawn from earth at his ascension, to return only at his parousia, meanwhile exercising his authority over the churches by remote control through their heavenly representatives, the angels. The first characteristic of Christ revealed by John in his vision is that he is present among the earthly congregations of his people, and whatever John has later to say about the coming of Christ must be interpreted in the light of this salient fact' (Caird). The Son of Man wears the long robe of priesthood. (Ex. 28 : 4; 29 : 5) and the golden cincture of royalty (1 Mac. 10 : 89).

14. What is said of the Ancient of Days (God) in Dn. is here applied to the Son of Man. The white hair symbolizes eternity; eyes like a flame of fire represent his divine knowledge.

15. The feet of 'bronze'—*chalkolibanos* is an unidentified metal alloy—suggest stability and, perhaps, should be seen in contrast to the fragile feet of iron and clay of Nebuchadnezzar's dream image (Dn. 2 : 33f.). His voice is the voice of the God of Israel (Ezek. 43 : 2).

16.   He holds in his right hand (in his power), the seven stars which are the 'angels of the seven churches' (1 : 20). The sharp two-edged sword (cf. 2 : 16; 19 : 15, 21; Heb. 4 : 12) issuing from his mouth is a symbol of his judicial authority (cf. Is. 49 : 2; Wis. 18 : 15f.). The final detail is very close to Mt. 17 : 2—'and he was transfigured before them, and his face shone like the sun'.

17f.   The overall effect of the vision is one of terrifying majesty : the Son of Man has entered into his glory. John's reaction is that of Daniel (Dn. 10 : 8f.). Yet, this Son of Man remains the Jesus of the gospel, and John hears again his comforting 'Fear not' (cf. Mk. 6 : 50; Mt. 28 : 10). Just as descriptive details of the vision pointed to the assimilation of the Son of Man to Yahweh, so, too, his own words do likewise. He is 'the first and the last' (Is. 44 : 6; 48 : 12), as the Lord God has said of himself in Ap. 1 : 8. Besides, he is the living one; 'As the Father has life in him-self, so he has granted the Son also to have life in himself' (Jn 5 : 26; cf. 1 : 4; 5 : 21). Because he is the living one, though he had died, his risen life is henceforth concurrent with his divine life : 'we know that Christ being raised from the dead will never die again' (Rom. 6 : 9). He is master of death and of the abode of the dead : 'the hour is coming when all who are in the tombs will hear his voice' (Jn 5 : 28; cf. 5 : 25-29). v. 18 'sets forth the threefold conception of Christ in John : the ever abiding life he had independently of the world; his humiliation even unto physical death, and his rising to a life not only ever-lasting in itself but to universal authority over life and death' (Charles). 'Death and Hades', cf. 20 : 13f.

19.   John is bidden to write 'what he sees' (the vision of the Son of Man), 'what is' (the condition of the churches, chapters 2-3), and 'what is to take place hereafter' (cf. Dn. 2 : 28) (the apoca-lyptic visions—the rest of the book).

20.   'Mystery' is the inner meaning of a symbolic vision, as in Dn. 2 : 47; cf. Ap. 17 : 7. The obvious difficulty in this verse is the meaning of the 'angels' of the seven churches. *angelos* occurs very frequently in Ap., always in the sense of a superhuman being; the presumption is that it has the same meaning here. It seems best, then, to regard the 'angels' as the heavenly guardians

or representatives of the churches. Angels appear as the guardians of nations in Dn. 10 : 13, 20, 21; 11 : 1; 12 : 1 in accordance with a view current in contemporary and later Judaism. Ap. itself speaks of 'the angel of water' (16 : 4). It may be, however, that the author has borrowed his 'seven stars' from the synagogue liturgy. Cf. *Targum of Pseudo-Jonathan* Ex. 40 : 4—'And you shall bring in the lampstand . . . and you shall kindle the seven lamps corresponding to the seven stars [or planets] which resemble the just that shine unto eternity in their righteousness'. We see that the seven lamps first represent the seven planets and these in turn represent the just who shall shine like stars forever (cf. Dn. 12 : 3). This would suggest that in Ap. 1 : 20 the 'angels' are the human representatives of the community or those in charge of the communities.[29] Yet, the other view seems preferable. At any rate, the presence and authority of the Son of Man are asserted : he walks among the lampstands, the churches, and holds in his power the stars, the angel guardians or representatives of the churches.

The vision of the Son of Man effectively brings out the oracular character of the first part of Ap., for it is closely parallel to the inaugural visions of the prophets. But where the latter proceeded to speak in the name of Yahweh ('thus says Yahweh'), John will make known the 'revelation of Jesus Christ'. And since, in the eyes of the inspired writer, the seven churches represent the universal church, his message—the message of the Lord—has meaning for the church until the end of time.

(3) THE LETTERS TO THE SEVEN CHURCHES (2-3)

The letters to the seven churches have the same literary characteristics as the properly apocalyptic part of Ap. and are the work of the same author. Originally, they may have been independent of the rest, to be joined later to the apocalypse proper; as such they form an integral part of the work as we know it. But the links between the letters and the rest are so close that the independent existence of the former seems unlikely.

Each church receives a judgment which is based upon an

[29] M. McNamara, *op. cit.*, 198f.

accurate knowledge of its conditions, both external (there are several topical references) and spiritual. The churches receive praise or blame (or both), usually with some qualifications, and in this there seems to be a definite plan and progression. Ephesus receives censure and commendation; then, Smyrna, Thyatira and Philadelphia (the even numbers) are praised, the latter with marked warmth, while Pergamum, Sardis, and Laodicea are censured, the last very severely. Their chief faults are a cooling of first fervour and a decline in charity, together with indulgence of, or concessions to, Nicolaitanism, a Gnostic heresy similar to that in question in the Johannine epistles.

The seven letters follow a common plan. All open with the formula: 'To the angel of . . . write'. Next comes 'The word of (*tade legei*) . . .'—the speaker is Christ whose titles, mostly taken from the preceding vision of the Son of Man, are relevant to the local situation in each case. His message always begins: 'I know . . .', leading to an outline of virtues or faults, with corresponding praise or blame, and to a final recommendation. All close with the promise: 'To him who conquers. . . .' The stereotyped formula, 'He who has an ear let him hear what the Spirit says to the churches', precedes the promise to the conqueror in the first three letters and follows it in the other four.

I. Letter to Ephesus (2: 1-7)

> *Gen. 2: 9: And out of the ground the Lord God made to grow every tree . . . the tree of life also in the midst of the garden.*

1. 'To the angel of the church in Ephesus write: "The words of him who holds the seven stars in his right hand, who walks among the seven golden lampstands. 2. I know your works, your toil and your patient endurance, and how you cannot bear evil men but have tested those who call themselves apostles but are not, and found them to be false; 3. I know you are enduring patiently and bearing up for my name's

sake, and you have not grown weary. 4. But I have this against you, that you have abandoned the love you had at first. 5. Remember then from what you have fallen, repent and do the works you did at first. If not, I will come to you and remove your lampstand from its place, unless you repent. 6. Yet this you have, you hate the works of the Nicolaitans, which I also hate. 7. He who has an ear, let him hear what the Spirit says to the churches. To him who conquers I will grant to eat of the tree of life, which is in the paradise of God." '

Ephesus, which lay at the mouth of the River Cayster, was the capital city of the province of Asia, though the Roman provincial governor resided at Pergamum. It was a wealthy city, the chief port and market centre of Asia and one of the great cities of the age. Because of the extensive silting caused by the Cayster, the shoreline has receded and the ancient gulf of Ephesus is now a swampy plain. Ephesus was famed for its Artemision—the temple of Artemis (Diana)—one of the seven wonders of the world; from the time of Augustus the temple became associated with the imperial cult. Ephesus was a natural centre of missionary activity. Paul visited the city for the first time towards the close of AD 52 on his way to Jerusalem at the end of the second missionary journey (Ac. 18 : 19-21). He was back during his third journey (53-58) for a long stay of almost three years (Ac. 19-20). From there he sent his disciples to the other cities of Asia. Hence, it is not surprising that the city stands first among those to which the messages are sent.

1. Because Ephesus was the most important church of the province (in a sense, the metropolitan church which represented the others), the Lord appears under titles which express his relation to the churches generally (cf. 1 : 13, 16, 20).

2f. Because he has seen with his eyes 'like a flame of fire' (1 : 14), the Lord 'knows' the 'works'—good (2 : 2f., 6) and bad (2 : 4)—of his church. The praiseworthy works of this church are its 'toil' in resisting and overcoming false teachers and its 'patient endurance', for the sake of Christ, in the labour and trials of the effort. For the 'false apostles' cf. 2 Cor. 11 : 5-13. In both passages 'apostle' is understood in the wide sense of Christian preacher. The difference is, of course, that Paul's 'false apostles' are juda-izers (that is, converts from Judaism who held that full observance of the Mosaic Law was necessary for salvation), whereas, in our text, they are Nicolaitans (Ap. 2 : 6). Paul had put forward the criterion of genuine apostleship : 'The signs of a true apostle were performed among you in all patience, with signs and wonders and mighty works' (2 Cor. 12 : 12); measured by some such stan-dards, the false apostles at Ephesus were shown in their true colours. Paul had foreseen that false teachers would seek to trouble the Ephesian church (Ac. 20 : 29f.). However, Ignatius attests that the Ephesians had a reputation for their immunity to false teaching.

4f. Yet, they had not emerged unscathed : they had preserved orthodoxy, but their love had waned. 'Love' is *agapē*—fraternal charity, a love which is self-giving, which seeks the good of others. Its source is God, who has first loved us (I Jn 4 : 19) and who has given his Son in order to reconcile sinners with himself (Jn 3 : 16f.). The love of Christians is to be modelled on this love of Father and Son. In the days of Paul's ministry at Ephesus their *agapē* was fervent (cf. Ac. 20 : 37)—'the love you had at first'. The admonition holds an invitation. *Remember . . . repent . . . do* 'answer to three stages in the history of conversion' (Swete). But there is also a threat if the invitation is not heeded : Ephesus will lose its rank as religious capital and may well disappear altogether.

6. 'Yet' (*alla*) modifies the 'but' (*alla*) of v. 4—though the loss of their first love is grievous, yet these Ephesians still have in their favour that they hate the deeds which Christ also hates (cf. Is. 61 : 8; Zech. 8 : 17). The Nicolaitans are named again in 2 : 15 and we learn more of them in 2 : 20-23. Attempts to connect the sect with the Nicolaus of Ac. 6 : 5 (one of the seven 'deacons') lack foundation. The cult of Artemis (originally a fertility god-dess) involved licentious practices; it may be that sexual immorality was a feature of the Nicolaitan trend.

'The one charge against the Ephesians is that their intolerance of imposture, their unflagging loyalty, and their hatred of heresy had bred an inquisitorial spirit which left no room for *love*. They had set out to be defenders of the faith, arming themselves with the heroic virtues of truth and courage, only to discover that in the battle they had lost the one quality without which all others are worthless. John has much to tell us about the demonic process by which all that is noble and good can be distorted into opposition to God, but nothing more eloquent than this simple statement that zeal for Christian truth may obliterate the one truth that matters, that God is love. John is a rigorist who shares the hatred of heresy which he attributes both to the church of Ephesus and to the church's Lord; but he recognizes the appalling danger of a religion prompted more by hate than by *love*. The only legitimate hatred is a revulsion against all that thwarts the operations of love; and how easily that hatred can turn into something less innocent! For all its apparent strength and vigour, this church is in danger of losing its *lamp*, of ceasing to be a real church' (Caird).

7. The formula 'He who has an ear . . .' recalls a saying of Jesus found in the synoptic gospels: 'He who has ears, let him hear' (Mt. 13 : 9, 43; 11 : 15, par.); each hearer of the message is called upon to appropriate to himself the warnings and promises addressed to the churches. Though in Ap. 2 : 1 it is evident that the speaker is Christ, here the Spirit of Christ is named: the Spirit whom Christ sends and who makes his words known and understood (Jn 15 : 26; 16 : 7, 13f.). 'He who conquers' appears in all the letters. He is one who 'keeps my words until the end' (Ap. 2 : 26), who has shared the victory of Christ (3 : 21). Elsewhere in the book the martyrs are those who, clothed in the white robes of victory, have come out of the great tribulation and have washed their robes in the blood of the Lamb (7 : 13f.), they have conquered Satan by the blood of the Lamb (12 : 11), they have conquered the beast and his image (15 : 2). Hence, in the letters, 'he who conquers' is, first and foremost, the martyr—one who has won the victory, as Christ has won the victory, by the laying down of his life. This is not to say that John expected all Christians to suffer martyrdom, or that he believed that only martyrs shared the blessedness of Christ. Always, the purpose of his book

must be kept in mind. He writes to encourage his readers in an hour of imminent peril. Persecution looms and there will be martyrs : it is a prospect that all must face. The martyr's reward is immortality (the 'tree of life', cf. Gen. 2 : 9) in the heavenly Jerusalem (cf. Ap. 22 : 2). It is perfectly natural that the earthly paradise of Gen. 2 should become a symbol of heavenly blessedness.

II. Letter to Smyrna (2: 8-11)

Dn. 1: 12, 14: 'Test your servants for ten days' . . . so he tested them for ten days.

8. 'And to the angel of the church in Smyrna write : "The words of the first and the last, who died and came to life.

9. ' "I know your tribulation and your poverty (but you are rich) and the slander of those who say that they are Jews and are not, but are a synagogue of Satan. 10. Do not fear what you are about to suffer. Behold, the devil is about to throw some of you into prison, that you may be tested, and for ten days you will have tribulation. Be faithful unto death, and I will give you the crown of life. 11. He who has an ear, let him hear what the Spirit says to the churches. He who conquers shall not be hurt by the second death." '

Smyrna (modern Izmir) lay 35 miles N. of Ephesus, at the head of a splendid harbour. Ancient Smyrna was destroyed at the beginning of the 6th century BC and was not rebuilt as a city until the time of Alexander the Great, three centuries later. In Roman times it was one of the most prosperous cities of Asia, second only to Ephesus—though it proudly described itself as the 'First of Asia'. It was a faithful ally of Rome and in AD 26 a temple to Tiberius was built there. Nothing is known of the origin of the Christian community in Smyrna.

8. The titles of Christ, based on 1 : 17f., fit neatly in a letter addressed to a 'first' city which had risen again from its ruins; they are calculated to inspire confidence within a church threatened by persecution and death.

9. The Christians are beset by trials and, in a wealthy city, are materially poor; but they are rich in spiritual goods, in faith. Cf. Jas 2 : 5—'Has not God chosen those who are poor in the world to be rich in faith?' Jews were strong in Smyrna and their hostility to Christians (attested throughout Ac.) was particularly virulent; later, they were to take a leading part in the martyrdom of Polycarp (*c.* AD 155). Yet, despite their claim, these are not really Jews; Christians are now the true Israel : 'It is not the children of the flesh who are the children of God, but the children of the promise are reckoned as descendants' (Rom. 9 : 8; cf. 2 : 28f.; Gal. 6 : 15). Because of their slanderous accusations they are 'a synagogue of Satan'; cf. 'You are of your father the devil ... for he is a liar, and the father of lies' (Jn 8 : 44).

10. In fact, the hostile Jews are agents of Satan who will use them to intensify the campaign against the church. False accusation laid before the magistrates will lead to the arrest and imprisonment of some Christians; in prison they await trial which may well end in death. 'Ten days' (cf. Dn. 1 : 12) suggests a short, limited period—but a testing-time for all that. They are not to fear, because this persecution will not last, and because those who stand firm (even if this means death) will be rewarded. Cf. Jas 1 : 12—'Blessed is the man who endures trials, for when he has stood the test he will receive the crown of life which God has promised to those who love him.'

11. The Lord himself suffered death, death on a cross; some, at least, of his disciples will follow him and die a violent death as he died : he will not prevent it. 'Do not fear those who kill the body, and after that have no more that they can do ... fear him who, after he has killed, has power to cast into hell' (Lk. 12 : 4f.; cf. Mt. 10 : 28). The expression, 'the second death', occurs again in Ap. 20 : 6, 14; 21 : 8—it is the 'lake of fire', final punishment; the conqueror is immune from this definitive death.

III. Letter to Pergamum (2: 12-17)

Num. 31: 16: Behold, these [the Midianite women] caused the people of Israel, by the counsel of Balaam, to act

treacherously against the Lord in the matter of Peor, and so the plague came among the congregation of the Lord.
Is. 62: 2: The nations shall see your vindication, and all the kings your glory; and you shall be called by a new name which the mouth of the Lord will give.

12. 'And to the angel of the church in Pergamum write; "The words of him who has the sharp two-edged sword.
13. ' "I know where you dwell, where Satan's throne is; you hold fast my name and you did not deny my faith even in the days of Antipas my witness, my faithful one, who was killed among you, where Satan dwells. 14. But I have a few things against you : you have some there who hold the teaching of Balaam, who taught Balak to put a stumbling block before the sons of Israel, that they might eat food sacrificed to idols and practise immorality. 15. So you also have some who hold the teaching of the Nicolaitans. 16. Repent then. If not, I will come to you soon and war against them with the sword of my mouth. 17. He who has an ear, let him hear what the Spirit says to the churches. To him who conquers I will give some of the hidden manna, and I will give him a white stone, with a new name written on the stone which no one knows except him who receives it." '

Pergamum lay 40 miles N. of Smyrna. The city came under Roman control in 133 BC and became the administrative centre of the province of Asia. It was noted for the cult of the healer god Asclepius. But John is more concerned with Pergamum as a centre of emperor-worship. In 29 BC it had a temple dedicated to Rome (the *Dea Roma*) and Augustus—the first of the cities of Asia in which the cult was established.

12. The 'sword' (cf. 1 : 16) will serve a purpose, 2 : 16.

13. The church of Pergamum, at the centre of the imperial cult ('Satan's throne'), is in a particularly difficult situation. Yet, the Christians have 'held fast my name'; they refused to give the divine title *kyrios* ('Lord') to Caesar, but reserved it for their Lord, the *kyrios Iēsous* (cf. 1 Cor. 12 : 3). Reference to the slaying of the faithful witness Antipas (of whom nothing further is

known) suggests a specific persecution in which the Christians had stood firm.

14f. While the church had withstood dangers from without, it had dealt less effectively with false doctrine within itself. We learn something more of the Nicolaitans (2 : 6). Jewish tradition, based on Num. 31 : 16, presented Balaam as the man who had enticed the Israelite into idolatry and licentiousness, and as a covetous man (cf. Jude 11; 2 Pet. 2 : 15). Here the point of comparison is that, as Balaam seduced the Israelites by his counsel, so the Nicolaitans, by their teaching, entice the churches to idolatrous practices. Though the Jewish tradition referred to would seem to suggest that *porneuein* (to commit fornication) should be taken in the literal sense, the metaphorical meaning (idolatry), common in the Bible, is the regular usage in Ap. The eating of food sacrificed to idols (cf. 1 Cor. 8 : 7-13; 10 : 20-30) here implies some connivance in the imperial cult; John regards such ambiguous conduct as a tacit approval of pagan sacrifice. Some later Gnostic sects held that it was permissible, as a merely external gesture, to offer sacrifice to idols, since true profession of faith was in the heart; and also that fornication, since it affected only the body and not the spirit, was a matter of indifference. But it is not at all clear that the Nicolaitans held such views.

16. The 'some' of the previous verses are the false teachers. Now the Christians of Pergamum are bidden 'repent' : they had been remiss in harbouring the Nicolaitans. 'The fault of Pergamum is the opposite of the fault of Ephesus; and how narrow is the safe path between the sin of tolerance and the sin of intolerance!' (Caird). If they fail to repent, Christ will come as judge and smite them with the sharp sword of his word (cf. 19 : 13, 15)—perhaps by means of persecution or calamity : the 'trial' (3 : 10), the 'great tribulation' (7 : 14).

17. The 'hidden manna' : a reference to a Jewish apocalyptic tradition (attested in 2 Mac. 2 : 4-8) according to which the manna, hidden with the ark by Jeremiah, will reappear as the food of the messianic kingdom—here, the food of the heavenly kingdom. More generally, there is abundant evidence, in later

Jewish documents, of a popular expectation that in the latter days God would again provide manna. While a *white* stone (white being the colour of victory and of joy) is suitably given to the conqueror, its precise significance is obscure—though the general sense is clear enough. The 'new name' symbolizes new life (cf. Is. 62 : 2), here the new life given by Christ (cf. Ap. 3 : 12) to the conqueror, who alone can receive it. Hence, the 'white stone' is the pledge of the divine favour which bestows participation in the life of the risen Christ. Cf. 2 Bar. 6 : 7-10; 29 : 8—'And it shall come to pass at that self-same time that the treasures of manna shall again descend from on high'.

IV. Letter to Thyatira (2: 18-29)

2 Kg. 9: 22: When Joram saw Jehu, he said, 'Is it peace, Jehu?' He answered, 'What peace can there be, so long as the harlotries and the sorceries of your mother Jezebel are so many?'
Jer. 11: 20: O Lord of hosts, who judgest righteously, who triest the heart and the mind.
Ps. 2: 7-9: I will tell of the decree of the Lord: he said to me, 'You are my son, today I have begotten you. Ask of me and I will make the nations your heritage, and the ends of the earth your possession. You shall break them with a rod of iron, and dash them in pieces like a potter's vessel.'

18. 'And to the angel of the church in Thyatira write: "The words of the Son of God, who has eyes like a flame of fire, and whose feet are like burnished bronze.
19. ' "I know your works, your love and faith and service and patient endurance, and that your latter works exceed the first. 20. But I have this against you, that you tolerate the woman Jezebel, who calls herself a prophetess and is teaching and beguiling my servants to practise immorality and to eat food sacrificed to idols. 21. I gave her time to repent, but she refuses to repent of her immorality. 22. Behold, I will throw

her on a sickbed, and those who commit adultery with her I will throw into great tribulation, unless they repent of her doings; 23. and I will strike her children dead. And all the churches shall know that I am he who searches mind and heart, and I will give to each of you as your works deserve. 24. But to the rest of you in Thyatira, who do not hold this teaching, who have not learned what some call the deep things of Satan, to you I say, I do not lay upon you any other burden; 25. only hold fast to what you have, until I come. 26. He who conquers and who keeps my works until the end, I will give him power over the nations, 27. and he shall rule them with a rod of iron, as when earthen pots are broken in pieces, even as I myself have received power from my Father; 28. and I will give him the morning star. 29. He who has an ear, let him hear what the Spirit says to the churches." '

Some 40 miles SE of Pergamum, Thyatira lay on the River Lycus, at the frontier of Mysia and Lydia. The town was a thriving centre of trade and was remarkable for the number of its guilds. It appears that the purple dye industry was one of the most important, and the guild of dyers figures on a number of inscriptions. The first of Paul's converts at Philippi was 'Lydia, from the city of Thyatira, a seller of purple goods' (Ac. 16 : 14). Near the town was the Sambatheion, the shrine of an oriental Sibyl. We know nothing about the foundation of the church in Thyatira.

18.   For the attributes of Christ cf. 1 : 14f. 'Son of God' appears only here in Ap. The burning eyes befit one who 'searches mind and heart' (2 : 23).

19.   Cf. the 'works' of the church of Ephesus. In Thyatira, *agapē* is not only present but comes first, and the fervour of this church has continued to increase. For the kind of service intended by *diakonia* cf. Rom. 15 : 25, 31; 1 Cor. 16 : 15; 2 Cor. 8 : 4; 9 : 1; Heb. 6 : 10.

20.   'Jezebel', clearly a Nicolaitan, is most probably a woman in the church of Thyatira who, in emulation of the Sibyl of the Sambatheion, claimed the gift of prophecy and exercised it in

the interests of her party. A burning question was the presence of Christians at the dinners of the trade guilds, since these were, in fact, religious functions. The Nicolaitans regarded such participation as justifiable; for John it was idolatry—the context does suggest that *porneia* (lit. 'fornication') should be taken in its metaphorical sense. Hence, this woman is named 'Jezebel' after the wife of Ahab who attempted to lead Israel into idolatry by the introduction of the cult of Baal. Significantly, in 2 Kg. 9 : 22, Jehu speaks of the 'harlotries and sorceries' (certainly referring to idolatrous practices) of Jezebel. The one fault of the Thyatiran church is that it tolerated the presence of this 'prophetess'.

21-23. Though she had been warned in the past, the woman had not changed her ways. Now is the time of judgment : 'sickbed' suggests that some affliction will befall her, but the word is also ironic in its immediate context. Her punishment will be shared by those who have been influenced by her. 'Those who commit adultery with her' are they who have been seduced by her teaching and have been misled; her 'children' are her spiritual progeny—the Nicolaitans. These 'children' are doomed like those of Ahab (2 Kg. 10 : 7). News of due punishment would repair the scandal that had been given and would be a salutary warning. 'I am he who searches mind and heart'—like Yahweh in Jer. 11 : 20. The concluding phrase of v. 23 recurs in a slightly different form in Ap. 22 : 12 (cf. Mt. 16 : 27).

24f. The Nicolaitans were Gnostics of some sort : those who claimed a special *gnōsis* (knowledge or wisdom), and who called their knowledge the 'deep things of God' (cf. 1 Cor. 2 : 10). John retorts that their vaunted wisdom comes not from God but from Satan. The Lord has no special task for the faithful ones of Thyatira; they are to hold fast to what they have (v. 19). 'I do not lay upon you any other burden'; cf. Ac. 15 : 28—'It has seemed good to the Holy Spirit and to us to lay upon you no greater burden . . . than that you abstain from what has been sacrificed to idols . . . and from *porneia*.' It seems that John had the decree of Ac. 15 in mind. 'Until I come' : he comes to reward his faithful ones just as he comes in judgment (2 : 5, 16; 3 : 3).

26-28.   v. 27a ('and he shall rule . . . pieces') is a parenthesis; the whole passage is inspired by Ps. 2 : 7-9 (cf. Ap. 12 : 5; 19 : 15). The Son, who has received power from his Father, imparts that power to the conqueror who has shared his own victory over the enemies of God (cf. Ap. 17 : 14). He will give him 'the morning star'—which is himself (22 : 16). The conqueror will not only win 'the victory that overcomes the world' (1 Jn 5 : 4) by sharing Christ's triumph : he is to possess Christ.

V.   Letter to Sardis (3: 1-6)

Ex. 32: 32f.: Moses said, 'If thou wilt forgive their sin— and if not, blot me, I pray thee, out of the book which thou hast written.' But the Lord said to Moses, 'Whoever has sinned against me, him will I blot out of my book.'
Ps. 69: 28: Let them be blotted out of the book of the living; let them not be enrolled among the righteous.

1. 'And to the angel of the church in Sardis write : "The words of him who has the seven spirits of God and the seven stars.

' "I know your works; you have the name of being alive, and you are dead. 2. Awake, and strengthen what remains and is on the point of death, for I have not found your works perfect in the sight of my God. 3. Remember then what you received and heard; keep that, and repent. If you will not awake, I will come like a thief, and you will not know at what hour I will come upon you. 4. Yet you have still a few names in Sardis, people who have not soiled their garments; and they shall walk with me in white, for they are worthy. 5. He who conquers shall be clad thus in white garments, and I will not blot his name out of the book of life; I will confess his name before my Father and before his angels. 6. He who has an ear, let him hear what the Spirit says to the churches." '

About 30 miles SE of Thyatira lay Sardis, the former capital of Lydia. Under Croesus, it was taken by Cyrus (546 BC) and became the administrative capital of the Persian satrapy of Asia Minor. The acropolis of the town had never fallen to assault but had twice been taken by stealth, without resistance: once by Cyrus and again by Antiochus the Great in 218 BC. It was a prosperous town, noted for its handicrafts, but had a bad name for luxury and licence.

1a. For the titles cf. 1 : 16. Christ has not only the seven stars but 'the seven spirits of God' (cf. 5 : 6): he is the one who has and gives the life-giving Spirit (cf. Jn 7 : 39). He alone can restore life to a dead church.

1b-2. For the first time in these letters, the 'works' are not praiseworthy but rather meet with severe censure (cf. 3 : 15). The Christians of Sardis are either spiritually dead (cf. Mt. 8 : 22; Lk. 15 : 24; Jn 5 : 25; Rom. 6 : 13) or in a spiritual torpor (1 Thess. 5 : 6; Rom. 13 : 11). Cf. especially Eph. 5 : 14—'Awake, O sleeper, and arise from the dead, and Christ shall give you life'—part of an early baptismal hymn. Life is not quite extinct after all; but they must come fully awake and carefully tend the spark of life that does remain, lest it should really be extinguished. The lamentable state of the church shows itself in its half-hearted living of the Christian life.

3. 'Remember . . .' (the same recommendation as to the Ephesians, 2 : 5): let them look back to the time when they had willingly listened to the preaching of the gospel and had gladly come to believe. Let them cling now to that faith and promptly turn from their past neglect. If they will not be urged, let them listen to a warning, then. Their city had twice been taken by stealth: the Son of Man will come in the same way. Cf. Mt. 24 : 43f.—'If the householder had known in what part of the night the thief was coming, he would have watched. . . . Therefore you also must be ready, for the Son of Man is coming at an hour you do not expect.'

4. A faithful remnant remains, unsullied by the sin that issued from the religious and moral lassitude of the rest. For the first time, others than the conqueror are explicitly promised blessedness; clothed in white, symbol of purity and victory, these faithful ones will dwell with Christ.

5.   In the OT white apparel denotes festivity (Qoh. 9 : 8), victory (2 Mac. 11 : 8), the heavenly (Dn. 7 : 9). All these associations meet in the 'white garments' here and in the previous verse, but the emphasis is on victory. It may be that the 'white garments' also symbolize the heavenly bodies after the resurrection (cf. 2 Cor. 5 : 4). The 'book of life'—the divine register of men—is mentioned in the OT (Ex. 32 : 32f.; Ps. 69 : 28; Is. 4 : 3; Mal. 3 : 16); the 'living' are the righteous. To be blotted out of this book meant death (Ps. 69 : 28). In Ap. 20 : 12 we read of 'books' and the 'book of life'. These are, respectively, the books in which men's deeds are recorded and in the light of which they are judged, and the book of life which contained the names of the elect (20 : 15). In our verse we learn that election is conditional : while a man cannot earn the right to have his name in this book, he can forfeit it. The closing statement of the verse is a reminiscence of a saying of Jesus : 'Everyone who acknowledges me before men, I will also acknowledge before my Father who is in heaven' (Mt. 10 : 32); '. . . the Son of Man also will acknowledge before the angels of God' (Lk. 12 : 8).

VI.   Letter to Philadelphia (3: 7-13)

Heb. 3: 3: God came from Teman, and the Holy One from Mount Paran.

Is. 22: 22: I will place on his shoulder the key of the house of David; he shall open, and none shall shut; and he shall shut, and none shall open.

Is. 60: 14: The sons of those who oppressed you shall come bending low to you; and all who despised you shall bow down at your feet.

Is. 43: 4: Because you are precious in my eyes, and honoured, and I love you.

Ezek. 48: 35: And the name of the city henceforth shall be, 'Yahweh is there'.

7. 'And to the angel of the church in Philadelphia write : "The words of the holy one, the true one, who has the key of

David, who opens and no one shall shut, who shuts and no one opens.

8. ' "I know your works. Behold I have set before you an open door, which no one is able to shut; I know that you have but little power, and yet you have kept my word and have not denied my name. 9. Behold, I will make those of the synagogue of Satan who say that they are Jews and are not, but lie—behold, I will make them come and bow down before your feet, and learn that I have loved you. 10. Because you have kept my word of patient endurance, I will keep you from the hour of trial which is coming on the whole world, to try those who dwell upon the earth. 11. I am coming soon; hold fast what you have, so that no one may seize your crown. 12. He who conquers, I will make him a pillar in the temple of my God; never shall he go out of it, and I will write on him the name of my God, and the name of the city of my God, the new Jerusalem which comes down from my God out of heaven, and my own new name. 13. He who has an ear, let him hear what the Spirit says to the churches." '

Founded by Attalus II of Pergamum (159-138 BC) as a centre for the spread of Greek culture in Lydia and Phrygia, Philadelphia (its Greek name means 'brotherly love'), a prosperous town, lay 30 miles SE of Sardis. It was subject to earthquakes and, together with Sardis and other towns, had been destroyed in the great earthquake of AD 17. It was rebuilt by Tiberius and named Neocaesarea (later, under Vespasian, 'Flavia' was added)—but the old name persisted.

7. The titles of Christ this time do not reflect details of the opening vision, but they have relevance to the situation in Philadelphia. 'The holy one' is a divine title (Heb. 3 : 3; Is. 40 : 25; cf. Ap. 4 : 8; 6 : 10), here applied to Christ (cf. Ap. 3 : 14; 19 : 11; Ac. 3 : 14). 'The true one' (cf. Is. 65 : 16): *alēthinos* ('true') is a Johannine word (10 times in Ap., 9 times in Jn, 4 times in 1 Jn; elsewhere in the NT, 3 times in Heb., once in Lk. and once in 1 Thess. 1 : 9). It has the meaning of both genuineness and permanence. It carries, too, the OT idea of faithfulness, con-

sistency. 'The Head of the church is characterized at once by absolute sanctity (cf. Heb. 7 : 26) and by absolute truth; he is all that he claims to be, fulfilling the ideals which he holds forth and the hopes which he inspires' (Swete). The 'key of David'—cf. Is. 22 : 22. In Is. the key entrusted to the steward Eliakim indicated his complete control over the royal household; here it symbolizes the authority of the risen Christ, set over the house of God (Eph. 1 : 22; Heb. 3 : 6), and exercising all authority in heaven and on earth (Mt. 28 : 18) and over death and Hades (Ap. 1 : 18). The title lends force to the promise of the following verse.

8.   The 'open door' is a Pauline metaphor : 'a wide door for effective work has opened to me' (1 Cor. 16 : 9); 'a door has opened for me in the Lord' (2 Cor. 2 : 12); 'pray . . . that God may open to us a door for the word' (Col. 4 : 3)—in each case the context shows that Paul means a good opportunity for missionary activity. Philadelphia will indeed be a centre for the spread not of Greek culture, but of the gospel. Since it is 'he who has the key of David' who has opened the door, the Philadelphian Christians are assured of efficacious preaching—especially in regard to the Jews in their midst (Ap. 3 : 9). The church had little power, little influence (cf. 1 Cor. 1 : 26), in Philadelphia— but Christ works through human weakness (2 Cor. 12: 9). Fidelity to the word and name of Christ points to a period of trial in the past (cf. v. 10).

9.   As at Smyrna, the opposition came from the Jews—Jews in name only (cf. Ap. 2 : 9; Rom. 9 : 8). But there is promise of the conversion of the Jewish opposition in Philadelphia. John has turned prophetic declarations on the homage of the gentiles to Israel into a promise of the homage of Jews to this small and weak, but loyal, church (cf. Is. 60 : 14; 43 : 4). 'I have loved you', a hebraism meaning 'I love you'. Here, for the first time in these letters, in relation to this little but faithful church, we find explicit mention of the love of Christ (but cf. 3 : 19).

10.   Because they keep his word with the steadfastness which is marked by patient endurance, they will reap their reward : they will be kept safe through the 'great tribulation' (7 : 14)—the persecution which is about to break on the church. It is clear

that Jesus 'kept safe' the Philadelphians not only because of their steadfastness, but because they were little and weak and knew it, thus letting Christ work through their weakness (v. 8), thus leaning on him. It is clear from the rest of the book that the expressions, 'the whole world' and 'those who dwell upon the earth' (cf. 6: 10; 8: 13; 11: 10; 13: 8, 14; 17: 8), mean the unbelieving world.

11. 'I am coming soon'. In 2: 16 Christ warned the Christians of Pergamum that he would 'come to you soon and war against them'—that is, those who had held the teaching of the Nicolaitans. He comes here to Philadelphia too, but not as judge. His promised preservation of them during the 'hour of trial' is both a reward for their fidelity and an assurance of the crown that awaits them : the 'crown of life' (2: 10).

12. 'Pillar'. Cf. 1 Tim. 3: 15, where it is more likely that it is Timothy (rather than the Church) who is a 'pillar and bulwark of the truth'. In Gal. 2: 9, James and Cephas and John are 'reputed to be pillars'. The conqueror will have a prominent and permanent place in the new Temple of God. 'Never shall he go out of it'—for Jesus has kept all whom the Father has given him and none of them is lost (Jn 17: 121 18: 9). The promised stability has special point for a town prone to earthquakes. 'Temple', no less than 'pillar', is used metaphorically; the text is not inconsistent with 21: 22 where it is said that there is no temple in the heavenly Jerusalem. The three names written on the 'pillar' mark the conqueror as the property of God and of Christ and as a citizen of the heavenly city. 'The name of my God' (cf. 2: 17; 14: 1); 'the name of the city' (cf. Ezek. 48: 35); 'the new Jerusalem' (cf. Ap. 21: 2, 10). 'My own new name'— he will share, in fulness, the life of Christ (2: 17; cf. 19: 12). The emphasis on 'name' and 'new name' may have reference to the name of Neocaesarea given to Philadelphia. Like Smyrna, Philadelphia receives no word of reproof. Yet, here the language is warmer, and the Philadelphian Christians receive the assurance : 'I love you'.

VII. Letter to Laodicea (3:14-22)

Is. 65: 16: He who blesses himself in the land shall bless himself by the God of truth, and he who takes an oath in the land shall swear by the God of truth.

Hos. 12: 9: Ephraim has said, 'Ah, but I am rich, I have gained wealth for myself.'

Prov. 3: 12: For the Lord reproves him whom he loves, as a father the son in whom he delights.

14. 'And to the angel of the church in Laodicea write: "The words of the Amen, the faithful and true witness, the beginning of God's creation.

15. ' "I know your works: you are neither cold nor hot. Would that you were cold or hot! 16. So, because you are lukewarm, and neither cold nor hot, I will spew you out of my mouth. 17. For you say, I am rich, I have prospered, and I need nothing; not knowing that you are wretched, pitiable, poor, blind, and naked. 18. Therefore I counsel you to buy from me gold refined by fire, that you may be rich, and white garments to clothe you and to keep the shame of your nakedness from being seen, and salve to anoint your eyes, that you may see. 19. Those whom I love, I reprove and chasten; so be zealous and repent. 20. Behold, I stand at the door and knock; if any one hears my voice and opens the door, I will come in to him and eat with him, and he with me. 21. He who conquers, I will grant him to sit with me on my throne, as I myself conquered and sat down with my Father on his throne. 22. He who has an ear, let him hear what the Spirit says to the churches." '

Laodicea, 40 miles SE of Philadelphia, in the valley of the Lycus, was founded by Antiochus II (261-246 BC), but developed under later Roman rule and became a centre of commercial activity. It was a banking centre, a manufacturer of clothing and carpets of the native glossy-black wool, and the seat of a medical school noted for its eye ointment. Laodicea was an opulent city, and

after the disastrous earthquake of AD 60 it rose from its ruins
without the aid of an imperial grant. Laodicea was quite near
Colossae and Hierapolis and there was close contact between
these towns (cf. Col. 4 : 15f.). Paul's disciple Epaphras, who had
envangelized Colossae (Col. 1 : 7), most likely preached the gospel in Laodicea also (4 : 12). It is practically certain that Paul
had not visited the towns (cf. 2 : 1) and that he knew of their
Christian communities only by hearsay (1 : 4, 9). Paul wrote a
letter to Laodicea (4 : 16), which may perhaps be Ephesians—
if we take this to have been a circular letter destined for several
churches, including Laodicea.

14.   Christ is the 'Amen'—the one who is faithful to his word.
Cf. Is. 65 : 16—'God of truth' is literally 'God of Amen'. The
designation 'faithful and true witness' (cf. Ap. 1 : 5; 3 : 7) brings
out the full meaning of 'Amen': Christ is the witness whose
testimony never falls short of the truth. 'The beginning of God's
creation', cf. Col. 1 : 15, 18—'He (Christ) . . . is the first-born of
all creation . . . he is the beginning'; the passage may have been
familiar to the church of Laodicea (cf. Col. 4 : 16). The idea is
that of Ap. 1 : 17—'I am the first and the last' (cf. Jn 1 : 3).

15f. Water from the hot springs of Hierapolis, by that time
become lukewarm, flowed over the cliff opposite Laodicea; the
sulphurous water was nauseating. It would seem that these factors
lie behind and give further weight to these striking verses.

17f. Cf. Hos. 12 : 9. The material prosperity of the city is
reflected in the attitude of the church which believes itself rich in
spiritual possessions and in want of nothing (cf. 1 Cor. 4 : 7f.).
The rebuttal is emphatic: 'You are the wretched (cf. Rom. 7 :
24) and pitiable (cf. 1 Cor. 15 : 19) one *par excellence*'. It is also
'poor, blind, and naked'—ironic allusions to the banking-business,
eye-ointment, and clothing industry of Laodicea, objects of its
self-complacency.

18.   The spiritual conditions of the Laodiceans as set forth in
the closing words of the preceding verse ('poor, blind, and
naked'), are made the subject of an admonition calculated to cure
their precarious state. Christ can give the true wealth: faith. Cf.
1 Pet. 1 : 7—'the genuineness of your faith, more precious than

gold which though perishable is tested by fire'. He can give them the spiritual garments (cf. Ap. 3 : 5)—better than their own vaunted woollen products. Cf. 2 Cor. 5 : 4—'While we are still in this tent, we sigh with anxiety; not that we would be un-clothed, but that we would be further clothed, so that what is mortal may be swallowed up by life.' He alone can give them the eye-ointment which can heal their dangerous blindness. Cf. Jn 9 : 38—'For judgment I came into this world, that those who do not see may see, and that those who see may become blind.'

'This is the church in an affluent society, without either *hot* enthusiasm or *cold* antagonism towards religious matters. Even open hostility would be preferable to this *lukewarm* and repulsive indifference, for it would at least suggest that religion was some-thing to be *in earnest* (RSV, "be zealous") about. Spiritually, the church is *poor, blind and naked,* and not all the banks, phar-macies and looms in Laodicea can provide for its need; for it has failed to find in Christ the source of all true wealth, splendour and vision. Of this church alone the heavenly scrutineer has nothing good to say' (Caird).

19.   Cf. Prov. 3 : 12; Heb. 12 : 6. The severity of the rebuke, with its implied threat, is really a sign of Christ's concern, of his love. He who loves the humble, faithful Philadelphians (Ap. 3 : 9) also loves the self-sufficient, lukewarm Laodiceans. Reproof and chastisement can be evidence of love. Though love is never cruel, it can be severe : it can inflict pain, but never hurt. These Christians must not only repent (cf. 2 : 5; 3 : 3), but 'be zealous', shake themselves out of their lethargy.

20.   Here the lover turns from the church to the individual Christian : he comes to each one and seeks an entrance into his heart. The true disciple will hear the voice of his friend. Cf. Jn 10 : 3f.—'the sheep hear his voice . . . for they know his voice', the voice of the Good Shepherd; 18 : 37—'Every one who is of the truth hears my voice'. And the friend will enter by the open door. Cf. Jn 14 : 23—'If a man loves me, he will keep my word, and my Father will love him, and we will come to him and make our home with him' (cf. Eph. 3 : 17). There is a eucharistic flavour about the promise of a meal shared by Christ and the

Christian; the eucharistic interest is very much at home in a
Johannine writing. Cf. Jn 6 : 56—'He who eats my flesh and
drinks my blood abides in me, and I in him'. There is also a
promise of the messianic feast. Cf. Mt. 26 : 29—'I shall not
drink again of this fruit of the vine until that day when I drink
it new with you in my Father's kingdom'. Swete puts the message of the verse thus : 'If any individual gives heed to the call of
Christ and opens the door, Christ will enter the dwelling and
exchange with such a one the fellowship of intimate communion
in that endless feast of Love of which the Eucharist is the
earnest.'

21.   Cf. 2 : 26f. Here, explicitly, the conqueror is one who has
shared the victory of Christ; one who has followed him along the
road to that victory, the way of the cross. In Lk. 22 : 28-30, as
here, enthronement follows immediately on mention of the
heavenly feast—'You are those who have continued with me in
my trials; as my Father appointed a kingdom for me, so do I
appoint for you that you may eat and drink at my table in my
kingdom, and sit on thrones judging the twelve tribes of Israel.'
As Christ through suffering entered into his glory, so the disciples, the companions of his trials will share his glory—that is
their reward. 'As I myself conquered'; cf. Jn 16 : 33—'I have
overcome the world'. The victory of Christ is the victory of the
Father who sent him, and the victory of the conqueror is the
victory of Christ (cf. Ap. 5 : 9f.; 7 : 14; 12 : 11). 'As I . . . sat
down with my Father on his throne'—cf. 'the throne of God and
of the Lamb' (22 : 1, 3).

THE CHRIST OF THE LETTERS

At a time of need, when persecution made it tempting to the
early Christians to 'abandon the love' they had at first, the Christ
of this first part of the Apocalypse appears as the one who can
answer all their needs : the Christ of love. He is the one who first
drew them to the faith they are now asked to keep; he it is who
stands amongst them and walks with them as their companion,
who cares so much about his church that he yearns to strengthen

its weaknesses by opening and entering the heart of every believer. He who speaks to John and tells him not to fear says the same to all his children in this hour of trial; and, although here and in the rest of the Apocalypse the Christians receive the triumphant proclamation that Christ's return as Saviour and judge is near, they first need the quiet certainty that Jesus himself is near to them—near to each personally as the friend who wishes simply that he might 'come in to him and eat with him, and he with me'. If, in promising them the morning star, Christ has promised the Christians himself and participation in his own final victory, they also need to know that each morning, each day, they *do* have him and *can* find him here and now: 'Behold, I stand at the door and knock.'

The Christians have this certainty of Christ's constant presence and support because they have the assurance of his love. In this *agapē*, he 'reproves and chastens' because he himself suffers when his followers tolerate idolatry and false prophets or are Christians, 'alive', in name only. And if this Christ is he who 'searches mind and heart', who unveils their wretchedness, blindness, and nakedness, he is such because his Father's great love sent him to share men's conditions, their infirmities and sufferings. The Christians' 'toils and works', their 'tribulation and poverty', are not undertaken or accepted in vain or in solitude: their Lord 'knows' these things because he himself has partaken in them. Because he loves his own, he cannot endure their indifference, their being 'neither cold nor hot'; but also because he loves them, they have every reason to believe, to hope, to stand steadfast with 'patient endurance'—to place unwavering confidence in this love of Jesus at a time when wavering, yielding to certain imperial commands, would have removed them from trial and danger.

The picture of Christ in the letters to the seven churches is a picture of the friend who cares—who not only promises 'hidden manna', but also gives daily bread; whose 'voice like the sound of many waters' can not only thunder majestically, but also whisper soothingly and refreshingly, 'Do not fear what you are about to suffer'. The seven churches collectively emerge from

John's words with all the virtues and faults, hopes and fears, of Christians then and now; but in the very midst of our humanness, our eras and their changes, stands the man Jesus—the 'first and the last' and our peace on earth, the Son of God who will not leave us alone because he 'loves us and has freed us'.

The Prophetical Visions and Epilogue
(4: 1 — 22: 21)

PART I—THE CHURCH AND ISRAEL (4-11)

We may divide the central section of the Apocalypse into two parts: 4-11 and 12: 1—21: 8. Though chapters 4-11 fit into the integral plan of the whole work, they can, in a true sense, be regarded as forming a complete apocalypse. Swete remarks that 'had all our manuscripts broken off at Apocalypse 11: 19 and no vestige of the last eleven chapters survived, it is conceivable that the loss might never have been suspected'. In Ap. 12: 1 the author makes a fresh beginning for which the reader had been prepared in 10: 11; and, again, we come to an ending at 21: 8. We have, then, two apocalypses, each of which stretches to an end. From chapter 12 onwards, John is concerned with the church and pagan Rome, while in chapters 4-11 he is preoccupied with the church's relation to the chosen people. His work has about it something of the structure of the Old Testament prophetical books: first, oracles against Israel and then, oracles against the nations.

I. GOD TRANSMITS TO THE LAMB THE SEALED SCROLL (4-5)

Vision of the throne of God (4)

> *1 Kg. 22: 19: I saw the Lord sitting on his throne, and all the host of heaven standing beside him on his right hand and on his left.*
> *Is. 6: 1-5: In the year that King Uzziah died I saw the Lord*

*sitting upon a throne, high and lifted up; and his train filled
the temple.*

*2. Above him stood the seraphim; each had six wings, with
two he covered his face, and with two he covered his feet,
and with two he flew.*

*3 And one called to another, and said: 'Holy, holy, holy
is the Lord of hosts; the whole earth is full of his glory'.*

*4. And the foundations of the thresholds shook at the voice
of him who called and the house was filled with smoke.*

*5. And I said: 'Woe is me: For I am lost; for I am a man of
unclean lips, and I dwell in the midst of a people of unclean
lips; for my eyes have seen the King, the Lord of hosts.'*

*Dn. 7: 9f.: As I looked, thrones were placed and one that
was ancient of days took his seat; his raiment was white as
snow, and the hair of his head like pure wool; his throne
was fiery flames, its wheels were burning fire. A stream of
fire issued and came forth from before him; a thousand
thousands served him, and ten thousand times ten thousand
stood before him; the court sat in judgment, and the books
were opened.*

*Is. 24: 23: The Lord of hosts will reign on Mount Zion and
in Jerusalem . . . and before his elders he will manifest his
glory.*

*Zech. 4: 2, 10: I see, and behold, a lampstand all of gold
. . . and seven lamps on it. . . . These seven are the eyes of
the Lord, which range through the whole earth.*

*Ps. 29: 1; 96: 7: Ascribe to the Lord glory and honour
(LXX).*

*Dn. 4: 34: I blessed the Most High, and praised and
honoured him who lives for ever and ever.*

1. After this I looked, and lo, in heaven an open door. And the
first voice, which I had heard speaking to me like a trumpet,
said: 'Come up hither, and I will show you what must take
place after this.' 2. At once I was in the Spirit, and lo, a throne
stood in heaven, with one seated on the throne! 3. And he
who sat there appeared like jasper and carnelian, and round

the throne was a rainbow that looked like an emerald. 4. Round the throne were twenty-four thrones, and seated on the thrones were twenty-four elders, clad in white garments with golden crowns upon their heads. 5. From the throne issue flashes of lightning, and voices and peals of thunder, and before the throne burn seven torches of fire which are the seven spirits of God. 6. And before the throne there is as it were a sea of glass like crystal.

And round the throne, on each side of the throne, are four living creatures, full of eyes in front and behind: 7. the first living creature like a lion, the second living creature like an ox, the third living creature with the face of a man, and the fourth living creature like a flying eagle. 8. And the four living creatures, each of them with six wings, are full of eyes all round and within, and day and night they never cease to sing:

> 'Holy, holy, holy, is the Lord God Almighty,
> who was and is and is to come!'

9. And whenever the living creatures give glory and honour and thanks to him who is seated on the throne, who lives for ever and ever, the twenty-four elders fall down before him who is seated on the throne and worship him who lives for ever and ever; they cast their crowns before the throne, singing:

> 'Worthy art thou, our Lord and God,
> to receive glory and honour and power,
> for thou didst create all things,
> and by thy will they existed and were created.'

1. The formula, 'after this, I looked', which occurs again in 7 : 1, 9; 15 : 5; 18 : 1, serves to introduce a fresh vision of special importance (cf. Dn. 7 : 6). The conception of the opened heavens is found in Ezek. 1 : 1, but the more precise idea of a door standing open reflects current apocalyptic phraseology (cf. 1 Enoch 14 : 15—'and the entire portal stood open before me'). The 'first voice' is that of Ap. 1 : 10—John forges a link between the letters and the rest of the book. That same voice which had bidden him: 'Write what you see in a book and send it to the

seven churches' (1 : 10) now bids him, 'Come up hither, and I
will show you what takes place after this'. In the preceding vision
of 1 : 10-20, the seer was on earth; now he is spiritually translated to heaven. Compare what Paul says of his own experience :
'I know a man in Christ who . . . was caught up to the third
heaven' (2 Cor. 12 : 2). However, John does not enter fully into
heaven, but is left standing at the door. 'What must take place
after this' : cf. Dn. 2 : 28.

2.   'At once I was in the Spirit'—John is in a prophetic trance
(cf. 1 : 10). Cf. 'I know that this man was caught up into paradise—whether in the body or out of the body I do not know, God
knows' (2 Cor. 12 : 2). The throne of God in heaven is frequently referred to in the Old Testament (cf. 1 Kg. 22 : 19; Is.
6 : 1; Ezek. 1 : 26; Ps. 47 : 8; Dn. 7 : 9). John's vision is dominated by this symbol of divine sovereignty. It is the 'great white
throne' from which the judge speaks the sentence (Ap. 20 : 11);
in the final scene, it is the 'throne of God and of the Lamb' (22 :
1, 3). The 'one seated on the throne' is henceforth named frequently : God as king and judge.

3.   Now it becomes clear that John had not really *seen* God; the
one seated on the throne *appeared like* brilliant jewels. In his
description, John carefully avoids anthropomorphic details; he
simply conveys the impression of dazzling light—brightness which
at once shows and hides the presence of God. Ezekiel, too, had
sought to convey an impression of the invisible God, but one has
only to compare the texts to see how far John has surpassed his
model. The rainbow is immediately suggested by Ezek. 1 : 28; it
may, perhaps, be a reminder of God's covenant with Noah (Gen.
9 : 12-17)—the judge is mindful of his mercy.

4.   The great throne does not stand alone but is surrounded by
twenty-four other thrones; on these thrones sit twenty-four elders
wearing the white robes of victory and crowned as kings. They
are absorbed in the glorification of God and the Lamb (4 : 9f.;
5 : 8-11, 14; 11 : 16-18; 19 : 4); they offer to God the prayers
of the saints (5 : 8). Hence, they have a cultic role. Who are
these elders? Though many have suggested that they are angels
of some kind, it does not seem that this is John's intention. Cer-

tainly, the presence of angels in apocalyptic is commonplace; but there is no indication at all that these figures are angels, while the title 'elder', applied to angels, is unusual, to say the least. Besides, in 5 : 11, the elders and the angels are carefully distinguished. It seems that the elders of the Apocalypse must be taken as men (not angels), as representatives of the people of God—like the elders of Ex. 24 : 9 and Is. 24 : 23. Some commentators, making an appeal to 21 : 12-14, have taken the 'twenty-four elders' as a symbol of the whole church: the old Israel (twelve patriarchs, or twelve tribes) and the new Israel (the twelve apostles). This interpretation cannot be sustained because in 5 : 8-14; 14 : 3; 15 : 2-4, the elders are distinguished from the Christian faithful, and in 19 : 4-9 they are distinguished from the bride of the Lamb.

It seems best, then, to find in these elders the figure of the saints of the Old Testament. The privileged position of the just of Israel is recognized elsewhere in the New Testament. Cf. Lk. 13 : 28—'Then you will weep and gnash your teeth, when you see Abraham and Isaac and Jacob and all the prophets in the kingdom of God and you yourselves thrust out'. Heb. 11 : 2 designates as *presbyteroi* (elders) the long list of Old Testament saints put forward as an example to Christians. The number twenty-four is suggested by I Chr. : twenty-four classes of priests (24 : 1-19), each class headed by a 'chief man' or 'officer'—elsewhere called the *presbyteroi* ('elders') of the priests (2 Kg. 19 : 2). In 1 Chr. 25, the temple musicians (levites) were also divided into twenty-four classes, and in Ap. 5 : 8 the elders hold harps with which they accompany their 'new song' (5 : 9). All in all, the background of 1 Chr. is one John could have in mind. The place of these elders (the saints of the Old Testament) in Ap. with their implied interest in the destiny of Christians, suggests a viewpoint shared by the author of Hebrews: 'Therefore, since we are surrounded by so great a crowd of witnesses [the Old Testament saints of Heb. 11] . . .' (12 : 1).

Our interpretation neatly fits the immediate context. In Ap. 4 : 11 the elders sing the praises of God the Creator in terms which have nothing specifically Christian about them. In 5 : 5

one of them names Jesus the 'lion of the tribe of Judah, the root of David'. It would not be easy to imagine the disciples of the Lamb (if they were represented by the elders) praising their Saviour in the detached manner of 5 : 9f. More generally, our interpretation accords with the view that Ap. 4-11 is concerned with the place of the chosen people in God's plan, and with the fate of Jerusalem.

5-6a.—'Flashes of lightning, and voices and peals of thunder'— reminiscent of the theophany of Ex. 19 : 16, a passage which had already inspired Ezek. 1 : 13f. (cf. Ap. 8 : 5; 11 : 19; 16 : 18). 'Seven torches of fire, which are the seven spirits of God'; cf. Zech. 4 : 2, 10. The burden of Zechariah's vision is that what is to be accomplished will be wrought 'not by might, nor by power, but by my Spirit' (Zech. 4 : 6). In Ap. 5 : 6, the seven eyes of the Lamb are 'the seven spirits of God sent out into all the earth', a manifest echo of Zech. 4 : 10. And in Ap. 1 : 4 the 'seven spirits who are before his throne' symbolize the sevenfold Spirit. Thus, whereas the view that the 'seven torches of fire' are the seven 'angels of the presence' (the seven archangels of Jewish tradition; cf. Ap. 8 : 2) is at first sight attractive, it seems more satisfactory to admit the influence of Zech. The 'sea of glass' like crystal may be the waters above the firmament of Gen. 1 : 7; Ps. 104 : 3. But the immediate inspiration would be the current apocalyptic imagery. Cf. 2 Enoch 3 : 3—'They showed me [in the first heaven] a very great sea, greater than the earthly sea'. However, it is natural to suppose that this 'sea of glass' is the same as the 'sea of glass mingled with fire' of Ap. 15 : 2; and this latter, as we shall see, is probably the heavenly Red Sea.

6b. The 'four living creatures' are akin to the cherubim of Ezekiel; but, again, the immediate source lies in the apocalyptic tradition; cf. 1 Enoch 71 : 7; 39 : 12; 61 : 11f.; 2 Enoch 19 : 16. The 'living creatures' are the four angels responsible for directing the physical world; therefore they symbolize the whole created cosmos. To the familiar cherubim and seraphim, the apocalyptic writers had added the egregoroi, who never close their eyes, and the ophanim, who are covered back and front, inside and out,

with eyes. Typically, in his description, John has combined
several of these elements.

7f.   The cherubim of Ezekiel (inspired by the winged sphinx of
the ancient Near East), human in form, have four faces—those of
man, lion, ox and eagle—four wings and human hands. John has
simplified the complicated imagery of Ezekiel. The identification
of the 'living creatures' with the evangelists, apparently originat-
ing with Irenaeus, is wholly fanciful. The 'six wings' come from
the seraphim of Is. 6 : 2 (Ezekiel gave each of his creatures four
wings, 1 : 6). 'Full of eyes all round and within', like the
ophanim. In apocalyptic literature the task of the cherubim,
seraphim, ophanim and egregoroi is to sing the praises of God.
Cf. 1 Enoch 39 : 12—'Those who sleep not . . . stand before thy
glory and bless, praise and extol, saying : "Holy, holy, holy is the
Lord of Spirits"'. In 2 Enoch 19 : 6 cherubim and seraphim,
with six wings and many eyes, stand before the throne singing :
'Holy, holy, holy is the Lord God of Sabaoth : heaven and earth
are full of thy glory'. John is obviously heir to this apocalyptic
tradition. In our text, as in the others, the canticle is based on
Is. 6 : 3. It is the unceasing song of nature in praise of its Creator
(cf. Ps. 19 : 1-6). 'Who was and is and is to come'; cf. 1 : 4, 8.

9f.   'Glory and honour', cf. Ps. 29 LXX; 96 : 7. 'Thanks'
(*eucharistia*) is a New Testament word. Swete observes that 'while
"glory" and "honour" have regard to the divine perfections,
"thanks" refers to the divine gifts in creation and redemption'.
'Who lives for ever and ever', cf. Dn. 4 : 34. The elders, in keeping with their cultic role throughout Ap., join in the worship of
God. Just as vassal kings removed their crowns when coming into
the presence of the emperor, these kings lay their diadems of victory before their Lord : their victory and their glory were from
him.

11.   Whereas the living creatures addressed the Creator simply
as 'Lord God Almighty' (4 : 8), the elders see him as 'our Lord', the
Yahweh of revelation, and as 'our God'. 'They existed and were
created'—the order is unexpected, but the idea of God's universal
creation is quite clear. This heavenly canticle is the first of many
in Ap. Doubtless, all of them are modelled on, or reflect, early

Christian hymns. However, the little hymn of 4 : 11, which has nothing specifically Christian about it, is fitting in the mouths of the elders—the saints of the Old Testament. 'So the chapter ends with the emphasis on God the Creator. We turn now to God the Redeemer' (Turner).

The Lamb receives the sealed scroll (5)

Ezek. 2: 9f.: When I looked, behold, a hand was stretched out to me, and, lo, a written scroll was in it; and he spread it out before me; and it had writing on the front and on the back, and there were written on it words of lamentation and mourning and woe.

Dn. 4: 13f.: Behold, a watcher, a holy one ('an angel of strength'—LXX) came down from heaven. He cried aloud and said. . . .

Ex. 20: 4: . . . anything that is in the heaven above, or that is in the earth beneath, or that is in the water under the earth.

Gen. 49: 9f.: Judah is a lion's whelp. . . . The sceptre shall not depart from Judah, nor the ruler's staff from between his feet, until he comes to whom it belongs; and to him shall be the obedience of the peoples.

Is. 11: 1-2a, 4b, 10: There shall come forth a shoot from the stump of Jesse, and a branch shall grow out of his roots. And the Spirit of the Lord shall rest upon him. . . . And he shall smite the earth with the rod of his mouth, and with the breath of his lips he shall slay the wicked. . . . In that day the root of Jesse shall stand as an ensign to the peoples.

Is. 53: 7: Like a lamb that is led to the slaughter, and like a sheep that before its shearers is dumb, so he opened not his mouth.

Zech. 4: 10: These seven [lamps] are the eyes of the Lord, which range through the whole earth.

Ps. 141: 2: Let my prayer be counted as incense before thee, and the lifting up of my hands as an evening sacrifice.

Dn. 7: 10: A thousand thousands served him, and ten thousand times ten thousand stood before him.

1 Chr. 29: 11: Thine, O Lord, is the greatness, and the power, and the glory, and the victory, and the majesty.

1. And I saw on the right hand of him who was seated on the throne a scroll written within and on the back, sealed with seven seals; 2. and I saw a strong angel proclaiming with a loud voice, 'Who is worthy to open the scroll and break its seals?' 3. And no one in heaven or on earth or under the earth was able to open the scroll or to look into it. 4. And I wept much that no one was found worthy to open the scroll or look into it. 5. Then one of the elders said to me : 'Weep not; lo, the lion of the tribe of Judah, the root of David, has conquered, so that he can open the scroll and its seven seals.'

6. And between the throne and the four living creatures and among the elders I saw a Lamb standing, as though it had been slain, with seven horns and with seven eyes, which are the seven spirits of God sent out into all the earth; 7. and he went and took the scroll from the right hand of him who was seated on the throne. 8. And when he had taken the scroll, the four living creatures and the twenty-four elders fell down before the Lamb, each holding a harp, and with golden bowls full of incense, which are the prayers of the saints; 9. and they sang a new song, saying :

'Worthy art thou to take the scroll and to open its seals,
   for thou wast slain and by thy blood didst ransom men for
      God
from every tribe and tongue and people and nation,
10. and hast made them a kingdom and priests to our God,
   and they shall reign on earth.'

11. Then I looked and I heard around the throne and the living creatures and the elders the voice of many angels, numbering myriads of myriads and thousands of thousands, 12. saying with a loud voice : 'Worthy is the Lamb who was slain, to receive power and wealth and wisdom and might and honour and glory and blessing!' 13. And I heard every creature in heaven and on earth and under the earth and in the sea, and all therein, saying : 'To him who sits upon the throne and to the

Lamb be blessing and honour and glory and might for ever
and ever!' 14. And the four living creatures said 'Amen!' and
the elders fell down and worshipped.

5 : 1.   When he turned again to the one on the throne, John saw
a scroll lying on the open palm of his right hand. The apparent
inconsistency that John can see the hand of one whom he could
discern only through the effulgence of his glory (4 : 3) illustrates
the proper approach to these visions: they are not meant to be
visualized but, rather, to be interpreted intellectually. The 'right
hand' (as in 1 : 16) symbolizes the authority of the one concerned;
the scroll, as God's property, is in his possession. Like the scroll
of Ezek. 2 : 9f., this one (most likely a papyrus roll) had writing
inside and on the back. This was unusual and, together with the
fact that it was sealed, would suggest an official document: the
text was written within but a résumé of the text was given on the
outside. However, it seems best to take it, as in the case of Ezekiel, that the contents had overflowed to the *verso* of the crowded
papyrus. Indeed, it is the whole passage Ezek 2 : 1—3 : 9 which
provides not only the background but the key to the understanding of our scroll.

The vision of the scroll may well have been the inaugural vision
of Ezekiel; at any rate, it maps out his mission. He is told: 'Son
of man, go, get you to the house of Israel and speak with my
words to them' (3 : 4). The limits of his mission are drawn: 'You
are not sent to a people of foreign speech and a hard language,
but to the house of Israel—not to many peoples' (3 : 5f.). The
sealed scroll of Ap. 5 is the Lord's judgment on an unfaithful
Israel, just as in Ezekiel. But, in his own free manner, John has
taken up the mission which was forbidden to Ezekiel by turning
in the second part of Ap. to 'many peoples of foreign speech and
a hard language' (Ezek. 3 : 5; cf. Jer. 1 : 10). The scroll passage
of Ezekiel is reflected also in Ap. 10. There John is given a 'little
scroll' (Ap. 10 : 2) which he eats (Ap. 10 : 9f.; cf. Ezek. 3 : 1-3),
and he is bidden 'prophesy about many peoples and nations and
tongues and kings' (Ap. 10 : 11; cf. Ezek. 3 : 5f.). According to
our interpretation of the work, Ap. 10 is a new prophetic investi-

ture in which John is called to a new mission : he must prophesy as he had not done up to now. That is, he is no longer concerned with Israel.

We take it, then, that the scroll of Ap. 5 contains 'words of lamentation and mourning and woe' addressed to Israel, this time to an Israel which had rejected its Messiah. It is a *'sealed* scroll'. Again, official documents were sealed; a Roman prescription demanded that a will should be sealed with seven seals. However, in our case, the breaking of the seals not only discloses the contents of the scroll but brings them to pass : the breaking of the seals is a special, indeed an exclusive task which the Lamb alone can perform. What is this sealed scroll? The underlying Ezekiel text suggests that it is God's judgment on Jerusalem. But Ezekiel is not the only prophet or the only Old Testament voice that has warned Israel. The book of Deuteronomy, which has brought out the significance of Israel's election, emphatically underlines the obligation involved. It sets before Israel two ways : the way of the commandments which is the way of life, or the way of faithlessness which means death (Dt. 30 : 15). In short, we can say that the recognition of election as involving obligations for Israel is a recurrent theme in the Old Testament, and that the repudiation of these obligations was tantamount to the repudiation of election. The fate of Israel can be read in the Old Testament—by one who has eyes to see. For, already, Isaiah had complained that Israel could not understand its own scriptures : 'And the vision of all this has become to you like the words of a book that is sealed. When men give it to one who can read, saying, "Read this", he says, "I cannot, for it is sealed". And when they give the book to one who cannot read, saying, "Read this", he says, "I cannot read" ' (Is. 29 : 11f.). Paul, summing up the Christian attitude, can declare of his Jewish contemporaries : 'To this day, when they read the old covenant, that same veil remains unlifted, because only through Christ is it taken away. Yes, to this day whenever Moses is read a veil hangs over their minds; but when a man turns to the Lord the veil is removed' (2 Cor. 3 : 14-16). The Old Testament can be fully understood only by Christians who are enlightened by Christ, as the two disciples were on the road to Emmaus: 'Beginning with Moses and all the prophets, he interpreted to them in all the scriptures the things concerning himself' (Lk. 24 : 27). And so it was that in his last contact with his disciples before his ascension, Jesus gave them a new understanding of the Old Testament: 'he opened their minds to understand the scriptures' (24 : 45).

The sealed scroll of Ap. 5 has to do primarily with the destiny of the chosen people (while keeping in view the rest of mankind who have a religious dependence on Israel). It represents the Old Testament writings, especially the oracles of the prophets about Israel, enigmatic writings to which Christ alone can provide a key. It is concerned with the 'time of Israel', with the close of that epoch of salvation history. We shall see that Ap. 4-11 is guided by the synoptic apocalypse, especially by Luke's version of it; so, like Luke, John has perceived a distinction between the end of Jerusalem and the end of the world. The fall of Jerusalem in AD 70 was of great importance to Christians: it made manifest to all that the 'time of Israel', which had in reality ended with the ministry of Jesus and the founding of the Church, was indeed at an end.

We may regard Ap. 4-11, with its series of seals and of trumpets, as, in large measure, a development of the data of the synoptic apocalypse. It is an interpretation of the history of the events foretold in the synoptics: the Jewish war and the destruction of Jerusalem, events which, when Ap. was written, were events of the past, events of great significance. 'The destruction of Jerusalem and of its temple marked not the end of *the* world, but the end of *a* world. It indicated the final separation of Judaism from Christianity, of the synagogue from the church. Henceforth, the latter turned principally to the gentiles.'[30] Luke has distinguished three periods of salvation history: the time of Israel, the time of Christ, and the time of the Church.[31] Ap. is not a gospel, and the author does not mark out the specific time of Christ; but he does discern the time of Israel and the

[30] A. Feuillet, *Johannine Studies, op. cit.*, 229f.

[31] See W. J. Harrington, *The Gospel According to St Luke*, Westminster, Newman Press, London, Geoffrey Chapman, 19f.

time of the Church, each period closing with a divine judgment.

2.   A 'strong angel' (cf. Dn. 4 : 13f.) is referred to again in 10 : 1; 18 : 21 : 'Worthy'—in the sense not only of being morally fit, but of being able. 'To open . . . and break' : though the opening of the book demands the breaking of the seals, to be able to open the book is the first necessity and is mentioned first.

3f.   Cf. Ex. 20 : 4; and Phil. 2 : 10 : '. . . every knee should bow, in heaven and on earth and under the earth.' The threefold division embraces the whole of creation : no one at all can be found to open the scroll. John's tears are not tears of frustration; he does not weep merely because he sees himself thwarted in his expectation of looking into the future. In fact, the opening of the scroll is not only the revealing of God's purposes but the accomplishing of them. From John's apocalyptic standpoint, the events leading up to the destruction of Jerusalem still lie in the future; and God seeks an agent through whom he may act.

5.   One of the elders (cf. 7 : 13) comforts John by assuring him that all is well. 'Weep not'—an echo of the words of Jesus in Lk. 7 : 13; 8 : 52. 'Lion of the tribe of Judah', cf. Gen. 49 : 9f. 'Root of David', cf. Is. 11; 1-10; Ap. 22 : 16; Rom. 15 : 12. The messianic Old Testament texts point to the son of David who has dominion over the nations; he has conquered and so has the right to open the scroll. Cf. Jn 16 : 33—'I have overcome the world'; cf. Ap. 1 : 18; 3 : 21. The victory has been won through his death and resurrection (cf. Rom. 1 : 4; Ac. 3 : 26).

6f.   When John looks up to find the lion of Judah, he sees a Lamb (cf. Is. 53 : 7; Ac. 8 : 32). We are at once reminded of Jn 1 : 29—'Behold the Lamb of God, who takes away the sin of the world' (cf. 1 : 36). In Jn the 'Lamb of God' is not only the suffering servant who, as an offering for sin, has borne the iniquity of mankind (Is. 53 : 5f., 10); he is also the Passover Lamb (Jn 19 : 36). The Lamb has been slain, and yet it is alive and standing erect (cf. Ap. 1 : 18). Ac. 2 : 24—'God raised him up, having loosed the pangs of death, because it was not possible for him to be held by it'. It is significant that the wounds of Christ (like the wound-bearing Lamb) figure in the Johannine tradition (Jn 20 :

25, 27; cf. Lk. 24: 40). The horn is a symbol of power; the seven horns of the Lamb symbolize the fulness of his power as the victorious Christ. Cf. Mt. 28: 18—'All authority in heaven and on earth has been given to me'; Jn 17: 2—'thou hast given him power over all flesh'. The seven eyes of the Lamb stand for the fulness of his knowledge (cf. Ap. 1: 14). Yet, at the same time, the eyes are 'the seven spirits of God sent out into all the earth'—like the 'eyes of the Lord' in Zechariah. The text not only echoes Zech. 4: 10, but also recalls to mind Is. 11: 2—the sevenfold Spirit of the Lord resting on the root of Jesse. Jesus, as glorified Messiah, pours forth the Spirit—a thoroughly Johannine idea. Cf. Jn 7: 39—'As yet the Spirit had not been given, because Jesus was not yet glorified'; 15: 26—'When the Counsellor comes, whom I shall send to you from the Father, even the Spirit of truth, who proceeds from the Father, he will bear witness to me' (cf. Ac. 2: 33). The Lamb, who had won the right to break the seven seals, went up to the throne to receive the scroll: it is a transfer of power.

8. The living creatures and the elders, whom we had heard worshipping God (4: 8-10), here acknowledge the divinity of the Lamb. The elders, in accordance with their cultic function, hold harps (like the levites of 1 Chr. 25) and censers; and they exercise the priestly office of mediation, offering the prayers of the faithful to God. Cf. Ps. 141: 2; Ap. 8: 3; Lk. 1: 10. That the saints of the Old Testament should offer to God the prayers of the Christian faithful is not incompatible with the New Testament understanding of the place of the saints of Israel (cf. Heb. 12: 1). Besides, the prayers in question had to do with the opening of the scroll; for Christians, too, the fate of Jerusalem, God's holy city, was a disturbing problem.

9f. A 'new song' is mentioned several times in the Psalms: 33: 3; 40: 4; 96: 1; 98: 1; 144: 9; 149: 1. Originally denoting simply a fresh song of praise, the phrase lent itself especially to songs composed for great occasions (cf. Is. 42: 10; Jdt. 16: 13). Here, the occasion for the new song is the redemption wrought by Christ. He is worthy to take the book because of his saving sacrifice. Only in Ap. is Jesus said to have been 'slain' (cf. 5 : 6, 9, 12; 13 : 8)—showing, perhaps, the influence of Is. 53 : 7. *agorazō* ('to ransom') is a Pauline word (1 Cor. 6 : 20; 7 : 23; Gal. 3 : 13; 4 : 5; cf. Ap. 14 : 3f.; 2 Pet. 2 : 1). The Lamb has ransomed men at the cost of his blood. 'Every tribe and tongue and people and nation', based on a phrase which recurs in Daniel (Dn. 3 : 4, 7; 5 : 19; 6 : 25), is found frequently in Ap. (7 : 9; 11 : 9; 13 : 7; 14 : 6). Christ has made those whom he has ransomed a kingdom of priests unto God (cf. 1 : 6; 20 : 6). 'To be a Christian is to be both king and priest, but with a sovereignty and priesthood derived from Christ, as his were derived from God. John does not think of Christ as having withdrawn from the scene of his earthly victory, to return only at the parousia. In and through his faithful followers he continues to exercise both his royal and priestly functions' (Caird). While this is so, 'earth' looks rather to the 'new earth' (21 : 1) in which 'they shall reign for ever and ever' (22 : 5). The tone of the canticle is impersonal ('didst ransom *men*', 'hast made *them*', '*they* shall reign') and would sound strangely in the mouths of those who had been ransomed by the blood of the Lamb; it is appropriate in the mouths of the Old Testament saints.

11f.   A new feature is introduced : the praise of the countless host of angels (cf. Dn. 7 : 10; 1 Enoch 40 : 1). The doxology (cf. 1 Chr. 29 : 11), addressed to the Lamb, is fuller than that which the elders have offered to the Creator (Ap. 4 : 11); but in 7 : 12 the attributes of 5 : 12 are again found (though in a different order, and with 'thanksgiving' instead of 'wealth') in a doxology addressed to God.

13f.   The whole of creation, without any exception, joins in the great canticle of praise; the threefold division of 5 : 3 now becomes fourfold; the sea is added. John *hears* the voice of the great acclamation; to it the four living creatures, heavenly representatives of the created universe, give their 'Amen'—and the elders worship as in 4 : 9f. The conjunction of God and Lamb, which recurs in 7 : 10; 21 : 22; 22 : 1, 3 cf. 3 : 21, represents an advanced christology : the same worship is addressed to God and Lamb—just as the throne of both is one and the same.

The doxologies offered to God by the living creatures (4 : 8) and

E

by the elders (4 : 11) dwell on the manifestation of God's glory in creation. The doxologies of the living creatures and elders (5 : 9f.) and of the host of angels (5 : 12) dwell on the redemption of the world by the Lamb. The climax comes when the worship offered to God (ch. 4) and to the Lamb (5 : 1-12) are united in the closing doxology (5 : 13), in which all created things throughout the entire universe acclaim together God and the Lamb (Charles).

II. THE OPENING OF THE SEVEN SEALS (6 : 1—8 : 1)

The breaking of the seals unleashes a series of plagues (6 : 1—8 : 1), a series which follows the pattern of events in the synoptic apocalypse (Mk 13, par.): war, strife among nations, famine, pestilence, persecution, phenomena (earthquakes, eclipses, etc.). On the whole, John is closest to Luke who, unlike Mark and Matthew, lists pestilence and whose 'distress of nations' (21 : 25) is the equivalent of Ap. 6 :15-17. On the other hand, Mk 13 : 24 and Mt. 24 : 29 develop the 'signs in the sun and moon and stars' (Lk. 21 : 25) in almost the same language as Ap. Evidently, John is building on the tradition which underlies the synoptic passages. It is of significance for our interpretation of this first part of Ap. that the synoptic apocalypse (most obviously in Luke) is concerned with the fate of Jerusalem.

The first four seals (6: 1-8)

> *Zech. 1: 8-11: I saw in the night and behold, a man riding upon a red horse: he was standing among the myrtle trees in the glen; and behind him were red, sorrel and white horses. Then I said, 'What are these, my Lord? The angel who talked with me said to me, 'I will show you what they are'. So the man who was standing among the myrtle trees answered, 'These are they whom the Lord has sent to patrol the earth'. And they answered the angel of the Lord who was standing among the myrtle trees, 'We have patrolled the earth, and behold, all the earth remains at rest.'*

Zech. 6: 1-8: And again I lifted my eyes and saw, and behold, four chariots came out from between two mountains, and the mountains were mountains of bronze. The first chariot had red horses, the second black horses, the third white horses and the fourth chariot dappled grey horses. Then I said to the angel who talked with me, 'What are these, my Lord?' And the angel answered me, 'These are going forth to the four winds of heaven, after presenting themselves before the Lord of all the earth. The chariot with the black horses goes toward the north country, the white ones go toward the west country, and the dappled ones go toward the south country'. When the steeds came out, they were impatient to get off and patrol the earth. And he said, 'Go, patrol the earth'. So they patrolled the earth. Then he cried to me, 'Behold, those who go toward the north country have set my Spirit at rest in the north country.'
Ezek. 14: 21: For thus says the Lord God: How much more when I send upon Jerusalem my four sore acts of judgment, sword, famine, evil beasts and pestilence to cut off from it man and beast.

1. Now I saw when the Lamb opened one of the seven seals, and I heard one of the four living creatures say, as with a voice of thunder: 'Come!' 2. And I saw, and behold, a white horse, and its rider had a bow, and a crown was given to him, and he went out conquering and to conquer.

3. When he opened the second seal, I heard the second living creature say, 'Come!' 4. And out came another horse, bright red; its rider was permitted to take peace from the earth, so that men should slay one another; and he was given a great sword.

5. When he opened the third seal, I heard the third living creature say 'Come!' And I saw, and behold, a black horse, and its rider had a balance in his hand; 6. and I heard what seemed to be a voice in the midst of the four living creatures saying, 'A quart of wheat for a denarius, and three quarts of barley for a denarius, but do not harm oil and wine!'

7. When he opened the fourth seal, I heard the voice of the fourth living creature say, 'Come!' 8. And I saw, and behold, a pale horse, and its rider's name was death, and Hades followed him; and they were given power over a fourth of the earth, to kill with sword and with famine and with pestilence and by wild beasts of the earth.

Though John follows the pattern of the synoptic apocalypse, he still quarries his descriptive material from the Old Testament. For the first four plagues he has turned to Zech. 1 : 8-11; 6 : 1-8. The four horsemen of Zech. 1 : 8-11 (horsemen because riders are implied in v. 11) are the angels who have the world under their surveillance; their dispatch symbolizes judgment on the nations. In 6 : 1-8 the four chariots presage the destruction of Babylon. They represent the messengers of God, going out from his heavenly council, travelling in different directions to patrol the earth. In 6 : 5 they are the personification of the four winds of heaven (cf. Ap. 7 : 1) which stand before the throne of God to carry out the decrees of his justice. Zechariah has suggested the horses and their colours, but John has altered their functions to suit his own purpose; typically, also, he has borrowed from two distinct visions.

6 : 1. The scroll had been sealed with seven seals and so, in fact, could not be unrolled until *all* the seals were broken. With fine dramatic effect, John presents the very breaking of a seal as a revelation : the loosing of the seals is a symbolic action. At first sight the fourfold 'Come' (6 : 1-7) might seem to be no more than the summoning of the particular plague. Rather, it seems to anticipate the 'Come' of the Spirit and the bride, of the hearer of the book, and of its writer (22 : 17, 20). Nature, too, awaits the coming of Christ, and the repeated 'Come' of the living creatures represents the 'eager longing of creation', cf. Rom. 8 : 19. For, indeed, the breaking of the seals is the work of the Lamb; because this work—which he alone can do—will mean that things will be brought to pass, revealed.

2. Some have identified this rider on the white horse with him of 19 : 11-16, and have seen him as a symbol of the victorious

course of the gospel. In reality, all that the two visions have in common is the *white* horse—the colour of victory. It is evident that, in our passage, the four horsemen must be taken together; they represent war and its attendant evils—the war, strife, famine, and pestilence of the synoptic apocalypse. The white horse signifies triumphant warfare; the horseman rides on his career of conquest. Mention of the bow points to the Parthians, the only mounted archers of the ancient world. The Parthians, along the eastern frontier of the Empire, were the great contemporary threat to Rome (they are in mind again in 9 : 14 and 16 : 12). As in the letters to the churches, John's symbolic language can be topical.

3f.   Like the first two woes of the synoptic apocalypse (wars and international strife, cf. Lk. 21 : 9f.), the first two horsemen are not clearly distinguished. The second horse is the colour of slaughter and his rider wields a great sword. He has been given power to take peace from the earth and to make men slaughter one another : the complementary sides of warfare.

5f.   War carries famine in its train : the rider on the black horse with his pair of scales. Swete suggests that the voice from the midst of the living creatures is 'the protest of Nature against the horrors of famine'. A denarius is the daily wage and a quart of wheat the average daily consumption of a workman. However, by buying barley (three quarts for a denarius) the workman could have something for his family as well. The conditions are near-famine, but the situation is not yet catastrophic. There is no rationing of oil and wine—a reference, perhaps, to the time of Domitian when there was a scarcity of bread and an abundance of wine. It seems unlikely that wine and oil should be regarded as luxury commodities, since wheat, barley, oil and wine were staple items in Palestine and Asia Minor.

7f.   The rider on the pale horse is a symbol of pestilence—*thanatos* ('death') can also mean 'pestilence' (cf. 2 : 23; 18 : 8); but he stands, too, as an epitome of the four plagues. Hades, the abode of the dead, swallows up the victims of the pestilence. Undoubtedly, Ezek. 14 : 21 lies behind this verse of Ap.; significantly, Ezekiel's text is directed against Jerusalem. The restriction to a 'fourth part of the earth' is to be understood in the same way as in the plagues of 8: 7-12, which strike only *one-third* of the earth and of the heavenly bodies. The reason for the restriction (which must be understood symbolically) in each case is that the plague of seals and trumpets are directed to Israel; there is no such qualification in the plagues of bowls which are aimed at the pagan world.

THE LAST THREE SEALS (6: 9—8: 1)

The four horsemen have not exhausted the plagues: 'this is but the beginning of the sufferings' (Mt. 24: 8; Mk 13: 8). Whereas the first four seals have been described in a few verses, the others are unfolded at greater length and are interspersed with other visions. The same procedure will be followed in the presentation of the seven trumpets (8-11).

The fifth seal (6: 9-11)

> *Zech. 1: 12: O Lord of hosts, how long wilt thou have no mercy on Jerusalem ...?*

9. When he opened the fifth seal, I saw under the altar the souls of those who had been slain for the word of God and for the witness they had borne; 10. they cried out with a loud voice, 'O Sovereign Lord, holy and true, how long before thou wilt judge and avenge our blood on those who dwell on the earth?' 11. Then they were each given a white robe and told to rest a little longer, until the number of their fellow servants and their brethren should be complete, who were to be killed as they themselves had been.

9. At the breaking of the fifth seal the martyrs appear; the pattern is still the synoptic apocalypse (Mt. 24: 9-14; Mk 13: 9-13; Lk. 21: 12-19). But, in Ap. these are the martyrs of the Old Testament. The striking imagery is suggested by Lev. 4: 7— 'The rest of the blood . . . he shall pour out at the base of the altar of burnt-offering'; and since 'blood is the life' (Lev. 17:

11), the 'souls' of the martyrs are where their life-blood is found. The martyrs are presented as sacrificial victims; underneath the heavenly altar, they are safely in the presence of God (the heavenly throne-room has become a temple). It was a current rabbinical belief that the souls of the righteous were under the altar in heaven. These had been slain 'for the word of God'; for their fidelity to the one God. Though the phrase 'for the witness they had borne' would suggest 'the testimony of Jesus' of 1 : 2, 9, it does not necessarily do so; it is still possible to remain within an Old Testament context.

10. Cf. Gen. 4 : 10—'The voice of your brother's blood is crying to me from the ground.' There is, too, the remarkably apposite text of Lk. 11 : 50f.—'. . . that the blood of all the prophets, shed from the foundation of the world, may be required of this generation, from the blood of Abel to the blood of Zechariah . . . Yes, I tell you, it shall be required of this generation' (cf. Mt. 23 : 35f.). 'How long?' re-echoes throughout the Old Testament (Ps. 6 : 3; 13 : 1f.; 35 : 17; 74 : 9f.; 79 : 5; 80 : 4; 89 : 46; 90 : 13; 94 : 3f.; Is. 6 : 11; Jer. 47 : 6; Heb. 1 : 2). Cf. especially Zech. 1 : 12. The words of the prayer assert the principle of divine retribution, which forbids the exercise of personal revenge. So Paul in Rom. 12 : 19 (referring to Lev. 19 : 18 and Dt. 32 : 35) : 'Beloved, never avenge yourselves, but leave it to the wrath of God; for it is written, "Vengeance is mine, I will repay, says the Lord".' Cf. Lk. 18 : 7f.—'Will not God vindicate his elect, who cry to him day and night? Will he delay long over them? I tell you he will vindicate them speedily.' 'Those who dwell upon the earth' (cf. Ap. 3 : 10; 8 : 13; 11 : 10; 13 : 8, 12, 14; 17 : 2-8); throughout the book these are the enemies of God.

11. These martyrs have already received the white robe of victory, and they are bidden to *rest* a little longer. Here we meet with an assertion that is subsequently made several times and in various ways: martyrs (whether of Israel, as here, or Christian martyrs as elsewhere in the book) are at peace from the moment of their martyrdom (cf. 7 : 9-17; 12 : 10f.; 14 : 1-5, 13f.; 15 : 2-4; 19 : 4; 20 : 4-6). They are to rest until the roll of martyrs is complete; their 'fellow servants and their brethren' are the Chris-

tian martyrs. The idea that the end would come when the roll of martyrs is complete was current in later Judaism. Cf. 4 Ezra 4: 35f.—'Did not the souls of the righteous in their chambers ask about these matters saying, "How long are we to remain here? And when will come the harvest of our reward?" And Jeremiel the archangel answered them and said, "When the number of those like yourselves is completed".'

The sixth seal (6: 12-17)

Jl 2: 31: The sun shall be turned to darkness, and the moon to blood, before the great and terrible day of the Lord comes.

Is. 13: 10: For the stars of the heavens and their constellations will not give their light; the sun will be dark at its rising and the moon will not shed its light.

Is. 34: 4: All the host of heaven shall rot away, and the skies roll up like a scroll. All their host shall fall, as leaves fall from the vine, like leaves falling from the fig tree.

Ps. 2: 2: The kings of the earth set themselves, and the rulers take counsel together, against the Lord.

Is. 2: 10, 19: Enter into the rock, and hide in the dust from before the terror of the Lord, and from the glory of his majesty. . . . And men shall enter the caves of the rocks and the holes of the ground from before the terror of the Lord.

Hos. 10: 8: And they shall say to the mountains, 'Cover us', and to the hills, 'Fall upon us'.

Zeph. 1: 14f.: The great day of the Lord is near . . . a day of wrath is that day.

Nah. 1: 6: Who can stand before his indignation? Who can endure the heat of his anger?

12. When he opened the sixth seal, I looked, and behold, there was a great earthquake; and the sun became black as sackcloth, and the full moon became like blood. 13. And the stars of the sky fell to the earth as the fig tree sheds its winter fruit when shaken by the wind; 14. the sky vanished like a scroll

that is rolled up, and every mountain and island was removed from its place. 15. Then the kings of the earth and the great men and the generals and the rich and the strong, and every one, slave and free, hid in the caves and among the rocks of the mountains, 16. calling to the mountains and rocks, 'Fall on us and hide us from the face of him who is seated on the throne, and from the wrath of the Lamb; 17. for the great day of their wrath has come, and who can stand before it?'

12-14. At the opening of the sixth seal the cosmic phenomena appear. The close parallel with the synoptic apocalypse is maintained, but the Old Testament has provided the imagery of the common tradition. Cf. *Assumption of Moses*, 10: 4f.—'And the earth shall tremble: to its confines shall it be shaken. And the high mountains shall be made low and the hills shall be shaken and fall. And the horns of the sun shall be broken and he shall be turned into darkness; and the moon shall not give her light, and be turned wholly into blood.' Earthquakes belong to the traditional apocalyptic scheme (cf. Ap. 8: 8; 9: 2; Ezek. 38: 19; Jl 2: 10; Lk. 21: 11 par.). And, also in keeping with traditional imagery, the earthquake is followed by cosmic phenomena. Cf. Jl 2: 31; Is. 13: 10; 34: 4. For the removal of mountain and island, cf. Ap. 16: 20. How aesthetically pleasing are the images of the fig tree with its winter fruit and the sky vanishing like a rolled-up scroll !

15-17. Cf. Ps. 2: 2. v. 15 shows that all classes of society will be terror-stricken by the signs: kings, magistrates, military authorities, wealthy, strong, slaves and free. Social distinctions will be forgotten in the frantic attempt to escape. Cf. Is. 2: 10, 19; Hos. 10: 8. Also Lk. 23: 30—'Then they will begin to say to the mountains, "Fall on us," and to the hills, "Cover us" '—in reference to the destruction of Jerusalem by the Romans. In 5: 5f. we have noted the irony of the contrast: 'Lo, the Lion . . . I saw a Lamb'; here (v. 16) we have the conscious paradox, 'the wrath of the Lamb'; for this Lamb is the Son of Man to whom judgment has been given (ch. 5), and he is the rider on the white horse who is terrible to his enemies (19: 11-21). God's 'wrath' or 'anger' is his judgment on the world, the hostile world. Here the Lamb, again assimilated to the Father, is the wielder of wrath. Indeed, in v. 17, 'their wrath' is the wrath of him who is seated on the throne *and* of the Lamb. Caird notes that the phrase 'the wrath of the Lamb' is put in the mouths of the terrified 'inhabitants of the earth'; it indicates their total misconception of Christ; for they have been deceived by Satan, 'the deceiver of the entire world' (Ap. 12 : 9; cf. 2 : 9; 3 : 9). 'They are men to whom a lie has become second nature, so that, faced with the love and forgiveness of the sacrificed Lamb, they can see only a figure of inexorable vengeance. "The wicked man runs though no one pursues" (Prov. 28 : 1). To him no doubt the terror is real enough, perhaps even the only and ultimate reality; but it is nevertheless a travesty of the truth about Christ.' For v. 17, cf. Zeph. 1 : 14f.; Nah. 1 : 6.

The remnant of Israel (7: 1-8)

Ezek. 9: 4-6: The Lord said to him [*the man with the writing case in heaven*], *'Go through the city, through Jerusalem, and put a mark upon the foreheads of the men who sigh and groan over all the abominations that are commited in it'. And to the others* [*six angels*] *he said in my hearing, 'Pass through the city after him and smite . . . but touch no one upon whom is the mark'.*

Zech. 6: 5: These [*the four chariots*] *are going forth to the four winds of heaven, after presenting themselves before the Lord of all the earth.*

1. After this I saw the four angels standing at the four corners of the earth, holding back the four winds of the earth, so that no wind might blow on earth or sea or against any tree. 2. Then I saw another angel ascend from the rising of the sun, with the seal of the living God, and he called with a loud voice to the four angels who had been given power to harm earth and sea, 3. saying, 'Do not harm the earth or the sea or the trees, till we have sealed the servants of God upon their

foreheads.' 4. And I heard the number of the sealed, a hundred and forty-four thousand sealed, out of every tribe of the sons of Israel, 5. twelve thousand sealed out of the tribe of Judah, twelve thousand of the tribe of Reuben, twelve thousand of the tribe of Gad, 6. twelve thousand of the tribe of Asher, twelve thousand of the tribe of Naphtali, twelve thousand of the tribe of Manasseh, 7. twelve thousand of the tribe of Simeon, twelve thousand of the tribe of Levi, twelve thousand of the tribe of Issachar, 8. twelve thousand of the tribe of Zabulun, twelve thousand of the tribe of Joseph, twelve thousand sealed out of the tribe of Benjamin.

Before the last seal was broken, the servants of God were signed with the seal of the living God, one hundred and forty-four thousand of them (7 : 1-8): the saved remnant of Israel. The opening of the last seal unleashes the plagues of trumpets (8 : 6-11 : 19) which are modelled on the plagues of Egypt. The sealing of the elect, symbolizing their immunity, reflects the immunity of the Israelites to the plagues which struck the Egyptians.

7 : 1. The four chariots of Zech. 6 went forth to 'the four winds of heaven' (Zech. 6 : 5); John, who had utilized the image of the chariots (transformed into horsemen), here makes use of the reference to the four winds. The idea that angels guarded elemental forces was current; cf. Ap. 14 : 18, 'the angel who has power over fire', and 16 : 5, 'the angel of water'. In Jewish tradition the winds which blew from the four angles or corners of the earth square in form (as distinct from the winds which blew from the sides) were harmful. Besides, it was expected that a great storm would usher in the end. Cf. Mt. 24 : 31—'And he will send out his angels with a loud trumpet call, and they will gather his elect from the four winds, from one end of heaven to the other'. The winds which will hurt the earth are restrained until God has gathered his elect to him.

2f. Cf. Ezek. 9 : 4-6—the prophet has in mind the imminent destruction of Jerusalem by Nebuchadnezzar. In Ap. the servants of God will be preserved by him from the plagues which will strike the others (cf. 9 : 4). 'The seal of the living God' : the divine signet ring, like that of an oriental monarch (cf. Gen. 41 : 42; Est. 3 : 10; 8 : 2, 8, 10; Dn. 6 : 17; 1 Mac. 6 : 15), which marked the sealed as his property. Cf. 2 Tim. 2 : 19—'God's firm foundation stands, bearing this seal : "The Lord knows those who are his".' The four angels who are in charge of the destructive winds are themselves depicted as the devastators of land and sea. 4-8. John has not witnessed the sealing, but he learns the number of the sealed and their description. 'A hundred and forty-four thousand' : a thousand signifies an immense number, and 144 is the square of 12 (the twelve tribes)—therefore the countless elect of Israel. The solemn (rather tedious) enumeration is typical of apocalyptic (cf. Ap 21 : 12f., 19f.). Judah comes first in the list because the Messiah came from that tribe (cf. 5 : 5). The list includes *both* Joseph *and* Manasseh (whereas we should expect *either* Joseph *or* Ephraim/Manasseh)—so another tribe has to go : Dan has been dropped. We cannot say why the list should have taken just this form.

The Christian martyrs (7: 9-17)

Ps. 3: 9: Salvation belongs to the Lord (LXX).
Is. 49: 10: They shall not hunger or thirst, neither scorching wind nor sun shall smite them, for he who has pity on them will lead them, and by springs of water will guide them.
Is. 25: 8: The Lord God will wipe away tears from all faces.

9. After this I looked, and behold, a great multitude which no man could number, from every nation, from all tribes and peoples and tongues, standing before the throne and before the Lamb, clothed in white robes, with palm branches in their hands, 10. and crying out with a loud voice, 'Salvation belongs to our God who sits upon the throne, and to the Lamb!' 11. And all the angels stood round the throne and round the elders and the four living creatures, and they fell on their faces before the throne and worshipped God, 12. saying, 'Amen! Blessing and glory and wisdom and thanksgiving and honour and power and might be to our God for ever and ever! Amen.'

13. Then one of the elders addressed me, saying, 'Who are these, clothed in white robes, and whence have they come?' 14. And I said to him, 'Sir, you know.' And he said to me, 'These are they who have come out of the great tribulation; they have washed their robes and made them white in the blood of the Lamb.

'15. Therefore are they before the throne of God,
and serve him day and night within his temple;
and he who sits upon the throne will shelter them with his presence.

16. They shall hunger no more, neither thirst any more;
the sun shall not strike them, nor any scorching heat.

17. For the Lamb in the midst of the throne will be their shepherd,
and he will guide them to springs of living water;
and God will wipe away every tear from their eyes.'

9. This other group, a countless multitude from all nations, are Christian martyrs, the 'fellow servants and brethren' of the Old Testament martyrs of 6: 9-11. The vision is proleptic, that is, it anticipates the victory of those who will come triumphantly through the great tribulation. Thus, side by side with the elect of Israel, and by anticipation, John places the Christian martyrs. In keeping with his consistent outlook, they are presented as happy here and now; they stand before God and the Lamb, celebrating a heavenly Feast of Tabernacles. As martyrs they have immediately received their white robes (cf. 6: 11). The palm branches are a symbol of victory and joy after war (cf. 1 Mac. 13: 51; 2 Mac. 10: 7). The Feast of Tabernacles was celebrated in the seventh month, after the harvest; it was an occasion of great rejoicing (cf. Lev. 23: 33-36; Neh. 8: 13-18) when palm branches were carried and used in the booths raised on the flat house-tops. In Zech. 14: 16-19 the Feast of Tabernacles is set in the messianic era. The symbolism is clear; in our terms we might depict these martyrs as celebrating, in heaven, a perpetual Christmas.

10. As Christians they address their song of praise to God and

to the Lamb. Cf. Ps. 3 : 9; Ap. 12 : 10; 19 : 1. 'Salvation' has here the nuance of 'victory'; they attribute their victory to God and to the Lamb.

11f.   The angels, the countless host of 5 : 11, join in the heavenly liturgy, first by adding their 'Amen' to the prayer of the martyrs, and then by their own prayer. The wording of this hymn, with its seven features, is very like their praise of the Lamb in 5 : 12.

13f.   As in 5 : 5, an elder intervenes to interpret the vision. For the form of the dialogue cf. Zech. 4 : 2, 5; 6 : 4f. The 'great tribulation'—cf. Dn. 12 : 1 : 'And there shall be a time of trouble, such as never has been since there was a nation till that time'; Mk 13 : 19—'For in those days there will be such tribulation as has not been from the beginning of creation which God created until now, and never will be'; cf. Mt. 24 : 21. A 'great tribulation' was expected to precede the end; but, for John, the tribulation through which the martyrs come triumphantly is imminent persecution (cf. Ap. 3 : 10; 13 : 7-10). These are the conquerors of the letters (cf. 2 : 7, etc.). The white robes symbolize not only victory but purity too : they have been washed in the blood of the Lamb (cf. 1 : 5; 5 : 9). The striking paradox ('made them *white* in the *blood* of the Lamb') has a strange beauty. The martyrs have 'washed' and 'made white'—theirs is an active and not merely passive role : by the shedding of their blood they have joined their sacrifice to that of the Lamb.

15.   In their priestly role (1 : 6) the martyrs serve God, adding their unceasing service to the prayer of creation (4 : 8; cf. 22 : 3). In their heavenly Feast of Tabernacles there is no need for the martyrs to construct their own booths : God himself will be their tabernacle. There is also reference here to the shekinah—the immediate presence of God in the temple (cf. Ap. 21 : 3).

16f.   Cf. Is. 49 : 10; 25 : 8; Ap. 21 : 4. The texts of Isaiah, which refer to the happy return from the Exile, find their fulfilment in the shepherding of the Lamb who leads his own sheep to the unfailing fountains of life—(cf. Ap. 21 : 4). For, in startling and beautiful paradox, the Lamb has become a shepherd. In the Fourth Gospel the Lamb of God (Jn 1 : 29, 36) is also the good shepherd (10 : 14-16). Indeed, some texts of John form the best comment on our verses. Cf. Jn 6 : 35—'he who comes to me shall not hunger, and he who believes in me shall never thirst'; 7 : 37f.—'If any one thirst let him come to me, and let him who believes in me drink. As the scripture has said, 'out of his heart shall flow rivers of living water'. Cf. Jn 4 : 14.

The seventh seal (8:1)

1. When the Lamb opened the seventh seal, there was silence in heaven for about half an hour.

8 : 1. The Lamb breaks the last of the seals. The new series of plagues is preceded by a dramatic pause; it may be that there is a pause in the unceasing prayer of heaven (4 : 8; 7 : 15) to allow the prayers of the saints to be heard (8 : 4).

III. THE SEVEN TRUMPETS (8 : 2—11 : 19)

The first four trumpets (8: 2-13)

The opening of the seventh seal marks a beginning rather than an end; it heralds a fresh series of plagues. The trumpets are presented in much the same manner as the seals: the first four (8 : 7-12) are described in a few verses, while the others are disclosed at greater length, interspersed with other visions. The elect have been sealed (7 : 4-8), and their 'fellow servants and brethren' have appeared (7 : 9-17). Now comes the climax, the end—the end of *a* world. As he will do later on with Babylon (Rome), John lingers over the fate of Israel.

The prelude (8: 2-6)

Tob. 12: 15: I am Raphael, one of the seven holy angels who present the prayers of the saints and enter into the presence of the glory of the holy one.
Jl 2: 1: Blow the trumpet in Zion; sound the alarm on my holy mountain: let all the inhabitants of the land tremble, for the day of the Lord is coming, it is near.

Ezek. 10: 2: Go in among the whirling wheels underneath the cherubim; fill your hands with burning coals from between the cherubim and scatter them over the city.

2. Then I saw the seven angels who stand before God, and seven trumpets were given to them. 3. And another angel came and stood at the altar with a golden censer; and he was given much incense to mingle with the prayers of all the saints upon the golden altar before the throne; 4. and the smoke of the incense rose with the prayers of the saints from the hand of the angel before God. 5. Then the angel took the censer and filled it with fire from the altar and threw it on the earth; and there were peals of thunder, loud noises, flashes of lightning, and an earthquake.

6. Now the seven angels who had the seven trumpets made ready to blow them.

8 : 2.   These are the 'angels of the presence' (cf. Is. 63 : 9—'the angel of his presence'), the seven 'archangels' (cf. 1 Enoch 20 : 1-8) of Jewish tradition who serve God, namely, Michael, Gabriel, Raphael, Uriel, Raguel, Sariel and Remiel. Cf. Tob. 12 : 15; and Lk. 1 : 19—'I am Gabriel, who stand in the presence of God'. In the Old Testament, the trumpet announces God's judgment (cf. Jl 2 : 1; Zeph. 1 : 16; Is. 27 : 13). In the New Testament, trumpet blasts, sounded by angels, proclaim the final judgment (Mt. 24 : 31; 1 Cor. 15 : 52; 1 Thess. 4 : 16).

3f.   'Another angel' (cf. 7 : 2; 10 : 1; 14 : 6, 8f.; 18 : 1) took his place at the altar—this time the altar of incense and not the altar of holocausts as in 6 : 9; in 14 : 18 this angel is 'the angel who has power over fire'. However, it may be that John visualizes a single altar which can serve a double purpose. Cf. Lk. 1 : 11—'And there appeared to him [Zechariah] an angel of the Lord standing on the right side of the altar of incense'. However, in our text, the angel officiates as priest in the heavenly temple and offers the incense. In Ap. 5 : 8 we read of 'the golden bowls full of incense, which are the prayers of the saints', but the metaphor is not quite the same here. It appears that the prayers of the saints are represented by the coals on the altar of holocausts; that is, they are the prayers of the martyrs of 6 : 9f. The meeting of incense and the coals produces the ascending smoke, the symbol of divine acceptance (cf. Ezek. 8 : 11).

5.   Cf. Ezek. 10 : 2. The martyrs had prayed : '. . . how long before thou wilt judge and avenge our blood on those who dwell upon the earth?' (6 : 10); now their prayer, which had gone up to God (8 : 4), returns to the earth in wrath. (But see the comment on 11 : 19.) The thunder, loud noises, lightning and earthquakes sound in heaven (cf. 4 : 5; 11 : 19): they are the warning signs of a great visitation. Cf. Wis. 19 : 13—'The punishments did not come upon the sinners without prior signs in the violence of thunder'.

6.   The angels of the presence had been waiting for the heavenly sign : now they make ready to sound their trumpets.

The four trumpets (8: 7-12)

Ex. 9: 23-26: Then Moses stretched forth his rod toward heaven; and the Lord sent thunder and hail, and fire ran down to the earth. And the Lord rained hail upon the land of Egypt; there was hail, and fire flashing continually in the midst of the hail, very heavy hail, such as had never been in all the land of Egypt since it became a nation. The hail struck down everything that was in the field throughout all the land of Egypt, both man and beast; and the hail struck down every plant of the field, and shattered every tree of the field. Only in the land of Goshen, where the people of Israel were, there was no hail.

Jl 2: 30: And I will give portents in the heavens and on the earth, blood and fire and columns of smoke.

Ex. 7: 20f.: In the sight of Pharoah and in the sight of his servants, he lifted up the rod and struck the water that was in the Nile, and all the water that was in the Nile turned to blood. And the fish in the Nile died; and the Nile became foul, so that the Egyptians could not drink water from the Nile; and there was blood throughout all the land of Egypt.

Jer. 9: 15: Behold, I will feed this people with wormwood, and give them poisonous water to drink.

Ex. 10: 21-23: Then the Lord said to Moses, 'Stretch out your hand toward heaven that there may be darkness on the land of Egypt, a darkness to be felt'. So Moses stretched out his hand toward heaven, and there was thick darkness in all the land of Egypt three days; they did not see one another, nor did any rise from his place for three days; but all the people of Israel had light where they dwelt.

7. The first angel blew his trumpet, and there followed hail and fire, mixed with blood, which fell on the earth; and a third of the earth was burnt up, and a third of the trees were burnt up, and all green grass was burnt up.

8. The second angel blew his trumpet, and something like a great mountain, burning with fire, was thrown into the sea; 9. and a third of the sea became blood, a third of the living creatures in the sea died, and a third of the ships were destroyed.

10. The third angel blew his trumpet, and a great star fell from heaven, blazing like a torch, and it fell on a third of the rivers and on the fountains of water. 11. The name of the star is Wormwood. A third of the waters became wormwood, and many men died of the water, because it was made bitter.

12. The fourth angel blew his trumpet, and a third of the sun was struck, and a third of the moon, and a third of the stars, so that a third of their light was darkened; a third of the day was kept from shining, and likewise a third of the night.

The plagues of 8 : 7-12 strike only *one-third* of the earth and of the heavenly bodies, and again, in 9 : 15, only one-third of mankind is stricken by the sixth plague. We have seen that the seals struck 'a fourth of the earth' (6 : 8). We may seek the reason for this limitation in the prophetic doctrine of the remnant; with that superb freedom of his, John might have in mind the saved 'third' (cf. Ezek. 5 : 1-4; Zech. 13 : 8f.). Perhaps, more directly, he thinks of the immunity of Israel from the plagues of Egypt; for John has modelled his plagues of trumpets (and bowls) on the plagues of Egypt. According to our interpretation, the seals, modelled on the synoptic apocalypse, are concerned with God's judgment on Jerusalem. They are closely connected with the trumpets, to which they form the prelude and preparation, and the latter must be understood in the same sense as the former. Though the first four trumpets apply to nature, men are the ultimate sufferers.

7. Cf. Ex. 9 : 23-26 (seventh plague). The combination of fire and blood in a context of judgment is found in Jl 2 : 30; cf. Ac. 2 : 19. The fire is like the sun which, in Mediterranean countries, quickly burns up the grass; cf. Jas 1 : 11—'the sun rises with its scorching heat and withers the grass'. Otherwise a third of trees and plants were destroyed.

8f. Cf. Ex. 7 : 20 (first plague). 'Something like a great mountain, burning with fire'; probably suggested by 1 Enoch 18 : 13— 'I saw there seven stars like great burning mountains'. The burning, red-hot mass turns the waters of the sea into blood. Again, the destruction is limited to one-third of the ocean with its fishes and ships.

10f. Cf. Ex. 7 : 20 (first plague). The Exodus text describes the turning of the Nile waters into blood—a single plague. In 8f. and 9f. John has transformed it into two plagues; above he has spoken of the ocean, now he turns to the rivers and springs. Like the burning mountain of v. 8, a burning star (cf. 1 Enoch 18 : 13) destroys a third of the fresh water supply. The plant wormwood (*artemisia absinthiaca*) has a bitter taste; it is a metaphor for divine punishment in Jer. 9 : 15; 23 : 15; Lam. 3 : 15, 19, and for disaster in Prov. 5 : 4. The plague is the reverse of the miracle of Marah (Ex. 15 : 23-25). Men who drink this water die, as the creatures of the sea perished in v. 9 (and, presumably, the crews of the wrecked ships).

12. Cf. Ex. 10 : 21-23 (ninth plague). A third of the sun's and moon's disc is darkened and a third of the stars are obscured. Strictly speaking, this would cause a partial darkness (a lessening of light), not a shortening of day and night as the second half of the verse suggests. 'There is an inconsistency here which shows the writers independence of the ordinary laws of thought; he is

content to produce a desired effect by heaping up symbolism without regard to the consistency of the details. Here his purpose is chiefly to emphasize the partial character of the visitation' (Swete).

The three woes (8: 13-11: 19): Prelude (8: 13)

13. Then I looked, and I heard an eagle crying with a loud voice, as it flew in midheaven, 'Woe, woe, woe to those who dwell on the earth, at the blasts of the other trumpets which the three angels are about to blow!'

13.   John saw a vision and heard a voice (cf. 5 : 11; 6 : 1). The eagle, a messenger of coming judgment, appears in the zenith, where the sun stands at midday. The eagle is said to be the only bird who gazes straight into the sun; and this, combined with its high flights, suggested that the eagle was acquainted with 'the things of eternity'. Perhaps, for 'eagle' (*aetos*) we should read 'vulture'. Thus, in Lk. 17 : 37, *aetoi* should be translated 'vultures' rather than 'eagles' : 'Where the body is, there the vultures will be gathered together'. A vulture is an obvious symbol of doom, and in Hos. 8 : 1 the presence of a vulture (LXX, *aetos*) calls forth the trumpet alarm : 'Set the trumpet to your lips, for a vulture is over the house of the Lord'. The triple woe has reference to the three remaining trumpet-blasts or, rather, to the visitations that will follow them. Earth and sea have been stricken by the former plagues; now it is the turn of those 'who dwell on the earth' (cf. Ap. 3 : 10; 6 : 10; 11 : 10; 13 : 8, 14; 14 : 6; 17 : 8). But the sealed of chapter 7 cannot be touched by these plagues.

The first woe (fifth trumpet) (9: 1-12)

Ex. 10: 12-15: Then the Lord said to Moses, 'Stretch your hand over the land of Egypt for the locusts, that they may come upon the land of Egypt, and eat every plant in the land, all that the hail has left'. So Moses stretched forth his

*rod over the land of Egypt, and the Lord brought an east
wind upon the land all that day and all that night; and
when it was morning the east wind had brought the locusts.
And the locusts came up over all the land of Egypt, and
settled on the whole country of Egypt, such a dense swarm
of locusts as had never been before, nor ever shall be again.
For they covered the face of the whole land, so that the
land was darkened, and they ate all the plants in the land
and all the fruit of the trees which the hail had left.*

*Jl 1: 6f., 15: For a nation has come against my land, power-
ful and without number; its teeth are lions' teeth, and it
has the fangs of a lioness. It has laid waste my vines, and
splintered my fig trees; it has stripped off their bark and
thrown it down; their branches are made white. . . . Alas
for the day ! For the day of the Lord is near, and as destruction from the Almighty it comes. . . .*

*Jl 2: 1-11: Blow the trumpet in Zion; sound the alarm on
my holy mountain! Let all the inhabitants of the land
tremble, for the day of the Lord is coming, it is near, a day
of darkness and gloom, a day of clouds and thick darkness!
Like blackness there is spread upon the mountains a great
and powerful people; their like has never been from of old,
nor will be again after them through the years of all
generations. Fire devours before them, and behind them a
flame burns. The land is like the garden of Eden before
them, but after them a desolate wilderness, and nothing
escapes them. Their appearance is like the appearance of
horses, and like war horses they run. As with the rumbling
of chariots, they leap on the tops of the mountains, like the
crackling of a flame of fire devouring the stubble, like a
powerful army drawn up for battle. Before them people are
in anguish, all faces grow pale. Like warriors they charge,
like soldiers they scale the wall. They do not jostle one
another, each marches in his path; they burst through the
weapons and are not halted. They leap upon the city, they
run upon the walls; they climb up into the houses, they
enter through the windows like a thief. The earth quakes*

*before them, the heavens tremble. The sun and the moon
are darkened, and the stars withdraw their shining. The Lord
utters his voice before his army, for his host is exceedingly
great; he that executes his word is powerful. For the day of
the Lord is great and very terrible; who can endure it?*

1. And the fifth angel blew his trumpet, and I saw a star
fallen from heaven to earth, and he was given the key of the
shaft of the bottomless pit; 2. he opened the shaft of the bottomless pit, and from the shaft rose smoke like the smoke of a
great furnace, and the sun and the air were darkened with
the smoke from the shaft. 3. Then from the smoke came locusts
on the earth, and they were given power like the power of
scorpions of the earth; 4. they were told not to harm the grass
of the earth or any green growth or any tree, but only those
of mankind who have not the seal of God upon their foreheads;
5. they were allowed to torture them for five months, but not
to kill them, and their torture was like the torture of a scorpion, when it stings a man. 6. And in those days men will seek
death and will not find it; they will long to die, and death will
fly from them.

7. In appearance the locusts were like horses arrayed for
battle; on their heads were what looked like crowns of gold;
their faces were like human faces, 8. their hair like women's
hair, and their teeth like lions' teeth; 9. they had scales like
iron breastplates, and the noise of their wings was like the noise
of many chariots with horses rushing into battle. 10. They
have tails like scorpions, and stings, and their power of hurting
men for five months lies in their tails. 11. They have as king
over them the angel of the bottomless pit; his name in Hebrew
is Abaddon, and in Greek he is called Apollyon.

12. The first woe has passed; behold, two woes are still to
come.

9: 1f. The 'fallen star' is a fallen angel; he is probably the
angel of 9: 11. Cf. Lk. 10: 18—'I saw Satan fall like lightning
from heaven'. The 'bottomless pit' (abyss) is, in Ap., the provi-
sional place of punishment for Satan and fallen angels (cf. 9: 1f.,

11; 11 : 7; 17 : 8; 20 : 1, 3). Cf. Lk. 8 : 31—'And they [many demons] begged him not to command them to depart into the abyss'. John pictures the abyss as entered by a shaft whose mouth is kept under lock and key; the angel is permitted to unlock it. Thick smoke rising from the abyss filled the atmosphere and obscured the sun. Cf. Jl 2 : 10; Ex. 19 : 18—'And the smoke of it went up like the smoke of a kiln'.

3-5.   Cf. Ex. 10 : 12-15 (eighth plague); Jl 1 : 6f., 15; 2 : 1-11. It is the Egyptian plague of locusts already greatly embellished by Joel. John, in his turn, not only outdoes the prophet, but explicitly presents his locusts as a demonic plague. Their hurtful power is like that of the scorpion—a creature, like the serpent, proverbially hostile to man and easily becoming a symbol of evil forces. Cf. Lk. 10 : 19—'I will give you authority to tread upon serpents and scorpions, and over all the power of the enemy'. Since they are not natural locusts, they do not harm vegetation; their target is the 'inhabitants of the earth', those who do not bear the seal of God (cf. 7 : 2f.). As Israel in Egypt was preserved from the plagues, so the remnant is immune from these plagues. A scorpion sting is not normally fatal, but it is exceedingly painful; so, these locusts are commissioned to torture men, but not to slay them. The 'five months' means a short period and, perhaps, reflects the locusts' life-span of five months.

6.   Cf. Job. 3 : 20f.—'Why is light given to him that is in misery—who longs for death, but it comes not'; Jer. 8 : 3— 'Death shall be preferred to life by all the remnant that remains of this evil family'. During these months of torture, men would prefer death itself to the agony of living; but death eludes them.

7-10.   This description of the locusts owes much to Joel. The heads of locusts bear a resemblance to those of horses. (In Italian locust is *cavalletta*, 'little horse', and in colloquial German *Heupferd*, 'hay-horse'.) They have the semblance of crowns on their heads, since they are invincible. Yet, they have human faces: 'Evil may take many sinister forms and ramify far beyond the immediate implications of individual sin; but in the last analysis it has a human face, for it is caused by the rebellion of human wills against the will of God' (Caird). 'Hair like women's hair' may be suggested by the antennae of the locusts—or, perhaps, the long-haired Parthians may be in mind (cf. 6 : 2). In his presentation John may have been influenced by the Book of Wisdom's midrashic treatment of the plagues of Egypt. Cf. Wis. 12 : 8f.— 'But even these thou didst spare, since they were but men, and did send wasps as forerunners of thy army . . . thou wast not unable to destroy them at a blow by dread wild beasts'.

11.   Cf. Prov. 30 : 27, 'the locusts have no king, yet all of them march in rank'. But these 'locusts' are demonic beings and they have a king. The 'angel of the bottomless pit' is most likely the fallen angel of 9 : 1. The Hebrew word *abaddon* ('destruction', 'perdition') is found almost exclusively in the wisdom literature (Job 26 : 6; 28 : 22; 31 : 12; Prov. 15 : 11; 27 : 20; Ps. 88 : 11) as a name for the region of the dead. John gives its Greek equivalent as Apollyon ('destroyer').

12.   The sixth and seventh trumpets have yet to be blown.

The second woe (sixth trumpet) (9: 13-21)

> *Ps. 115: 4f., 7: Their idols are silver and gold, the work of men's hands. They have mouths but do not speak; eyes but do not see. They have ears but do not hear . . . they have feet but do not walk.*
>
> *Dn. 5: 23: You have praised the gods of silver and gold, of bronze, iron, wood and stone, which do not see or hear or know.*

13. Then the sixth angel blew his trumpet, and I heard a voice from the four horns of the altar before God, 14. saying to the sixth angel who had the trumpet, 'Release the four angels who are bound at the great river Euphrates.' 15. So the four angels were released; who had been held ready for the hour, the day, the month, and the year, to kill a third of mankind. 16. The number of the troops of cavalry was twice ten thousand times ten thousand; I heard their number. 17. And this was how I saw the horses in my vision: the riders wore breastplates the colour of fire and of sapphire and of sulphur, and the

heads of the horses were like lions' heads, and fire and smoke and sulphur issued from their mouths. 18. By these three plagues a third of mankind was killed, by the fire and smoke and sulphur issuing from their mouths. 19. For the power of the horses is in their mouths and in their tails; their tails are like serpents, with heads, and by means of them they wound.

20. The rest of mankind, who were not killed by these plagues, did not repent of the works of their hands nor give up worshipping demons and idols of gold and silver and bronze and stone and wood, which cannot either see or hear or walk; 21. nor did they repent of their murders or their sorceries or their immorality or their theft.

13f. The golden altar is the altar of incense (8 : 3); the voice represents the prayers of the saints (8 : 4); the 'horns' are the raised corners of the altar. These four angels are angels of punishment (cf. 1 Enoch 66 : 1). The Euphrates marked the eastern frontier of Rome; beyond it lay the Parthians, the dreaded, and mysterious, enemy of Rome. John has the topical situation in mind, but his 'cavalry' are not the Parthians but another presentation of the demonic locusts of 9 : 3-11. Besides, the great powers, Assyrians and Babylonians, which had devastated Israel had come from beyond the Euphrates: an invasion from the east was an obvious symbol of woe for Jerusalem. Cf. Is. 8 : 7—'Behold, the Lord is bringing up against them the waters of the River [Euphrates], mighty and many, the king of Assyria and all his glory'.

15. The ministers of vengeance are set free to carry out their task. The fixing of their time of release, down to the precise hour, emphasizes the truth that the visitation had been prepared in the divine foreknowledge. Again its scope is limited, but this time 'a third' of mankind will be *killed*; a third, that is, of 'those of mankind who have not the seal of God upon their foreheads' (9 : 4).

16f. The vast forces at the disposal of the destroying angels numbered 200 millions; it is a host as great as the locust swarm of Exodus or Joel. The colours of the riders' armour, fiery red, smoky blue, and suphurous yellow, matched the colours of the fire, smoke, and sulphur breathed out of the horses' mouths. Cf.

Job's description of Leviathan (the crocodile); 'out of his mouth go flaming torches; sparks of fire leap forth. Out of his nostrils comes forth smoke. . . . His breath kindles coals, and a flame comes forth from his mouth' (41 : 19-21). But the horses of Ap. are demonic beings.

18f.   The deadly power of the visitation lay in the three plagues, the fire, the smoke, and the brimstone, that issued from the mouths of the demonic horses. For the limitation of their scope, cf. v. 15. v. 19 is modelled on 9 : 10. While the destructive power of the horses is in their mouths, they can also wound with the bite of their serpent tails. This last detail may well be a reference to the Parthians; their mounted archers fired a volley on the charge and another, backwards, as they immediately retired. But, for John, these serpent-like horses are emissaries of Satan, 'that ancient serpent' (12 : 9). Cf. Wis. 11 : 17f.—'For thy all-powerful hand . . . did not lack the means to send upon them . . . newly created unknown beasts full of rage, or such as breathe out fiery breath, or belch forth a thick pall of smoke, or flash terrible sparks from their eyes'.

20f.   'The rest of mankind', that is, the two-thirds of the unsealed (9 : 4) who had not been slain by the plague of the sixth trumpet (9 : 15, 18). Cf. Ps. 115 : 4f., 7; Dn. 5 : 23. Here, at least, it would seem that John cannot have Israel in view, not even unfaithful Israel: he could not accuse Israel of crass idolatry. Yet, he has already characterized Jews as 'a synagogue of Satan' (2 : 9; 3 : 9). It could well be that he is using the Old Testament polemic against idolatry as a particularly telling way of underlining the hardness of heart of these unrepentant people. 'They did not repent' (repeated)—the plagues were a salutary warning, but they were ignored. Cf. Zech. 1 : 4—'Thus says the Lord of hosts, "Return from your evil ways and from your evil deeds". But they did not heed or hear me, says the Lord.' We are still in the perspective of the destruction of Jerusalem; 11 : 13 will show a different reaction—the ultimate repentance of Israel. Wis. 12 : 3-5 links idolatry with sorcery and murder. Wis. 14 : 22-26 gives a long list of the vices and crimes that flow from idolatry and explicitly states in 14 : 27 that 'the worship of idols not to be

named is the beginning and cause and end of every evil'. Cf. 1
Cor. 6: 9—'Do not be deceived; neither the immoral, nor
idolaters . . . nor thieves . . . will inherit the kingdom of God'.

It is significant that the idolaters of v. 20 are not described as
'worshippers of the beast', those who appear throughout the
second apocalyptic part (12: 1-21: 8). Instead, they are like the
vague 'murderers, sorcerers, idolaters' of 21: 8 and 22: 15—
those who are excluded from the heavenly Jerusalem. So, we may
take it that the unrepentant 'rest of mankind', who have dis-
regarded the stern divine warning, are rebellious Jews who will
take their place among the outcasts of 21: 8 and 22: 15. Zephaniah provides an instructive parallel. In 1: 2—2: 3, the day of
Yahweh is presented as a judgment on Judah and Jerusalem, yet
it is set in the context of universal judgment. 'I will utterly sweep
away everything from the face of the earth,' says the Lord. . . .
'I will cut off mankind from the face of the earth,' says the Lord.
'I will stretch out my hand against Judah, and against all the
inhabitants of Jerusalem' (1: 2-4). And the crime which has
called forth the anger of the Lord is idolatry (1: 4-7).

The little scroll (10)

> *Dn. 10: 5f.: I lifted up my eyes and looked, and behold, a
> man clothed in linen, whose loins were girded with gold of
> Uphaz. His body was like beryl, his face like the appearance
> of lightning, his eyes like flaming torches, his arms and legs
> like the gleam of burnished bronze, and the sound of his
> words like the noise of a multitude.*
>
> *Dn. 12: 7: The man clothed in linen, who was above the
> waters of the stream, raised his right hand and his left hand
> toward heaven; and I heard him swear by him who lives for
> ever that it would be for a time, two times, and half a time;
> and that when the shattering of the power of the holy people
> comes to an end all these things will be accomplished.*
>
> *Dn. 8: 26: Seal up the vision, for it pertains to many days
> hence.*
>
> *Dn. 12: 4, 9: But you, Daniel, shut up the words, and seal*

*the book, until the time of the end. . . . Go your way, Daniel,
for the words are shut up and sealed until the time of the end.
Am. 3: 7: Surely the Lord God does nothing without
revealing his secret to his servants the prophets.*

*Ezek. 2: 8; 3: 1-3: 'But you, son of man, hear what I say
to you; be not rebellious like that rebellious house; open
your mouth and eat what I give you'. . . . And he said to me,
'Son of man, eat what is offered to you; eat this scroll, and
go, speak to the house of Israel.' So I opened my mouth,
and he gave me the scroll to eat. And he said to me, 'Son of
man, eat this scroll'. . . . and it was in my mouth as sweet
as honey.*

*Jer. 1: 10: See, I have set you this day over nations and
over kingdoms, to pluck up and to break down, to destroy,
and to overthrow, to build and to plant.*

1. Then I saw another mighty angel coming down from
heaven, wrapped in a cloud, with a rainbow over his head, and
his face was like the sun, and his legs like pillars of fire. 2. He
had a little scroll open in his hand. And he set his right foot on
the sea, and his left foot on the land, 3. and called out with a
loud voice, like a lion roaring; when he called out, the seven
thunders sounded. 4. And when the seven thunders had
sounded, I was about to write, but I heard a voice from heaven
saying, 'Seal up what the seven thunders have said and do not
write it down.' 5. And the angel whom I saw standing on the
sea and land lifted up his right hand to heaven 6. and swore
by him who lives for ever and ever, who created heaven and
what is in it, the earth and what is in it, and the sea and what
is in it, that there should be no more delay, 7. but that in the
days of the trumpet call to be sounded by the seventh angel,
the mystery of God, as he announced to his servants the
prophets, should be fulfilled.

8. Then the voice which I had heard from heaven spoke to
me again, saying, 'Go, take the scroll which is open in the hand
of the angel who is standing on the sea and on the land.' 9. So
I went to the angel and told him to give me the little scroll;
and he said to me, 'Take it and eat; it will be bitter to your

stomach, but sweet as honey in your mouth.' 10. And I took
the little scroll from the hand of the angel and ate it; it was
sweet as honey in my mouth, but when I had eaten it my
stomach was made bitter. 11. And I was told, 'You must again
prophesy about many peoples and nations and tongues and
kings.'

Just as the opening of the seventh seal was preceded by the two-
fold vision of chapter 7, so the visions of chapters 10 and 11 are
preparatory to the blowing of the last trumpet.

10: 1f. John is no longer in heaven (4 : 1) but on earth; he
saw an angel 'coming down from heaven'. 'Another angel', that is,
not one of the seven who sounded the trumpets, nor one of the
four of 9 : 14 (cf. 7 : 2; 14 : 6, 8f., 15, 17f.). A 'mighty' angel:
cf. Dn. 4 : 13; Ap. 5 : 2; 18 : 21. 'Wrapped in a cloud': the
'cloud' is the heavenly vehicle (cf. Dn. 7 : 13; Ps. 104 : 3; Ap. 1 :
7; 11 : 12; 14 : 14). The 'rainbow' over his head is from the sun-
brightness of his face against the cloud (cf. Ezek. 1 : 28). 'His
face was like the sun' recalls the description of the Son of Man
(Ap. 1 : 16). 'His legs like pillars of fire', cf. Dn. 10: 6; the
description may be a reference to Ex. 14 : 19, 24—'Then the
angel of God who went before the host of Israel moved . . . and
the pillar of fire moved.' 'The Lord in the pillar of fire and cloud
looked down upon the Egyptians.' Perhaps the details of the
description are meant to have a deeper significance. 'The angel
is wrapped in the *cloud* of the divine presence, and over his head
is the *rainbow* of the divine mercy (cf. Ap. 4 : 3). He bears the
delegated attributes of deity, but he is also the angel of Jesus
Christ, whose face John has seen shining *like the sun* (cf. 1 : 16).
The *legs like pillars of fire* are reminiscent of Israel's journeys in
the wilderness. This is the angel who is to guide the new Israel
through the darkness of its Exodus pilgrimage from Egypt to the
promised land' (Caird).

The angel holds a 'little' scroll, a small papyrus roll, 'open' in
his hand—a double contrast to the sealed scroll of 5 : 1 (cf. Ezek.
2 : 9). In Ap. 5 : 2 the invitation of a 'strong angel' led to the
opening of the sealed scroll: there is a parallel between angels

and scrolls of ch. 5 and ch. 10, but the differences are very
marked. The angel of ch. 10, with traits also of the Son of Man
of Daniel (Dn. 7 : 13), is more majestic than the other; of giant
stature, he stands on sea and land (cf. Ex. 20 : 4, 11; Ps. 69 : 34)
because his message is for all mankind. We have seen that, in the
passage 5 : 1-12, the titles given to Christ (the lion of the tribe
of Judah, the root of David) and the role of the twenty-four elders
(the saints of the OT) point to the chosen people. The sealed scroll
is the OT, especially the prophetic oracles, to which Christ had
supplied the key. On the other hand, the little scroll (less extensive than the OT, but open and universalist in scope) is the message of Jesus (cf. 2 Cor. 3 : 12; 4 : 6). Significantly, the angel who
is entrusted with the little scroll is by far the most impressive
angelic figure of this angel-studded book; the little scroll has an
importance beyond its size.

3.   A 'loud voice' is commonplace in Ap., so the voice of this
mighty angel has to be described in more impressive terms—it is
like the roaring of a lion. His call was a signal, at once answered
by the call of the 'seven thunders'—the voice of God. Cf. Ps.
29 : 3—'The voice of the Lord is upon the waters; the God of
glory thunders'; Jer. 25 : 30—'The Lord will roar from on high
. . . against all the inhabitants of the earth' (cf. Am. 1 : 2; 3 : 8;
Hos. 11 : 10). Cf. Jn 12 : 28f.—'Then a voice came from heaven,
"I have glorified it, and will glorify it again." The crowd standing by heard it and said that it thundered. Others said, "An
angel has spoken to him".'

4.   Cf. Dn. 8 : 26; 12 : 4, 9. In apocalyptic, visions which are
sealed are messages, communicated by God, which will be fulfilled only in the distant future. That is precisely why we read in
Ap. 22 : 10—'Do not seal up the words of the prophecy of this
book, *for the time is near*'. In 10 : 4, as in Daniel, John is bidden,
by a heavenly voice (cf. 14 : 2, 13; 18 : 4), to seal the message
communicated to him, a message concerning new events yet in
the future. It is typical of John's paradoxical style that the seer is
instructed to seal up what he *had not written*. Always, it is the
idea that matters, and the idea is clear.

5-7.   The angel, already standing on sea and land, now raises his

right hand to heaven: he touches the three parts of the universe
because he is going to swear by him who created them. Cf. Dn.
12: 7; Dt. 32: 40—'For I [Yahweh] lift up my hand to heaven
and swear'. 'That there should be no more delay'—the declaration stands in deliberate contrast to Dn. 12: 7—'that it would
be for a time, two times, and half a time' before all should be
accomplished. Cf. 1 Jn 2: 18—'Children, it is the last hour',
clearly meaning that this is the eleventh hour, the final, decisive
age of history. The 'mystery of God' (cf. Ap. 1: 20; 17: 5, 7) is
the definitive establishment of the kingdom of God, marked by
the destruction of all his enemies. The sounding of the seventh
trumpet will herald the end. 'His servants the prophets' (cf. Am.
3: 7)—here both OT and NT prophets. God 'evangelized'
(*euēngelisen*) the mystery to the prophets. This has reference to
the 'gospel' (*euangelion*) of 14: 6; we shall see that the passages
correspond.

In 10: 3-7, we find two antithetical scenes: one (vv. 3f.) signifies that the universal judgment is still far off ('Seal up what
the seven thunders have said'), and the other (vv. 5-7), that the
end is near ('there shall be no more delay'). Dn. 12: 4-9, which
has inspired the antithesis, also helps to explain it. Daniel had been
ordered to seal up the revelations he had received, and the angel
swore by the Creator that they will be accomplished after a
certain delay ('a time, two times, and half a time', that is, three
and a half years, the time of tribulation). John also seals what he
has heard, but now the angel swears by the Creator that there is
no more delay: the old situation has been transformed. The
Christian economy, which has replaced Judaism, is the final stage
of God's plan. The time of Israel has drawn to a close—it will end
at the blowing of the seventh trumpet. Then, at ch. 12, John
turns to the time of the church.

8-10. The heavenly voice which had ordered John not to seal
the message of the seven thunders now bids him take the little
scroll from the angel. The angel's words are inspired by Ezek.
3: 1-3, a prophetic investiture; the eating of the scroll symbolizes the prophet's digesting of the message which he has to
transmit. This message is bitter-sweet: sweet because it proclaims

the triumph of the Church, bitter because it must include the sufferings of Christians.

11.   This marks a new prophetical investiture, distinct from that of 1 : 9-20. John must 'again' prophesy, and this time about 'many peoples and nations and tongues and kings'. This means that he is called to a new mission : he must prophesy as he had not done up to now. The message of the sealed scroll bears directly on the chosen people (cf. 7 : 4-8), and it is only from ch. 12 onwards that there is question of 'peoples and nations and tongues' (cf. 12 : 5; 13 : 7; 14 : 6, 8; 14 : 4; 17 : 15). Whereas the mission of Ezekiel had been restricted to the house of Israel (Ezek. 3 : 4f.), John's mission breaks out of this restriction and is more like that of Jeremiah, who stands out as the prophet to the nations (cf. Jer. 1 : 10). 'We might say in brief that the new prophetic mission confided to John in ch. 10 is an echo of the investiture of Jeremiah as "prophet to the nations". By contrast, the preparatory vision at the opening of the book of the seven seals (chapters 4-5) recalls very closely the inaugural vision of Ezekiel, Jewish prophet *par excellence*. This confirms what we have said before, that the Apocalypse is concerned first with the chosen people (chapters 4-11) and then with the nations (chapter 12 ff.).'[32] It seems that the purpose of chapter 10 is to introduce the period of preaching to the gentiles and to bring out the paradox of the gospel : the end is near (we live in the last age), and yet the final episode may be long delayed.

The temple measured (11: 1f.)

> *Ezek. 40: 3: Behold, there was a man, whose appearance was like bronze, with a line of flax and a measuring reed in his hand [to measure the temple, 40: 5—42: 20].*
> *Zech. 2: 1f.: And I lifted up my eyes and saw, and behold, a man with a measuring line in his hand! Then I said, 'Where are you going?' And he said to me, 'To measure Jerusalem, to see what is its breadth and what is its length.'*

---

[32] A. Feuillet, *Johannine Studies, op. cit.,* 224.

1. Then I was given a measuring rod like a staff, and I was told: 'Rise and measure the temple of God and the altar and those who worship there, 2. but do not measure the court outside the temple; leave that out, for it is given over to the nations, and they will trample over the holy city for forty-two months.'

This is an episode not unlike that of the sealing of the servants of God (7 : 4-8).

11 : 1.   Cf. Ezek. 40 : 3; Zech. 2 : 1f. A 'measuring rod like a staff' means a long one; Ezekiel's reed was of six cubits, about nine feet. John himself becomes an actor in the drama he witnesses and is bidden to measure the temple he sees in vision. 'Temple' (*naos*) stands for the whole of the temple precincts except for the outer court, the court of the gentiles. He must measure temple and altar and worshippers—what is thus measured is under God's special protection (as in Ezek. and Zech.). The measuring not only of temple and altar but also of worshippers underlines the fact that we are dealing with symbols.

2.   But John must 'cast out the court which is outside the temple' (*tēn aulēn tēn exōthen tou naou ekbale exōthen*). This court is given over to the nations who 'will trample over the holy city for forty-two months'. Lk. 21 : 24 springs to mind at once: unbelieving Jerusalem 'will be trodden down by the gentiles, until the times of the gentiles are fulfilled'. Another text of Luke casts light on the enigmatic phrase, 'cast out the court which is outside'. In Lk. 13 : 25-28—the parable of the closed door—the unbelieving contemporaries of Jesus are represented as standing outside their Lord's door and knocking in vain for admittance (v. 25); and yet, a few verses later, they are 'thrust out' (*ekballomenous exō*, v. 28). In both cases we have the same paradox: those already outside are cast out. Swete has noted: 'If the temple represents the Church, the outer court is perhaps the rejected Synagogue; as in 2 : 9; 3 : 9; the tables are turned, and while the Church fills the court of the Israelites and worships at the Altar of the Cross (Heb. 13 : 10), Israel after the flesh is cast out (Mt. 8 : 12).' John refers to the final break between church and synagogue brought about by the catastrophe of AD 70. The true

F

temple of God, which Titus could not destroy, was constituted in the first place by the faithful Jews, the messianic remnant (cf. the 144,000 of 7 : 4-8). The unbelieving Jews, until then rather like the outer court of the true temple, were now no longer part of it. However, the prospect is not one of unrelieved gloom : the court will be trampled for 'forty-two months'; this is nothing else than the 'time, two times, and half a time' of Dn. 7 : 25, that is, three and a half years, the approximate duration of the persecution of Antiochus IV, and hence a symbol of a time of trial. In Ap. the expression or its equivalent (11 : 3; 12 : 6, 14; 13 : 5) is a symbolic designation of the time of trial which separates Christians from the perfect establishment of the kingdom of God. The tribulations of the unconverted Jewish world will last just so long —'until the times of the gentiles are fulfilled' (Lk. 21 : 24). Then, with Paul (Rom. 11 : 25f.), we can look to the salvation of Israel.

The two witnesses (11: 3-13)

Zech. 4: 2f., 11-14: He said to me, 'What do you see?' I said, 'I see, and behold, a lampstand all of gold, with a bowl on the top of it, and seven lamps on it, with seven lips in each of the lamps which are on the top of it. And there are two olive trees by it, one on the right of the bowl and the other on its left. . . . Then I said to him, 'What are these two olive trees on the right and the left of the lampstand?' And a second time I said to him, 'What are these two branches of the olive trees, which are beside the two golden pipes from which the oil is poured out?' He said to me, 'Do you not know what these are?' I said, 'No, my Lord.' Then he said, 'These are the two anointed who stand by the Lord of the whole earth.'

Dn. 7: 21: As I looked, this horn made war on the saints, and prevailed over them.

Ezek. 37: 10: So I prophesied as he commanded me, and the breath came into them, and they lived and stood upon their feet.

3. 'I will grant my two witnesses power to prophesy for one thousand two hundred and sixty days, clothed in sackcloth.'

4. These are the two olive trees and the two lampstands which stand before the Lord of the earth. 5. And if any one would harm them, fire pours from their mouth and consumes their foes; if any one would harm them, thus he is doomed to be killed. 6. They have power to shut the sky, that no rain may fall during the days of their prophesying, and they have power over the waters to turn them into blood, and to smite the earth with every plague, as often as they desire. 7. And when they have finished their testimony, the beast that ascends from the bottomless pit will make war upon them and conquer them and kill them, 8. and their dead bodies will lie in the street of the great city which is allegorically called Sodom and Egypt, where their Lord was crucified. 9. For three days and a half men from the peoples and tribes and tongues and nations gaze at their dead bodies and refuse to let them be placed in a tomb, 10. and those who dwell on the earth will rejoice over them and make merry and exchange presents, because these two prophets had been a torment to those who dwell on the earth. 11. But after the three and a half days a breath of life from God entered them, and they stood up on their feet, and great fear fell on those who saw them. 12. Then they heard a loud voice from heaven saying to them, 'Come up hither!' And in the sight of their foes they went up to heaven in a cloud. 13. And at that hour there was a great earthquake, and a tenth of the city fell; seven thousand people were killed in the earthquake, and the rest were terrified and gave glory to the God of heaven.

3. The duration of the ministry of the two witnesses (1,260 days =forty-two lunar months) is the same as the duration of the time of the gentiles (11 : 2), the whole time of the church (12 : 6, 14). The speaker is probably Christ (cf. 2 : 13; 21 : 6). These witnesses represent the church in her function of witness-bearing; cf. Ac. 1 : 8—'You shall by my witnesses in Jerusalem . . . and to the ends of the earth'. Acts describes the preaching to Israel: the apostles

are witnesses of Christ who must proclaim the events of his life from the baptism of John to the ascension of Jesus, especially the crowning event of the resurrection (Ac. 1 : 22; 2 : 32). Their preaching is accompanied by 'signs' (Mk 16 : 17; Ac. 4 : 30; 5 : 12; 16; 8 : 6 ff.). They meet with hostility (Ac. 4 : 2f.; 5 : 17 f.), like the OT prophets (Lk. 11 : 47-50; Ac. 7 : 51f.), but they are aided by the Holy Spirit (Ac. 4 : 27-31) and even miraculously delivered from death (5 : 19-21; 12 : 1-17). All of this is verified in the ministry of the two witnesses. 'Two' witnesses stem from Dt. 19 : 15—'Only on the evidence of two witnesses or of three witnesses shall a charge be sustained' (cf. Jn 8 : 17). 'Clothed in sackcloth' : perhaps a reference to the rough costume worn by ancient prophets (cf. 2 Kg. 1 : 8; Is. 20 : 2; Zech. 13 : 4; Mk 1 : 6), but also a sign that the witnesses were to preach a message of repentance (cf. Jn 3 : 5f.; Mt. 11 : 21).

4.   Cf. Zech. 4 : 2f., 11-14. In Zechariah the lampstand is Israel, and the olive trees are Zerubbabel the Davidic prince and Joshua the high priest. John freely adapts the text : now the two olive trees *and two* lampstands represent his two witnesses. Already, in 1 : 20, John's seven lamps (he had the same text of Zech. in mind) represented the seven churches of Asia and, in some fashion, the universal church. As 'olive trees' the two witnesses are anointed ones, that is, marked by the Spirit of God; as 'lampstands' they are the bearers of God's light, which shines before the people in Law and prophets (cf. v. 6).

5.   In late Judaism it was believed that Elijah would appear before the coming of the Messiah (cf. Mal. 3 : 24; Sir. 48 : 10); Jesus refers to this belief (Mk 9 : 11; cf. Lk. 1 : 17). Apocalyptic expectation looked to the coming of Elijah and Enoch. Yet, in Jn 1 : 21, it is interesting to note that in their question to the Baptist the priests associate Elijah and the prophet like Moses (Dt. 18 : 15-18). It is Moses and Elijah who figure in the synoptic scene of the transfiguration (cf. Mk 9 : 4), and it is they who are in question in our passage. 'Fire pours from their mouths'; cf. Num. 16 : 35—'And fire came forth from the Lord, and consumed the two hundred and fifty men offering the incense' (that is, those involved in the rebellion of Korah against Moses); 2 Kg.

1 : 10—'Elijah answered the captain of fifty, "If I am a man of God, let fire come down from heaven and consume you and your fifty" ' (cf. 1 : 12, 14; Lk. 9 : 54). Also Jer. 5 : 14—'Behold, I am making my words in your mouth a fire, and this people wood, and the fire shall devour them'. The witnesses cannot be silenced as long as their ministry lasts; those who try to stifle them bring destruction on themselves.

6. The two witnesses are modelled on Elijah (power to bring about drought) and Moses (power to turn water into blood and to smite the earth with every plague). 'During the days of their prophesying'—after v. 3, this is three and a half years. The drought proclaimed by Elijah is for 'three years' (1 Kg. 17 : 1); Ap. reflects a tradition also found in Lk. 4 : 25 and Jas 5 : 17. It appears that the witnesses are the incarnation of the testimony—from the Law and the prophets—borne to Christ by the church in the presence of the Jewish world. Moses and Elijah (Law and prophets) render witness to Jesus through the mouths of the apostles and their successors, showing to the Jews that Christianity is the fulfilment of the Old Covenant.

7. The witnesses are specially protected and immune from danger for as long as their allotted time of office lasts—that is, for three and a half years (11 : 13), the duration of the church right up to the moment of the great final assault. Their death (and glorification) is to occur in the future, at the end of the present epoch. The 'beast that ascends from the bottomless pit', abruptly introduced here, is described in 13 : 1—the great persecuting power, instrument of Satan (cf. Dn. 7 : 21). That this verse is best understood in terms of the final assault on the church is seen from its close correspondence with 20 : 7f.—'And when the thousand years are ended, Satan will be loosed from his prison and will come out to deceive the nations'. Ap. 20 : 7-9 is the final Satan-inspired rebellion of the nations against 'the camp of the saints and the beloved city'; but the enemy forces are destroyed by fire from heaven (20 : 9; cf. 11 : 5). In ch. 20 the assault is followed by judgment (20 : 11-15); the last judgment also figures in 11 : 18.

8. As an added indignity the witnesses' bodies will remain un-

buried (cf. Jer. 8 : 2; Tob. 1 : 17; 2 Mac. 5 : 10) and will be left
to lie in the streets of Jerusalem. Throughout the remainder of
the book, Rome is 'the great city' (16 : 19; 17 : 18; 18 : 10, 16,
18f., 21; cf. 14 : 8; 16 : 19; 17 : 5; 18 : 2). Some have suggested
that here too 'the great city' must be Rome and have explained
the phrase 'where their Lord was crucified', which points to Jerusalem, as a later scribal note. There is no textual evidence at all
to support this contention. In Is. 1 : 9f. Judah is compared to
Sodom; and Sodom and Egypt are alluded to in Wis. 19 : 14f. as
types of wickedness. Swete notes that the phrase 'where their
Lord was crucified' recalls the saying of Jn 15 : 20—'A servant
is not greater than his master. If they persecuted me, they will
persecute you'.

9f.   While the ministry of the two witnesses had been in Jerusalem, where they had also met their death, the perspective now
widens out to take in the wide world. 'Thus the whole world,
declared enemy of Christ, and including the incredulous Jews,
rejoices at the murder of the two witnesses. The reason is that we
are here, as also in 20 : 7ff., in the presence of the great final
revolt of the nations against Christ. However, in ch. 11, unlike the
parallel text in ch. 20, this revolt is considered particularly with
regard to the Jewish world, in accordance with the perspective of
the entire first prophetic part of the Apocalypse; in resisting and
persecuting Christ's Church the Jews really insult and reject the
Law and the Prophets.'[33] Cf. Jn. 5 : 39, 45-57. 'For three days
and a half'—in place of three and a half years—a brief triumph.
'The delight of the spectators is represented as at once fiendish
and childish' (Swete). The exchanging of gifts recalls Est. 9 : 19.
'Had been a torment'—the role of the witnesses to Christ in the
eyes of those who reject them; the cessation of their testimony,
rather than their death, was the cause of joy (cf. Wis. 2 : 12-20).

11.   The victory of the beast and the exultation of his followers
are ephemeral: after three and a half days the witnesses return
to life. Cf. Ezek. 37 : 10. 'The author wishes to express the truth,
so dear to primitive Christianity, that, if Christ's witnesses are
subjected to persecution and martyrdom, still the Church wins

[33] *Ibid.*, 248.

precisely in her martyrs, and rises again after the trial, just as Ezekiel had foretold of Israel during the period of Babylonian exile' (Feuillet, *op. cit.*, 245). 'Great fear fell on them'—a Lucan phrase (Lk. 1 : 12; Ac. 19 : 17; cf. Ac. 2 : 6, 12, 43; 5 : 5, 11).

12. As it was for their Lord, the resurrection of the witnesses is followed by their ascension; and, like their Lord, 'they went up to heaven in a cloud' (cf. Ac. 1 : 9). We are also to recall that Elijah 'went up by a whirlwind into heaven' (2 Kg. 2 : 11) and that, according to a Jewish tradition, Moses was removed from the sight of his followers by a cloud (cf. Josephus, *Ant.*, VI, 8, 48). Summoned by a heavenly voice (surely that of their Lord), they receive the recompense of their faithful witness.

13. 'A great earthquake' (cf. 6 : 12; Ezek. 38 : 19f.)—a familiar symbol of divine punishment. Yet here the chastisement is mitigated : a tenth of the city fell, in contrast to the quarters (6 : 8) and thirds (chapters 8-9) of the previous plagues. Seven thousand people (presumably one-tenth of the total) would suit the population of Jerusalem; at any rate it is a small figure (cf. the 144,000 of 7 : 4 and the 200 millions of 9 : 16). The visible triumph of the witnesses and this mitigated punishment were meant to bring men to their senses. The terrified survivors 'gave glory to the God of heaven'; (cf. Dn. 2 : 18f. for the title 'God of heaven'). In Ap. 16 : 11 the 'inhabitants of the earth', stricken by plagues, will 'curse the god of heaven' (cf. Ap. 14 : 7; 16 : 9). The phrase 'give glory to God' has its less usual meaning of repentance (cf. Jos. 7 : 19; Jer. 13 : 16) in this verse. 'In its present context it can only mean . . . the conversion of Israel to Christianity in the last days—an expectation that agrees with Rom. 11 : 25f., according to which this conversion is to follow when the full number of the gentiles has entered into Christ's kingdom' (Charles). Cf. Lk. 13 : 34f.—'O Jerusalem, Jerusalem, killing the prophets and stoning those who are sent to you! . . . Behold, your house is forsaken. And I tell you, you will not see me until you say, "Blessed is he who comes in the name of the Lord" '—a verse which joins Lk 21 : 24; Rom. 11 : 25f. and Ap. 11 : 2, 13 in heralding the salvation of Israel.

The last 'woe' (seventh trumpet) (11: 14-19)

> *Ps. 2: 1, 5: Why do the nations conspire, and the peoples plot in vain? . . . He will speak to them in his wrath and terrify them in his fury.*
>
> *Ps. 115: 13: He will bless those who fear the Lord, both small and great.*

14. The second woe has passed; behold, the third woe is soon to come.

15. Then the seventh angel blew his trumpet, and there were loud voices in heaven, saying, 'The kingdom of the world has become the kingdom of our Lord and of his Christ, and he shall reign for ever and ever.' 16. And the twenty-four elders who sit on their thrones before God fell on their faces and worshipped God, 17. saying,

> 'We give thanks to thee, Lord God almighty, who art and who wast,
>
> that thou hast taken thy great power and begun to reign.

18. The nations raged, but thy wrath came,
>
> and the time for the dead to be judged,
>
> for rewarding thy servants, the prophets and saints,
>
> and those who fear thy name, both small and great,
>
> and for destroying the destroyers of the earth.'

19. Then God's temple in heaven was opened, and the ark of his covenant was seen within his temple; and there were flashes of lightning, loud noises, peals of thunder, an earthquake, and heavy hail.

In Rom. 11 : 25f. the conversion of Israel, after the full number of the gentiles had come in, seems to mark the culminating point of the divine plan. The same is true here; now is the end. The punishment of the wicked is implied in the third 'woe' (v. 14); then the seventh trumpet can sound to announce the end of the world and the definitive inauguration of the kingdom of God and of his Christ.

14. The second woe is the sixth trumpet (9 : 13-21). Now the seventh trumpet follows without delay.

15. In contrast to the silence which followed the opening of the seventh seal (8 : 1), the sound of the last trumpet is answered by loud voices of praise in heaven—the voices, perhaps, of the living creatures or of the angelic choirs (4 : 8; 5 : 11f.). 'The words suggest the vision of a world-empire, once dominated by a usurping power, which has now at last passed into the hands of its true Owner and Imperator (cf. Mt. 4 : 8f.; Jn 14 : 30; Eph. 2 : 2; 6 : 12)' (Swete). The terms are not specifically Christian : 'our Lord' is the Father, and Christ is the Lord's 'anointed' (cf. Lk. 2 : 26; 9 : 20); cf. Ps. 2 : 2—'the Lord and his anointed'. 'He shall reign', because the rule of God and Christ is one (cf. 1 Cor. 15 : 27).

16-18. Significantly, the canticle (11 : 17f.) is put in the mouths of the twenty-four elders (the saints of Israel), for its language is thoroughly Jewish. Cf. Ps. 2 : 1, 5; Ps. 115 : 13. The elders thank and glorify God who has at last manifested his great power : the kingdom of God has come. Until now God is he 'who is and who was and who is to come' (1 : 4, 8; 4 : 8). But here there is no 'who art to come' (cf. 16 : 5): he has come, his reign has begun. 'Always up to this point God has reigned over a rebellious world. A king may be king *de jure*, but he is not king *de facto* until the trumpet which announces his ascension is answered by the acclamation of a loyal and obedient people' (Caird).

The close of the second prophetic part of Ap., a scene of final judgment (20 : 11-15), corresponds to the proleptic judgment-scene of 11 : 15-18. Yet, the differences are notable. In 20 : 12f. the judgment is shown as really taking place and its universality is underlined. In ch. 11 the universal judgment is presented in typically Jewish terms. The 'nations who raged' are those of Ps. 2. The time has come for judging, for rewarding, and for destroying; and three classes receive reward. 'Thy servants the prophets' (cf. Am. 3 : 7) are, primarily, the OT prophets. If the 'saints' and 'those who fear thy name' are to be distinguished, we may regard the 'saints' as Christians of Jewish origin. In Acts the 'God-fearers' (Ac. 13 : 43, 50; 17 : 4; cf. Rom. 2 : 19f.) are gentiles who, attracted to Judaism, accepted monotheism and certain Jewish practices and were admitted to synagogue worship. Thus, for John, 'those who fear thy name', in contrast to the 'saints', would appear to be Christians of pagan origin. The phrase 'great and small' (cf. Ap. 19 : 5, 18; 20 : 12) covers all sorts and conditions of men. Finally, victims of the divine wrath, all evil-doers will be destroyed.

19.   The heavenly temple (3 : 12; 7 : 15; 15 : 5-8; 21 : 22) was opened: the heavenly temple has come to take the place of the earthly sanctuary. And not only that: the holy of holies is thrown open and the ark of the covenant is visible. 'This last act is symbolical. As the earthly ark was witness to the covenant between God and Israel, the heavenly ark is a witness to the covenant between God and the Christian community, which is the true Israel' (Charles). The ark disappeared in the destruction of Solomon's temple by Nebuchadnezzar in 587 BC. But a Jewish legend, reflected in 2 Mac. 2 : 4-8, represents Jeremiah as having hidden both the ark and the altar of incense against the day of Israel's restoration. He declared that the hiding-place is to remain unknown 'until God gathers his people together again and shows his mercy. And then the Lord will disclose these things, and the glory of the Lord will appear' (2 : 7f.; cf. Ap. 2 : 17). Now is the end: the kingdom has come, the glory of the Lord has appeared. The open holy of holies indicates the restoration of perfect access to God through the glorification of the incarnate Son. Cf. Heb. 8 : 1f.—'We have such a high priest, one who is seated at the right hand of the throne of majesty in heaven, a minister in the sanctuary and the true tent which is set up not by man but by the Lord' 10 : 19—'we have confidence to enter the sanctuary by the blood of Jesus'.

The phenomena of Ap. 11 : 19b may be the usual symbols of majesty and power which attend theophanies (cf. Ex. 19 : 16; Ps. 29 : 3-9). However, we may recall that in Ap. 8 : 5 the prayer of the martyrs occasioned similar manifestations. And now, in the light of the enthronement of God as king, we may understand that their prayer was, basically, the petition of all Christians : thy kingdom come (Caird).

It seems, then, that the historical background of Ap. 11 (indeed of Ap. 4-11) is the catastrophe of AD 70 which brought about the final separation of church and synagogue. This explains the artificial antedating of Ap.; for (as we shall see), in Ap. 17 : 10f., the sixth of a list of seven emperors, the one in whose reign the writing is set, is, reasonably, Vespasian. By using the customary apocalyptic procedure, John can thus place himself before the destruction of Jerusalem.

But, whatever may be said of our interpretation of Ap. 4-11, it is at least certain that ch. 11 marks a climax, and that ch. 12 is a new departure. Swete (who does not, however, refer these chapters to Israel and the church) has made the point very clearly : 'With the seventh trumpet-blast the kingdom of God has come, and the general judgment is at hand. Thus, this section of the Apocalypse brings the course of history down to the parousia. If the book had ended here, it would have been within these limits complete. But the seer pauses for a moment only to take up his role again with a fresh presentation of the future, in which the vision is to be carried to its issue. A new prophecy begins in chapter 12, the contents of the open *biblaridion* (little scroll) which the seer had been directed to take from the hand of the angel and consume. Impelled by a fresh gift of prophetic energy, he feels himself bound to prophesy again to a larger circle of hearers and with wider aims (Ap. 10 : 11); and this second message occupies the remainder of the book.'

THE CHRIST OF PART I

The Christ of this first part of the Apocalyptic visions is the triumphant Messiah—the fulfilment of the law and the prophets, the first-born of the true Israel. Only he can provide the key to the sealed scroll which he 'went and took' from the hand of his Father; only he can unfold, and unleash, the events by which he removes the veil from the Old Law until finally the heavenly ark witnesses a new covenant with the Christian community. 'God's temple in heaven was opened' : for Christians facing the 'great tribulation' and in need not only of the friendship of Jesus, but also of the assurance of his divine help and sovereignty, John portrays Christ in the very midst of the heavenly Father's throne, 'the kingdom of our Lord and of his Christ' constitutes a single reign; the four living creatures, the elders, and the angels offer a united homage to God and to the Lamb. Christ has brought his followers so near to the Father that they may have confidence that 'he who sits upon the throne will shelter them with his presence'; and he has enlightened hearts and minds to understand the words of loving care which God had spoken to his people throughout the time of Israel.

But why is Christ 'worthy' to receive the sevenfold doxology, and why does the time of Israel give way to the victorious theme, the 'new song', that 'salvation belongs to our God and to the Lamb'? Indeed, the answer can be found in John's choice of the Lamb as the prevalent image in his portrait of Christ—the paschal lamb without a bone broken, Isaiah's suffering servant and silent lamb bearing the iniquity of mankind (and subconsciously evoked by the silent pause in heaven following the opening of the seventh seal). For, central to the triumph of Christ in this section, and unforgettable in a scene where both Christian and Jewish martyrs participate, is the fact that this living Lamb had been slain. 'Thou wast slain and by thy blood didst ransom men for God. . . .' The 'new song' is a song of redemption; the saints of the Old Testament, the brethren and martyrs of the new, can look with joyful confidence towards the person of Christ because each personally has been redeemed.

It is because this slain Lamb has overcome death that John no longer needs to weep : 'the lion of the tribe of Judah, the root of David, *has* conquered, so that he *can* open the scroll'. And those whose robes have been washed in his blood by sharing his sacrifice have also been made a kingdom of priests to share and to continue his royal and priestly acts. He is the Lamb who seems to be a vengeful lion to the Israel who has rejected him. These will seek to 'hide in caves among the rocks of the mountains' because the one commandment of love he has asked them to follow seems too threatening, and they have hardened their hearts to see only a lion's wrath. But he is the Lamb in whose very weakness and apparent defencelessness lies the power to determine the facts of Jerusalem and to proclaim a message so bitter, so hard for Israel to accept, that his witnesses will face sufferings and death 'where their Lord was crucified'. Just as the Lord has known his own and sealed them to himself, so only a chosen remnant are blessed enough to know him as he really is; the Christ, the triumphant Messiah, in this section of the Apocalypse, is not the Messiah Israel had expected.

But, ultimately, both the Old Testament saints and Christians know him as the Lamb who is merciful—who freely offers them, in a hand open and lit by a rainbow of promise, the little scroll containing his own message of love. This is 'sweet as honey' beyond all bitterness, and it promises that the end—the parousia —is near even though it will be delayed. Here is the Jesus whose invitation, 'Come up hither', to his witnesses stirs them to an even more fervent longing to hold fast the faith with their constant prayer to him, 'Come!' He is the good shepherd who will 'guide them to springs of living water' and 'wipe every tear from their eyes'. He is the gentle leader whose justice softens punishment and whose love embraces the conversion of all of Israel as the final coming of his Father's will, of his own kingdom.

The elder who sees Christ as the conquering 'root of David' understands him in terms of the prophecy in Isaiah 11. Perhaps in this section of the Apocalypse, relating the church to Israel, this same passage can define the portrait of Christ as it is delineated here.

We are told that the gifts of the Spirit rest upon him, that he shall provide for the 'meek of the earth' even as he shall smite the rebellious with the 'rod of his mouth'. And finally, he shall not only recover the chosen remnant of his people and be an 'ensign to the nations'; he will also 'assemble the outcasts of Israel and gather the dispersed of Judah from the four corners of the earth'. Thus all of Israel and the whole church shall be one: the 'wolf shall dwell with the Lamb', and Jesus is the 'little child' who shall lead us through the 'great tribulation' to his 'new earth', his peace which the world cannot give.

PART II. THE CHURCH AND PAGAN ROME (12: 1—20: 15)

This second part, although it offers its own particular problems, has met with a greater measure of agreement in its general interpretation than the preceding part. The historical background is undoubtedly the persecution of the church by Rome, and the precise occasion of the persecution is the church's refusal to countenance Caesar-worship; the two beasts of ch. 13 represent Rome and the religion of Rome. Here is John's answer to the blasphemous pretentions of the emperors, which must end in disaster: Rome will go the way of Babylon.

1. THE DRAMATIS PERSONAE (12: 1—15: 5)

The woman and the dragon (12)

Chapter 12 falls into three parts: (1) a diptych which introduces the two symbolical figures, the woman and the dragon (vv. 1-4a); (2) the assault on Christ and his victory (vv. 4b-12); (3) the persecution of Christians (vv. 13-17).

(1) The woman and the dragon (12: 1-4a)

Gen. 3: 14-16: The Lord God said to the serpent, 'Because you have done this, cursed are you above all cattle. . . . I will put enmity between you and the woman, and between your seed and her seed; he shall bruise your head, and you shall bruise his heel.' To the woman he said, 'I will greatly multiply your pain in childbearing; in pain you shall bring forth children.' Gen. 37: 9: Behold, the sun, the moon, and eleven stars were bowing down to me [Joseph].

164

Song 6: 10: Who is this that looks forth like the dawn, fair as the moon, bright as the sun.

Is. 66: 7f.: Before she was in labour she gave birth; before her pain came upon her she was delivered of a son. . . . For as soon as Zion was in labour she brought forth her son.

Dn. 7: 7: Behold, a fourth beast, terrible and dreadful and exceedingly strong. . . . It was different from all the beasts that were before it; and it had ten horns.

Dn. 8: 10: It [the little horn = Antiochus IV] grew great, even to the host of heaven; and some of the host of the stars it cast down to the ground, and trampled upon them.

1. And a great portent appeared in heaven, a woman clothed with the sun, with the moon under her feet, and on her head a crown of twelve stars; 2. she was with child and she cried out in her pangs of birth, in anguish for delivery. 3. And another portent appeared in heaven; behold, a great red dragon, with seven heads and ten horns, and seven diadems upon his heads. 4. His tail swept down a third of the stars of heaven, and cast them to the earth.

12 : 1f.   This new vision is described as a *sēmeion* ('sign', 'portent'), a term proper to this second part of Ap. (cf. 12 : 3; 13 : 13f.; 15 : 1; 16 : 14; 19 : 20). In the LXX *sēmeion* renders the Hebrew *oth*, which can refer to a heavenly sign like the rainbow (Gen. 9 : 12-17), or to the heavenly bodies (1 : 14), or to a miracle (Ex. 7 : 3); the first meaning suits the context here. Cf. 'a sign from heaven' (Mk 8 : 11; Mt. 16 : 1); 'the sign of the Son of Man in heaven' (Mt. 24 : 30). The portent appeared 'in heaven', that is, in the sky. The vision was projected on the screen of the sky, and this is why the woman is seen surrounded by heavenly bodies. The description recalls Gen. 37 : 9 and Song 6 : 10. 'Clothed with the sun'; cf. Ps. 104 : 2—'who coverest thyself with light as with a garment'. The 'twelve stars' (suggested, perhaps, by Gen. 37 : 9) symbolize the twelve tribes of Israel (and, it may be, the twelve apostles as well). In the very centre of a vision of splendour, this woman is with child and near to delivery. Her birth-pangs are those of Eve (Gen. 3 : 16); and

they are the pangs of travailing Israel, as described by the prophets. Cf. Is. 66 : 7f.; Mic. 4 : 10—'Writhe and groan, O
daughter of Zion, like a woman in travail'; Is. 26 : 17f.—'Like a
woman with child, who writhes and cries out in her pangs, when
she is near her time, so were we because of thee, O Lord; we
were with child, we writhed'. And, in rabbinical literature, 'the
birth-pangs of the Messiah' was a current phrase. Seen against this
background, the woman symbolizes the people of God which
brings forth the messianic age and the Messiah (cf. Ap. 12 : 5).
The following verses will identify her more clearly. 'Thus the
woman who gave birth to the Christ (v. 5) is afterwards identified
with her who after his departure suffered for her faith in him
(v. 12) and who is the mother of believers (v. 17; cf. Gal. 4 : 27)'
(Swete).

3-4a. In contrast to the woman stands another sign : a great
red dragon. In 12 : 9 and 20 : 2 we are informed that the dragon
is 'that ancient serpent, who is called the Devil and Satan'—
he is the serpent of Gen. 3. In Jewish tradition the serpent or
dragon symbolized the power of evil, the principle of all the
sufferings of Israel. Because he is hostile to God and to his people,
God will destroy him at the end of time (Boismard). But other
OT texts, too, stand behind the dragon-figure. Cf. Is. 27 : 1—
'In that day the Lord with his hard and great and strong sword
will punish Leviathan the fleeing serpent, Leviathan the twisting
serpent, and he will slay the dragon that is in the sea'; Ps. 74 : 14;
Is. 51 : 9—'O arm of the Lord . . . was it not thou that didst cut
Rahab in pieces, and didst pierce the dragon?'; Ps. 89 : 10f.;
Job 9 : 13; 26 : 12. Leviathan and Rahab ('the dragon') suggest the mythological monster of chaos which readily symbolizes the power of evil. For John, the 'serpent' of Gen. 3 has
become the dragon. The dragon is fiery red (cf. Ap. 6 : 4), the
colour of bloodshed and murder. Cf. Jn 8 : 44—'He was a murderer from the beginning'. The 'seven heads' suggest the multiple
heads of Leviathan (cf. Ps. 74 : 14—'Thou didst crush the heads
of Leviathan'); the 'ten horns' come from Dn. 7 : 7. In Ap. 13 : 1
the beast, who is the instrument of the dragon, has 'ten horns and
seven heads'. That beast is Rome, and it would seem that this

description of the dragon evokes that imperial incarnation of his own power. In a more general sense, the horns, symbolizing royal power, and the diadem-crowned heads suggest the arrogance of Satan, the 'ruler of this world' (Jn 12: 31; 14: 30; 16: 11; Lk. 4: 5f.). In Dn 8: 10 the 'stars' represent the faithful people of God, victims of the persecution of Antiochus IV; but John seems to have in mind the fall of the angels implicated in Satan's revolt and defeat (Ap. 12: 7-9). However, it could well be that the detail implies no more than the vast size of the monster, whose lashing tail drags along a third of the stars.

(2) The victory of Christ (12: 4b-12)

Jer. 51: 34: [*The inhabitants of Zion say*] '*Nebuchadnezzar the king of Babylon has devoured me, he has crushed me; . . . he has swallowed me like a monster.*'
Ps. 2: 9: You shall break them [*the nations*] *with a rod of iron, and dash them in pieces like a potter's vessel.*
Dn. 10: 13: The prince of the kingdom of Persia withstood me twenty-one days; but Michael, one of the chief princes, came to help me.

4b. And the dragon stood before the woman who was about to bear a child, that he might devour her child when she brought it forth; 5. she brought forth a male child, one who is to rule all the nations with a rod of iron, but her child was caught up to God and to his throne, 6. and the woman fled into the wilderness, where she has a place prepared by God, in which to be nourished for one thousand two hundred and sixty days.

7. Now war arose in heaven, Michael and his angels fighting against the dragon; and the dragon and his angels fought, 8. but they were defeated and there was no longer any place for them in heaven. 9. And the great dragon was thrown down, that ancient serpent, who is called the Devil and Satan, the deceiver of the whole world—he was thrown down to the earth, and his angels were thrown down with him. 10. And I heard

a loud voice in heaven, saying, 'Now the salvation and the power and the kingdom of our God and the authority of his Christ have come, for the accuser of our brethren has been thrown down, who accuses them day and night before our God. 11. And they have conquered him by the blood of the Lamb and by the word of their testimony, for they loved not their lives even unto death. 12. Rejoice then, O heaven and you that dwell therein! But woe to you, O earth and sea, for the devil has come down to you in great wrath, because he knows that his time is short!'

4b-5.   Once again, as in Gen. 3, the woman and the dragon are face to face. Cf. Jer. 51: 34. Swete observes: 'A greater sufferer than Jerusalem is here, and a greater foe than the king of Babylon. The seer looks back over the long period of expectation which followed the original sentence on the serpent (Gen. 3: 15).' The dragon seeks to destroy the child of the woman. Her 'male child' (cf. Is. 66: 7) is the Messiah, explicitly identified as such by the citation of Ps. 2: 9. 'Her child was caught up to God and to his throne': the 'male-child' was snatched out of the dragon's power to the throne of God—a reference to the ascension (cf. Ac. 1: 9, 'he was lifted up') and the triumph of Christ, which will bring about the fall of the dragon. The reference to Ps. 2 is significant. The anointed king of the Psalm is addressed by God not at his birth but at his enthronement: 'You are my son, today I have begotten you' (Ps. 2: 7). Cf. Ac. 13: 33—'This he has fulfilled . . . by raising Jesus; as also it is written in the second Psalm, "Thou art my Son, today I have begotten thee" ' —the text is applied to the resurrection (cf. Rom. 1: 4).

The idea behind this passage of Ap. is thoroughly Johannine: the death of Christ, which is his glorification, is also the moment of the assault of Satan and of his defeat. The Fourth Gospel has no temptation story at the beginning of the ministry: Satan makes his bid at its close. It is he who instigated Judas (Jn 13: 2, 27; cf. Lk. 22: 3). In his final discourse Jesus declared: 'I will no longer talk much with you, for the ruler of this world is coming. He has no power over me' (Jn 14: 30). Luke, who has many contacts with the Johannine tradition, reflects the same view-point. After the temptation story he adds : 'And when the devil had ended every temptation, he departed from him until an opportune time' (Lk. 4 : 13); the moment indicated by the 'oppor-tune time' is the moment of the passion (22 : 3, 53). 'The passion itself may be regarded as a conflict between Jesus and Satan.'[34] In Jn 3 : 14 we read of the Son of Man being 'lifted up'. The same expression occurs in 8 : 28 and 12 : 32f.; in the latter case a note explains that crucifixion is meant. The evangelist regards the 'elevation' of Jesus on the cross as a symbol of his 'elevation' to heaven by his resurrection and ascension. In John's eyes, the death, resurrection and exaltation of Christ are all aspects of one and the same event; hence, he can regard the elevation on the cross and the exaltation in glory as one movement. The Johannine background, then, fully justifies our seeing in the 'birth' of the Messiah his birth on Calvary, and in his being snatched out of the power of the dragon his victory over Satan won by his death and glorification.

6.   Meanwhile the woman (the people of God of the OT which, having given Christ to the world, thereby became the Christian church) found refuge in the desert where God cares for her for 1,260 days. This is the equivalent of forty-two months or three and one-half years—the earthly duration of the church. In the OT the wilderness is the traditional place of refuge for the per-secuted (Ex. 2 : 15; 1 Kg. 17 : 2f.; 19 : 3f.; I Mac. 2 : 29f.). But John seems to have in mind more than this; v. 14 certainly has the Exodus in view. The wilderness suggests the Sinai wandering : the desert was a place of freedom and safety after the bondage of Egypt. Besides, God's care, described as a nourishing, recalls the manna. The 1,260 days (cf. Dn. 7 : 25; 12 : 7; Ap. 11 : 2f.) is the time of trial before the final inauguration of the kingdom of God. 'Thus the conclusion seems obvious; the woman nourished by God in the desert is the Christian church, which God nourishes and protects during its earthly wandering, as it awaits the parousia.'[35]

---

[34] C. K. Barrett, *The Gospel According to St John,* New York, Seabury Press (S.P.C.K.), 1955, 392.

[35] A. Feuillet, *Johannine Studies, op. cit.,* 280.

7-9. The fall of the dragon is dramatized in 12: 7-12; and although Michael is represented as casting Satan out of heaven, it really is the victory of Christ (vv. 10f.). Cf. Dn. 10: 13, which refers to a struggle of Michael, protector of the people of God, with the angel of the Persians, a bad angel who championed a pagan people. The combat is symbolic : it represents the perpetual antagonism between the good and evil angels. In Jewish tradition Michael came to be the angelic representative of the power of goodness in the strife with evil : as such he fights with Satan. Thus, in Daniel, Michael is the protector of Israel, God's people (Dn. 10: 21; 12: 1) and in I Enoch 20: 5 he appears as the patron angel of the saints in Israel.

This battle between Michael and Satan and their followers does not refer to the original rebellion of Satan. It is a dramatic presentation of the defeat of Satan by the glorification of Christ. The best comment on it is provided by two gospel texts. In Lk. 10: 18 Jesus declares: 'I saw Satan fall like lightning from heaven'. He assures his disciples that their real cause for rejoicing is that the kingdom of God has come (cf. 11: 20; Mt. 12: 28). For Satan it is the beginning of the end—his fall will be lightning fast. In Jn 12: 31 we read: 'Now is the judgment of this world, now shall the ruler of this world be cast out [or, variant, 'cast down'].' Jesus had just said (12: 23) that the hour of his death (his glorification) had come; v. 31 describes it as the hour of judgment on the hostile world, the hour when the devil would be cast out of (or cast down from) his realm. The judgment of God, already begun in the work of Jesus, reaches its climax in his death and victory; his death is his victory over Satan. Thus we find the meaning of our passage : through his glorification by God, merited by his earthly work and his death, the Messiah has won a first and decisive victory over Satan. The latter's power is thus basically broken; it is limited in regard to place (the earth, v. 9) and time ('his time is short', v. 12). Although in John's thought the dragon is Satan, the prince of evil spirits, and the implacable enemy of God, the place of Satan in heaven reflects another strand of biblical tradition. In Job 1: 6ff.; 2: 1ff., Satan ('the adversary') is one of the angels in the heavenly court : he is a heavenly prosecutor whose function it is to test the genuineness of human virtue. Satan likewise appears as accuser in Zech. 3 : 1f. and I Chr. 21 : 1; and the same idea is vaguely present in I Pet. 5 : 8; Jude 9; I Tim. 3 : 6. But he can no longer exercise this office: he has lost his last case—'Now is the judgment of this world, now shall the ruler of this world be cast out'. The heaven from which the dragon is cast down is not God's heaven but one of the many 'intermediate heavens' between the throne of God and earth. In v. 9 the dragon is explicitly identified as the serpent of Gen. 3 (cf. Wis. 2 : 24). ' "That ancient serpent", the primeval serpent, identifies the dragon with the serpent of Gen. 3 : 1ff., while "who is called the Devil and Satan" declares him to be the person so named in the later books of the OT and in Jewish literature' (Swete). 'The deceiver of the whole world' : cf. Jn 8 : 44—'He [the devil] was a murderer from the beginning, and has nothing to do with the truth, because there is no truth in him. When he lies, he speaks according to his own nature, for he is a liar and the father of lies.'

10.   The heavenly hymn (vv. 10-12) gives the explanation of these events. The voice would seem to be that of one of the elders : as a representative of the OT saints he can speak of 'our brethren' —the Christian martyrs (v. 11). It is not Michael's victory but the Lord's. The downfall of Satan manifests afresh the saving power of God, exercised by the glorified Christ. 'Accuser of our brethren'; cf. Job 1 : 6; Zech. 3 : 1f. Cf. Lk. 22 : 31—'Simon, Simon, behold, Satan demanded to have you, that he might sift you like wheat' : Satan demanded to have Simon as he had sought to ruin Job. Our text still reflects the 'prosecuting counsel' role of Satan current in the OT and in Jewish tradition. The victory of Christ has brought this role to an end.

11.   The 'brethren' of v. 10 (as in 6 : 11) now stand forth as the Christian martyrs. They are those 'who have come out of the great tribulation' and 'have washed their robes . . . in the blood of the Lamb' (7 : 14). Here they are those who will shed their blood for Christ all through the time of the Church, which is a time of trial (vv. 12, 17). They have conquered Satan 'by the blood of the Lamb'—his victory is their victory too (cf. 5 : 9f.;

7 : 9-17). 'The heavenly chorus explains that the real victory has been won *by the life-blood of the Lamb*. Michael's victory is simply the heavenly and symbolic counterpart of the earthly reality of the cross. Michael, in fact, is not the field officer who does the actual fighting, but the staff officer in the heavenly control room, who is able to remove Satan's flag from the heavenly map because the real victory has been won on Calvary' (Caird). 'They loved not their lives even unto death'; cf. Jn 12 : 25—'He who loves his life loses it, and he who hates his life in this world will keep it for eternal life'; cf. Ap. 2 : 10.

12.   The martyrs share in the victory of Christ; death has set them free from the devil's power. So, in heaven, there is great rejoicing (cf. 19 : 1-9); but on earth, Satan can still, for a little while, give vent to his wrath. 'Earth and sea', as opposed to heaven, now remain the sole sphere of Satan's future operations. Smarting from his humiliating defeat, and knowing that his days are numbered, he is going to redouble his efforts on the stage and in the time left to him. 'His time is short'—it is the 'time, and times, and half a time' of v. 14 (cf. v. 6).

(3)   Persecution of the Church   (12: 13-18)

> *Ex. 19: 4: You have seen . . . how I bore you on eagles' wings and brought you to myself.*
> *Num. 16: 30: But if the Lord creates something new, and the ground opens its mouth, and swallows them up. . . .*
> *Num. 26: 10: And the earth opened its mouth and swallowed them up together with Korah.*

13. And when the dragon saw that he had been thrown down to the earth, he pursued the woman who had borne the male child. 14. But the woman was given the two wings of the great eagle that she might fly from the serpent into the wilderness, to the place where she is to be nourished for a time, and times, and half a time. 15. The serpent poured water like a river after the woman, to sweep here away with the flood. 16. But the earth came to the help of the woman,

and the earth opened its mouth and swallowed the river which
the dragon had poured from his mouth. 17. Then the dragon
was angry with the woman, and went off to make war on the
rest of her offspring, on those who keep the commandments of
God and bear testimony to Jesus. 18. And he stood on the sand
of the sea.

13f.   The dragon's attempt to destroy the woman, implicit in
12: 6, is described in vv. 13-16. The woman is protected for 'a
time, and times, and half a time' (cf. 12: 6): the church, as such,
is under God's special care throughout its historical duration. The
'two wings of the great eagle' recall the Exodus background and
are a symbol of the speed and effectiveness of the divine help. Cf.
Ex. 19: 4; Dt. 32: 11f.—'Like an eagle . . . spreading out its
wings, catching them, bearing them on its pinions, the Lord alone
did lead him'; Is. 40: 31—'They who wait for the Lord . . . shall
mount up with wings like eagles'.
15f.   The dragon is now the 'serpent', that is, the 'ancient serpent'
(v. 9). It is hardly necessary to observe that these verses are
obscure. The flood of water which the dragon pours from its
mouth is probably borrowed remotely from Mesopotamian mytho-
logy; for the dragon (Leviathan, Rahab) has some relation to the
cosmic serpent, the symbol of the powers of evil and darkness.
Thus, the water might be a flood of evil which would engulf the
woman (cf. Ps. 18: 4; 32: 6; 124: 4f.; Is. 43: 2). It may
symbolize an invading and persecuting power (cf. Is. 8: 7f.; Ap.
9: 14f.)—the Roman Empire which would swallow up the
church (Ap. 13). However, in view of the Exodus typology, the
flood may have been suggested by the crossing of the Red Sea; in
Ezek. 29: 3; 32: 2f., Pharaoh is 'like a dragon in the sea', a
water monster. 'The earth opened its mouth and swallowed'; cf.
Num. 16: 30; 26: 10; Dt. 11: 6.
17f.   The dragon, frustrated in his attempt to destroy the Messiah (vv. 4f.), is further enraged when he discovers that he cannot
touch the mother of the Messiah: the church as such is beyond
his reach (cf. Mt. 16: 18). However, the faithful on earth are
vulnerable: Satan, through his instruments, can make war on

them; they will be persecuted and put to death. 'The rest of her offspring' : cf. Gen. 3 : 15—'I will put enmity between you and the woman, and between your seed and her seed'. For indeed, Christians are brethren of the Messiah (cf. Rom. 8 : 29—'For those whom he foreknew he also predestined to be conformed to the image of his son, in order that he might be the firstborn among many brothers') and children of the church (cf. Gal. 4 : 26—'But the Jerusalem above is free, and she is our mother'). These faithful children keep the commandments of God (cf. Ap. 14 : 12) and they bear witness to Jesus (cf. 1 : 9; 19 : 10; 20 : 4). And the message of Ap. is precisely that those who are steadfast to the end share in the glorious victory of the Lamb. 'And he stood on the sand of the sea'; the variant, 'and I stood', would connect the sentence with 13 : 1. However, the former reading receives overwhelming support from the best manuscripts. The dragon, intent on his warfare against the offspring of the woman, is about to conjure up the terrible beast of ch. 13, the instrument of his malignant power.

Apropos of Ap. 12 we may ask if there is a basis in the text for a mariological interpretation. At the outset, it is well to be clear that the woman does not primarily signify Mary the mother of Christ, for the context and the OT background leave no doubt that the woman symbolizes the people of God which gives birth to the messianic age and to the Messiah. The only possibility is that the woman may also, and in a secondary sense, symbolize Mary. Many eminent exegetes believe that this is so. The most impressive argument in support of such a view would seem to be that which, recognizing in Ap. a Johannine writing, links Ap. 12 with a text of the Fourth Gospel : Jn 19 : 26f. The evangelist had already shown that Jesus had, at Cana, addressed his mother as 'woman' (2 : 4) and, by involving her in this 'the first of his signs' (2 : 11), the symbolic manifestation of his 'glory', had associated her with the whole of his work. Now he tells us that Jesus later used the same title, this time addressed to her at the foot of the cross : 'Woman, behold your son' (19 : 26). And now, too, the title takes on a new meaning if we see in it a reference to the woman of Gen. 3 : 15—Mary is the new Eve, the 'mother of all living' (3 : 20). At that moment beneath the cross the sword pierced her soul as Simeon had foretold (Lk. 2 : 35); united to the redemptive sacrifice of her Son, in the travail of Calvary, she became again a mother. For, in pointing out to her the disciple who stood there—'Woman, behold your son'—Jesus called her to a new spiritual maternity which will henceforth be hers towards the people of God. Henceforth, the mother of God is mother, too, of those other children of God, the brethren of her Son.[36] We have seen that the travail of the woman of Ap. 12 : 2 is the travail of Calvary, the birth of Christ to glory (12 : 5); and that the woman is mother not only of the Messiah but of the faithful of Christ (12 : 17). Thus it would seem not unreasonable to suppose that the author of Ap. does have Mary in mind when he speaks of the mother of the Messiah.

While this is so, I find that, personally, I share the hesitation of M.-E. Boismard. He writes: 'It is not sufficient to say that, in the eyes of a Christian, the "woman who brings forth the Messiah" must *necessarily* evoke Mary, the mother of Jesus. It remains for one to prove that the author of Apocalypse *intends* to attach a special importance to Mary as personal mother of Christ. More serious is the argument from Gen. 3: 15. It is certain, in fact, that the woman of Ap. 12 is described in terms of Eve: she is tried by Satan, the "ancient serpent" (Ap. 12 : 9; cf. Gen. 3 : 1ff.), she brings forth in anguish (Ap. 12 : 2; cf. Gen. 3 : 16), she is subject to the persecutions of Satan (Ap. 12 : 6, 14; cf. Gen. 3 : 15)—she and all her children (Ap. 12 : 17; cf. Gen. 3 : 15). The question is whether, *for the author of the Apocalypse,* the Eve of Gen. 3 : 15 pointed to Mary or simply stood for the people of God called to take its revenge on the serpent that had led it astray. In short, the woman of Ap. 12 represents certainly, and primarily, the people of God which brings forth the Messiah and the messianic times. Has the author of the Apocalypse intended that she should *also* represent Mary, the personal mother of the Messiah? It is possible, but the arguments in favour of this view do not quite carry conviction.'[37]

[36] See Vatican II, *Dogmatic Constitution on the Church*, 63.
[37] Robert-Feuillet, *Introduction à la Bible, op. cit.*, II, 738.

The two beasts (13): The first beast (13: 1-10)

Dn. 7: 2-8, 20f., 25: Daniel said, 'I saw in my vision by night, and behold, the four winds of heaven were stirring up the great sea. And four great beasts came up out of the sea, different from one another. The first was like a lion and had eagles' wings. Then as I looked its wings were plucked off, and it was lifted up from the ground and made to stand upon two feet like a man; and the mind of a man was given to it. And behold, another beast, a second one, like a bear. It was raised up on one side; it had three ribs in its mouth between its teeth; and it was told, "Arise, devour much flesh." After this I looked, and lo, another, like a leopard, with four wings of a bird on its back; and the beast had four heads; and dominion was given to it. After this I saw in the night visions, and behold, a fourth beast, terrible and dreadful and exceedingly strong; and it had great iron teeth; it devoured and broke in pieces, and stamped the residue with its feet. It was different from all the beasts that were before it; and it had ten horns. I considered the horns, and behold, there came up among them another horn, a little one, before which three of the first horns were plucked up by the roots; and behold, in this horn were eyes like the eyes of a man, and a mouth speaking great things . . . and concerning the ten horns that were on its head, and the other horn which came up and before which three of them fell, the horn which had eyes and a mouth that spoke great things, and which seemed greater than its fellows. As I looked, this horn made war with the saints, and prevailed over them. . . . He shall speak words against the Most High, and shall wear out the saints of the Most High, and shall think to change the times and the law; and they shall be given into his hand for a time, two times, and half a time.'

Dn. 11: 36: And the king shall do according to his will; he shall exalt himself and magnify himself above every god, and shall speak astonishing things against the God of gods. He shall prosper till the indignation is accomplished; for what is determined shall be done.

Jer. 15: 2: Thus says the Lord: 'Those who are for pestilence, to pestilence, and those who are for the sword, to the sword; those who are for famine, to famine, and those who are for captivity, to captivity.

1. And I saw a beast rising out of the sea, with ten horns and seven heads, with ten diadems upon its horns and a blasphemous name upon its heads. 2. And the beast that I saw was like a leopard, its feet were like a bear's, and its mouth was like a lion's mouth. And to it the dragon gave his power and his throne and great authority. 3. One of its heads seemed to have a mortal wound, but its mortal wound was healed, and the whole earth followed the beast with wonder. 4. Men worshipped the dragon, for he had given his authority to the beast, and they worshipped the beast, saying, 'Who is like the beast, and who can fight against it?'

5. And the beast was given a mouth uttering haughty and blasphemous words, and it was allowed to exercise authority for forty-two months; 6. it opened its mouth to utter blasphemies against God, blaspheming his name and his dwelling, that is, those who dwell in heaven. 7. Also it was allowed to make war on the saints and to conquer them. And authority was given it over every tribe and people and tongue and nation, 8. and all who dwell on earth will worship it, every one whose name has not been written before the foundation of the world in the book of life of the Lamb that was slain. 9. If any one has an ear, let him hear :

10.   If any one is to be taken captive,
      to captivity he goes;
      if any one slays with the sword,
      with the sword must he be slain.

Here is a call for the endurance and faith of the saints.

13 : 1.   Cf. Dn. 7 : 2-8. The beast was introduced in Ap. 11 : 7. In Daniel the four beasts, representing world empires, emerged from the 'great sea'; John also sees his beast emerge from the sea.

Cf. 4 Ezra 11 : 1—'Behold, there came up from the sea an eagle that had twelve feathered wings and three heads'; 12 : 11—'The eagle which you saw coming up from the sea is the fourth kingdom which appeared in a vision to your brother Daniel'. 'Sea' has something of the sense of the *tehom*, the 'deep' or 'abyss' of Gen. 1 : 2 (in Ap. 11 : 7 the beast came 'from the abyss'); and the 'sea' will be excluded from the new order (21 : 1). It is a hostile element and, fittingly, the home of monsters. In v. 11 John will describe another beast 'which rose out of the earth'. He follows the apocalyptic tradition that, on the fifth day, God had created two mythological creatures, Leviathan and Behemoth, one to inhabit the sea and the other the land. Cf. 4 Ezra 6 : 49-52—'Then thou didst keep in existence two living creatures; the name of the one thou didst call Behemoth and the name of the other Leviathan. . . . And thou didst give Behemoth one of the parts which had been dried up on the third day, to live in it . . . but to Leviathan thou didst give the seventh part, the watery part'; cf. I Enoch 60 : 7-10; 2 Bar. 29 : 4. The beast, like the dragon, (Ap. 12 : 3), has seven heads (cf. the many-headed Leviathan of Ps. 74 : 14) and ten horns. The ten horns with ten diadems symbolize kingly power (the ten horns of Daniel's fourth beast are ten kings, Dn. 7 : 24), and the seven heads stand for the fulness of might—a totalitarian state. The further significance of heads and horns will be explained in 17 : 9-14—they identify the power as the Roman Empire. The 'blasphemous names' on each of the heads are the divine titles assumed by the emperors, e.g. *kyrios* (Lord), *sebastos* = *Augustus* (worthy of reverence), *divus* (divine), *Dominus et Deus* (Lord and God—Domitian).

2. Already 4 Ezra had seen Rome in Daniel's fourth beast. John follows the same line, and he describes his beast in terms of the other three of Daniel—a fine example of his free use of sources. 'The description, however impossible to realize as a picture, is surely admirable as a symbol of the character of the foe which the Church found in the Empire, blending massive strength with feline dexterity, following up a stealthy and perhaps unobserved policy of repression with the sudden terrors of a hostile edict' (Swete). To the beast the dragon gave his own power, throne and

authority. Satan (though cast down from heaven) is still 'the ruler of this world' (Jn 12 : 31) for a short time (Ap. 12 : 12). He can still declare : 'To you I will give all this authority and their glory; for it has been delivered to me, and I give it to whom I will' (Lk. 4 : 6). John regards the Empire as the agent of Satan and the persecuting emperors as his vassals.

3.   The Beast is a parody of the Lamb (cf. 5 : 6). One of its heads had received a mortal wound, and the healing of a *mortal* wound is nothing less than a return from the dead. Nero's suicide in AD 68 was followed by a year of civil war which threatened the existence of the Empire; but, with Vespasian, the Beast came to life again. However, a 'head' of the Beast is an emperor; the head whose 'mortal wound was healed' is the 'beast that was, and is not, and is to ascend from the abyss' (17 : 8-11). John has in mind the current legend of *Nero redivivus*—Nero resurrected; in his eyes, Domitian, the second great persecutor of Christians, is Nero all over again. 'The whole earth' gaped in wonder on this Beast and its restored head (cf. 17 : 8); the world is amazed to see Nero return from the abyss.

4.   Emperor-worship is really worship of Satan. Cf. 1 Cor. 10 : 20—'I imply that what pagans sacrifice they offer to demons [and not to idols which are nothing]'. 'Who is like the beast?' (a parody of Ex. 15 : 11, 'Who is like thee, O Lord?') is ironic after Ap. 12 : 7-9—Satan's defeat by Michael, whose name signifies 'who is like God' (Boismard). 'Who can fight against it?' points to the motive which prompted the worship of the beast : not moral greatness but invincible power. In Asia, especially, emperor-worship was enthusiastically embraced.

5f.   Cf. Dn. 7 : 8, 20. The blasphemous claims of the emperors echo those of Antiochus IV (the 'little horn' of Daniel). The beast 'was allowed to exercise authority'. Cf. Lk. 4 : 6—'for it [all this authority and their glory] *has been delivered to me*' : God is the ultimate source of all authority and power, and Satan's activity is covered by God's permission. 'For forty-two months' : the beast's power endures as long as the time of the gentiles (Ap. 11 : 2), as long as the prophesying of the two witnesses (11 : 3), as long as the woman's abode in the wilderness (12 : 6, 14). In other

words, the beast, in one form or another, will survive as long as
the earthly duration of the church. The blasphemies of the beast
—cf. Dn. 7 : 25; 11 : 36. Likewise 'the man of lawlessness' (Antichrist) of 2 Thess. 2 : 4 'opposes and exalts himself against every
so-called god or object of worship, so that he takes his seat in
the temple of God, proclaiming himself to be God'. John identifies God's 'dwelling' with 'those who dwell in heaven', that is,
the martyrs who rejoice at the fall of Satan (Ap. 12 : 12); Satan's
frustrated rage ('blasphemy' in a broad sense) is aimed at
them.

7f. Cf. Dn. 7 : 6, 21. The beast is the dragon's instrument in
his warfare against the seed of the woman (12 : 17), and his
authority covered the inhabited world, the *orbis Romanus*. 'All
who dwell on the earth' (cf. 3 : 10; 6 : 10; 8 : 13; 11 : 10)—the
enemies of God; here they stand out clearly in contrast to the
followers of the Lamb. As again in 21 : 27, the 'book of life' is
said to belong to 'the Lamb that was slain'. The 'inhabitants of
the earth' are those whose names have not been written in this
book since the foundation of the world. Yet, in 3 : 5, Christ
assured the conqueror that he will not blot his name out of the
book of life; and in 20 : 12 there are record books to be opened as
well as the book of life. John does not assert that the worshippers
of the beast are predestined to damnation, but he is clear that
salvation is a free and unmerited gift of God.

9f. 'If any one has an ear, let him hear'—an admonition found
in each of the letters to the churches: John is again turning
directly to Christians with a special message for them. As in 2 : 7,
11, 17, this call to serious attention points ahead to the following
proclamation. In v. 10 John has combined part of Jeremiah's
oracle against Jerusalem (Jer. 15 : 2) with the saying of Jesus
found in Mt. 26 : 52—'All who take the sword will perish by
the sword'. 'The whole is a warning against any attempt on the
part of the Church to resist its persecutors. If a Christian is condemned to exile, as St John had been, he is to regard exile as his
allotted portion, and to go readily; if he is sentenced to death, he
is not to lift his hand against the tyrant; to do so will be to
deserve his punishment' (Swete). It is precisely this suffering with-

out resistance which calls for patient endurance and faith (cf. Ap. 1 : 9; 14 : 12). Caird's illuminating comment opens up a wider perspective: 'When one man wrongs another, the other may retaliate, bear a grudge, or take his injury out on a third person. Whichever he does, there are now two evils where before there was one; and a chain reaction is started, like the spreading of a contagion. Only if the victim absorbs the wrong and so puts it out of currency, can it be prevented from going any further. And this is why the great ordeal is also the great victory.'

The false prophet (13: 11-18)

Dn. 2: 5f.: You are to fall down and worship the golden image that king Nebuchadnezzar has set up; and whoever does not fall down and worship shall be cast into a burning, fiery furnace.

11. Then I saw another beast which rose out of the earth; it had two horns like a lamb and it spoke like a dragon. 12. It exercises all the authority of the first beast in its presence, and makes the earth and its inhabitants worship the first beast, whose mortal wound was healed. 13. It works great signs, even making fire come down from heaven to earth in the sight of men; 14. and by the signs which it is allowed to work in the presence of the beast, it deceives those who dwell on earth, bidding them make an image for the beast which was wounded by the sword and yet lived; 15. and it was allowed to give breath to the image of the beast so that the image of the beast should even speak, and to cause those who will not worship the image of the beast to be slain. 16. Also it causes all, both small and great, both rich and poor, both free and slave, to be marked on the right hand or on the forehead, 17. so that no one can buy or sell unless he has the mark, that is, the name of the beast or the number of its name. 18. This calls for wisdom : let him who has understanding reckon the number of the beast, for it is a human number, its number is six hundred and sixty-six.

11.   In 4 Ezra 6 : 51; 1 Enoch 60 : 7-10, Behemoth is a land monster (cf. Ap. 13 : 1); here likewise the second beast arises out of the earth. Perhaps of greater significance is the fact that, whereas in Daniel's vision the four beasts 'came up out of the sea' (Dn. 7 : 3), in the interpretation of the vision they 'arise out of the earth' (7 : 11). This second beast (called the 'false prophet' in 16 : 13, 19 : 20; 20 : 10), with the horns of a lamb and the voice of a dragon, is a wolf in sheep's clothing. Cf. Mt. 7 : 15 —'Beware of false prophets, who come to you in sheep's clothing but inwardly are ravening wolves'.

12.   The false prophet, who induces all the 'inhabitants of the earth' to worship the beast, is the imperial religion in the service of Rome. He is the interpreter and servant of the beast.

13-15.   As a false prophet, the second beast can work miracles. Cf. Mk 13 : 22—'False Christs and false prophets will arise and shows signs and wonders, to lead astray, if possible, the elect'; 2 Thess. 2 : 9f.—'The coming of the lawless one by the activity of Satan will be with all power and with pretended signs and wonders, and with all wicked deception for those who are to perish'. Thus, early Christian tradition expected that prodigies would precede the coming of Antichrist. John must have known of the magic and the fraudulent miracles of pagan cults, designed to impress and awe a superstitious people. Our only evidence that such practices were also features of the imperial cult is his word, but his claim is entirely credible. One of the prodigies, fire from heaven, aped the sign of the true prophet Elijah (cf. I Kg. 18 : 38; 2 Kg. 1 : 10). As a tool of Satan, 'the deceiver of the whole world' (Ap. 12 : 9), the false prophet deceives the inhabitants of the earth. The deception takes the precise form of emperor-cult : they must 'make an image for the beast'—a reference to the images, set up in temples of Rome and of the Empire, to which divine honours were rendered. 'So that the image of the beast should even speak'—speaking statues were engineered in various ways, e.g. by hiding somebody in a hollow statue or by the use of ventriloquism. John suggests that the voices could be used to instigate violent action against those who refused to accept the

Caesar-cult (cf. Dn. 3 : 5f.). 'Thus in the immediate view of the seer the second beast represents the sorcery and superstition of the age as engaged in a common attempt to impose the Caesar-cult upon the provinces, behind which lay the Satanic purpose of bringing ruin upon the rising Christian brotherhoods' (Swete).

16f. The false prophet causes the totality (cf. 6 : 15; 11 : 18; 19 : 5, 18; 20 : 12) of those who accepted the imperial cult to wear the mark of the beast. The marking of the emperor-worshippers on the right hand and forehead may be seen as a contrast to the practice of Jews of the first century who wore phylacteries on the left arm and on the brow (cf. Mt. 23 : 5) as an expression of their attachment and fidelity to God. It does not seem that visible distinguishing marks are in question. We have seen that the servants of God receive his seal upon their foreheads (Ap. 7 : 3), and the followers of the Lamb have his name and his Father's name written on their foreheads (14 : 1; cf. 3 : 12; 22 : 4). So, too, the servants of the beast are marked with the 'stamp' of the beast : it is a travesty of the seal of the living God (7 : 2). In each case the wearers of the mark are under divine protection —the former under the protection of God and the latter under the care of Satan. v. 17 envisages an economic boycott against those who stand aloof from the imperial cult. A totalitarian régime, especially in a sycophantic atmosphere, has many ways and means of bringing pressure to bear.

18. 'This calls for wisdom' (cf. 17 : 9), the shrewdness which can interpret this riddle. The number of the beast stands for its name, which can be discovered by the process of *gematria* (that is, by the addition of the numerical value of the letters of the name—in Hebrew and Greek, in place of numerals, the letters of the alphabet have a numerical value). The number of the beast (which is the number of its name) is a human number, representing a man's name. In other words, the beast (the Roman Empire) is here represented by an individual emperor (just as in Dn. 2 : 27f. Nebuchadnezzar stands for the Babylonian Empire). It is reasonable to believe that the emperor is Nero. And the Greek *Neron Kaisar,* transliterated into Hebrew script (*nrwn qsr*), gives 666. It is interesting, too, to observe that the Latin form

o

Nero Caesar (in Hebrew script *nrw qsr*) gives 616—which occurs as a variant reading.

The companions of the Lamb (14: 1-5)

> *Zeph. 3: 13: Those who are left in Israel . . . shall utter no lies, nor shall there be found in their mouth a deceitful tongue.*

1. Then I looked, and lo, on Mount Zion stood the Lamb, and with him a hundred and forty-four thousand who had his name and his Father's name written on their foreheads. 2. And I heard a voice from heaven like the sound of many waters and like the sound of loud thunder; the voice I heard was like the sound of harpers playing on their harps, 3. and they sing a new song before the throne and before the four living creatures and before the elders. No one could learn that song except the hundred and forty-four thousand who had been redeemed from the earth. 4. It is these who have not defiled themselves with women, for they are chaste; it is these who follow the Lamb wherever he goes; these have been redeemed from mankind as first fruits for God and the Lamb, 5. and in their mouth no lie was found, for they are spotless.

In deliberate and striking antithesis to the beast and his followers stand the Lamb and his companions, bearing on their foreheads the name of the Lamb and of his Father (14 : 1-5). The 144,000 are not those of 7 : 4-8, the remnant of Israel; they are instead the faithful remnant of the new Israel—the martyrs.

14 : 1. 'On Mount Zion stood the Lamb'. In 11 : 18 and 12 : 5 (cf. 2 : 27) John has made use of Ps. 2; he would seem to have that Psalm in mind here too. Cf. 'I have set my king on Zion, my holy hill' (Ps. 2 : 4); yet, John sees not a warrior king but the Lamb (cf. Ap. 5 : 5f.). In the prophetical writings, Zion (Jerusalem) was traditionally regarded as the place of assembly for the 'remnant', the kernel of messianic restoration (cf. 2 Kg. 19 : 30f.; Ob. 17; Jl 2 : 32; Zeph. 3 : 12f.) (Boismard). John arrives at 144,000 perhaps by taking the square of twelve (12 tribes and

12 apostles), multiplied by 1,000, a great multitude. Or, and this is more likely, he may have deliberately re-employed the symbol of the remnant of Israel in 7 : 4 to symbolize here the remnant of the new Israel. In Jl 2 : 32 (3 : 5) the remnant 'call upon the name of the Lord' (cf. Zeph. 3 : 12); and in Ac. 9 : 14, 21; Rom. 10 : 13; I Cor. 1 : 2, the 'saints' are those who call on the name of the Lord Jesus. This would appear to be the significance of the name of Lamb and Father written on their foreheads (cf. Ap. 3 : 12; 22 : 4).

2f. The 'voice' from heaven is the voice of the host of heaven (5 : 11). Much of the phraseology of v. 3 occurs elsewhere in Ap. 'I heard a voice from heaven' (10; 4; 14 : 15; 18 : 4); 'like the sound of many waters' (1 : 15; 19 : 6); 'like the sound of loud thunder' (19 : 6); 'harps' are mentioned in 5 : 8; 15 : 2. For 'a new song', cf. 5 : 9. Again, it is a heavenly liturgy, but this time the words of the hymn are not given : only the 144,000 could 'learn' (that is, hear and understand, cf. Jn 6 : 45) the new song. They are those who have been ransomed for God (5 : 9), redeemed from the earth. In 15 : 3-5 the conquerors of the beast will sing the 'song of Moses' (Ex. 15 : 1f.) which celebrated the deliverance from Egypt; this 'new song' celebrates the new deliverance of God's people. 'Earth' here corresponds to the 'world' of the Fourth Gospel : it is the pagan world (Boismard).

4f. The designation 'chaste' (literally, 'virgins') must be understood in a metaphorical sense. The OT prophets, especially Hosea, Jeremiah, and Ezekiel, had represented the covenant relationship as a marriage of God with his people (cf. Hos. 1-3; Jer. 2 : 1-4; 4; Ezek. 16; 23); therefore, all idolatry was regarded as adultery or fornication (and, in fact, Canaanite worship did involve ritual prostitution). And, in Ap., the church is the bride of the Lamb (19 : 7; 21 : 2-9), while Rome is presented as a harlot (17 : 4-6; cf. 14 : 8). The 144,000 are contrasted with the followers of the beast because they have refused to worship the beast and have remained faithful to the Lamb. In not giving themselves to the cult of the beast they have kept their virginity.[38]

---

[38] M.-E. Boismard, 'Notes sur l'apocalypse', *Revue Biblique,* 59 (1952), 161-72.

They are those 'who follow the Lamb wherever he goes'.
Cf. Mk. 8 : 34—'If any man would come after me, let him deny
himself and take up his cross and follow me'; cf. Mt. 10 : 38; Jn
21 : 19; Lk. 9 : 57—'I will follow you wherever you go'. The
martyrs have indeed followed the Lamb : they have shared his
sufferings and now share his glory (cf. Lk. 24 : 26). v. 4c interprets and amplifies 'who had been redeemed from the earth' (v.
3). If 'earth' is the Johannine 'world', it is likely that 'mankind'
means 'the inhabitants of the earth'. The 144,000 are 'firstfruits'
of the harvest of God and Lamb (cf. 14 : 14-16)—a fitting description of the martyrs. 'In their mouth no lie was found'—cf.
Zeph. 3 : 13; 1 Pet. 2 : 22—'He committed no sin; no guile was
found on his lips' (cf. Is. 53 : 9). Here the lie would consist in
acknowledging the claims of the beast. They are 'virgins' in their
attachment to the Lamb and truthful in 'holding fast his name'
(Ap. 2 : 13). 'They are spotless'—as martyrs, the 144,000 are
sacrificial victims (cf. 6 : 9). *Amōmos* ('spotless') is in the LXX a
levitical term for appropriate sacrifices. Elsewhere in the NT
Christ himself is so described : 'You have been ransomed with
the precious blood of Christ, like that of a Lamb without blemish
or spot' (1 Pet. 1 : 19); 'Christ . . . offered himself without blemish to God' (Heb. 9 : 14). In this, too, the martyrs are true followers of the Lamb.

THE HOUR OF JUDGMENT (14 : 6—16 : 21)

Proclamation of the hour of judgment (14: 6-13)

> *Ex. 20: 11: For in six days the Lord made heaven and earth,
> the sea, and all that is in them.*
> *Is. 21: 9: Fallen, fallen is Babylon.*
> *Dn. 4: 30: Is not this great Babylon?*
> *Jer. 51: 7f.: Babylon was a golden cup in the Lord's hand,
> making all the earth drunken; the nations drank of her wine,
> therefore the nations went mad. Suddenly Babylon has fallen
> and been broken.*
> *Jer. 25: 15: Take from my hand this cup of the wine of*

wrath, and make all the nations to whom I send you drink it.

Is. 51: 7: Stand up, O Jerusalem, you who have drunk at the hand of the Lord the cup of his wrath.

Is. 34: 10 (Judgment of Edom): Night and day it shall not be quenched; its smoke shall go up for ever.

6. Then I saw another angel flying in midheaven, with an eternal gospel to proclaim to those who dwell on earth, to every nation and tribe and tongue and people; 7. and he said with a loud voice, 'Fear God and give him glory, for the hour of his judgment has come; and worship him who made heaven and earth, the sea and the fountains of water.'

8. Another angel, a second, followed, saying, 'Fallen, fallen is Babylon the great, she who made all nations drink the wine of her impure passion.'

9. And another angel, a third, followed them, saying with a loud voice, 'If any one worships the beast and its image, and receives a mark on his forehead or on his hand, 10. he also shall drink the wine of God's wrath, poured unmixed into the cup of his anger, and he shall be tormented with fire and brimstone in the presence of the holy angels and in the presence of the Lamb. 11. And the smoke of their torment goes up for ever and ever; and they have no rest, day or night, these worshippers of the beast and its image, and whoever receives the mark of its name.'

12. Here is a call for the endurance of the saints, those who keep the commandments of God and the faith of Jesus.

13. And I heard a voice from heaven saying, 'Write this: Blessed are the dead who die in the Lord henceforth.' 'Blessed indeed,' says the Spirit, 'that they may rest from their labours, for their deeds follow them.'

Satan, the two beasts and their followers the 'inhabitants of the earth', the woman and her children, the Lamb and his companions—the dramatis personae of the great eschatological struggle—have all been introduced. Now comes the proclamation of the hour of judgment. Ch. 14 : 6-20 is wholly proleptic, that is, it anticipates events yet to come, and summarizes the coming judgments.

6.   Each of the angels who now appear in succession is designated 'another angel' (14 : 6, 8, 9, 15, 17f.); the first of them is thus distinguished from the angel of the seventh trumpet (11 : 15), the last-mentioned angelic being. The angel flies in midheaven (cf. 8 : 13) because his proclamation is of universal import. His 'eternal gospel' which must be 'evangelized' recalls 10 : 1f., 7; for it would seem that the 'little scroll' which contains the good news of the mystery of God revealed to the prophets (10 : 7) is the 'eternal gospel' proclaimed to 'those who dwell on the earth'. 'If the angel carried a *gospel* which was *eternal* good news *to every nation, tribe, tongue, and people,* it is hard to see how this could differ from *the* gospel. For John really believed in the gospel: he believed that Christ had ransomed for God men from every tribe, tongue, people and nation (5 : 9). This gospel had to be proclaimed if men were to have a chance of accepting it; "How can they believe in one they never heard of? How can they hear without someone to proclaim the news?" (Rom. 10 : 14)' (Caird).

7.   The invitation is addressed to all mankind, even to 'those who dwell on earth'. They are urged to 'fear God and give him glory' (cf. 11 : 13); they are invited to repent. Cf. Mk. 1 : 14f.— 'Jesus came into Galilee, preaching the gospel of God, and saying, "The time is fulfilled, and the kingdom of God is at hand; repent and believe in the gospel".' The proclamation is made to pagans, and so the terms resemble those of the proclamation addressed by Barnabas and Paul to the pagan people of Lystra : 'We bring you good news, that you should turn from these vain things to a living God who made the heaven and the earth and the sea and all that is in them' (Ac. 14 : 15; cf. Ex. 20 : 11). 'The hour of his judgment has come' : this announcement, too, is gospel, good news. Cf. Jn 12 : 31f.—'Now is the judgment of this world, now shall the ruler of this world be cast out; and I, when I am lifted up from the earth, will draw all men to myself'. The simple fact is that God wills the salvation of all men (cf. Tim. 2 : 4).

8.   Cf. Is. 21 : 9; Dn. 4 : 30. The second angel proclaims that the

hour of judgment will involve the fall of Babylon. She is already
judged by God and marked down for destruction; the chastisement of the great city will form the subject of Ap. 17: 1-19.

10. As in 1 Pet. 5: 12, 'Babylon' stands for Rome. Babylon
was depicted by the OT prophets as the ungodly power *par
excellence*, as an oppressive power and a symbol of idolatry and
immorality. Cf. Jer. 51: 7f. 'The wine of her impure passion':
already the picture of the 'great harlot' (Ap. 17: 1-6) is suggested. The image is OT. Thus Nahum, in reference to Nineveh,
speaks of 'the countless harlotries of the harlot . . . who betrays
nations with her harlotries' (Nah. 3 :4); similarly, Tyre is a harlot (Is. 23 : 16f.), and even Zion can deserve the title: 'How the
faithful city has become a harlot' (Is. 1 : 21). Rome, instrument
of the dragon in his warfare against mankind, has led the world
astray by her pagan religion, by her emperor-worship.

9-11.   Men are not compelled to follow the beast to destruction,
the third angel proclaims that God's wrath is aimed at those who
worship the beast (cf. 13 : 4, 16f.). Inveterate worshippers of the
beast will be given to drink the undiluted wine of God's wrath
which stands ready in the cup of God's anger. Cf. Jer. 25 : 15;
Is. 51 : 7. 'He shall be tormented with fire and brimstone': the
'lake of fire and brimstone' (19 : 20; 20 : 10) is the final punishment of the wicked (21 : 8). The image comes from the destruction of Sodom and Gomorrah (Gen. 19: 24-26), coloured by
Is. 30 : 33—'For a burning place has long been prepared for
you . . . the breath of the Lord, like a stream of brimstone,
kindles it' (cf. Ezek. 38 : 22). 'In the presence of the holy angels
and in the presence of the Lamb'—John cannot be said to share
the view of some apocalyptists who believed that a sight of the
torments of the damned would add to the bliss of the redeemed
(cf. 1 Enoch 27 : 3; 48 : 9; 4 Ezra 7 : 36). 'The simple fact is
that John really believed in heaven, the eternal bliss which he
endeavours to describe, even beyond the breaking point of
language, in his final chapters. If words fail in describing the possession of eternity, must they not also fail in describing the priva-
tion of it? To John heaven meant living eternally in the presence
of God; if even he could face that presence only in fear and

trembling, what must it mean for those who had flouted it all their lives? Jesus had spoken of the Son of Man repudiating before the angels those who repudiated him (Lk. 12 : 8), and what could such repudiation be but torment *in fire and brimstone'* (Caird). For v. 11 cf. Is. 34 : 10. The remorse of those who have deserted Christ for Caesar will never die or sleep. 'They have no rest, day or night' is the grim parody of the unceasing worship of the heavenly choir (Ap. 4 : 8).

12f.   Cf. 13 : 10. In Jn 12 : 31f. the hour of judgment is the hour of the 'glorification' of Christ—the hour of his death; so, too, the judgment just described here will involve the passion of the saints, the death of martyrs. These are the faithful ones who have kept the commandments of God and their faith in Jesus (cf. Ap. 1 : 2; 2 : 13; 12 : 17). And as the death of Jesus, though a judgment on the world, was in order to draw all men to him (Jn 12 : 31f.), so the sufferings of the martyrs is a witness to the world. Compare the reaction to the death and glorification of the two witnesses (Ap. 11 : 12f.). In v. 13 *ap'arti* ('henceforth') is better taken with the words which follow it than with the preceding words—as in *The New English Bible* : 'Happy are the dead who died in the faith of Christ! Henceforth, says the Spirit, they may rest from their labours', and in *The Jerusalem Bible* : 'Happy are those who die in the Lord! Happy indeed, the Spirit says; now they can rest for ever after their work.' The text shows John's continued concern for the fate of the martyrs (cf. 6 : 9-11; 7 : 9-17; 12 : 7-11; 14 : 1-5; 15 : 2-4; 19 : 9; 20 : 4-6); it is explicitly asserted that they have found rest, and found it here and now. If the tribulation calls for patient endurance, a voice from heaven, surely the voice of their Lord (cf. 11 : 12; 16 : 15), assures the faithful ones that they are about to enter into rest. Cf. 1 Cor. 15 : 18—'. . . those who have fallen asleep in Christ'. 'Those who die in the Lord' are, primarily, the martyrs, the first-fruits of the redeemed (Ap. 14 : 4), but the beatitude, in its widest sense, applies to all who die in Christ. The Spirit speaks, as in the letters to the churches; for the beatitude is addressed to Christians who find themselves on the verge of the great tribulation. The labours of the faithful ones now are over, but their works abide and go with them (cf. Mt. 25 : 31-46; Ap. 20 : 12). They have entered upon the fulness of rest promised by Jesus : 'Come to me, all you who labour and are heavy-laden, and I will give you rest' (Mt. 11 : 28).

Harvest and vintage of the earth (14: 14-20)

Jl 3: 12f.: Let the nations bestir themselves, and come up to the valley of Jehosaphat; for there I will sit to judge all the nations round about. Put in the sickle, for the harvest is ripe. Go in, tread, for the wine press is full. The vats overflow, for their wickedness is great.

Dn. 7: 13: Behold, with the clouds of heaven there came one like a son of man.

Is. 63: 3, 6: I have trodden the wine press alone, and from the peoples no one was with me; I trod them in my anger and trampled them in my wrath; their lifeblood is sprinkled upon my garments, and I have stained all my raiment. . . . I trod down the peoples in my anger, I made them drunk in my wrath, and I poured out their lifeblood on the earth.

14. Then I looked, and lo, a white cloud, and seated on the cloud one like a son of man, with a golden crown on his head, and a sharp sickle in his hand. 15. And another angel came out of the temple, calling with a loud voice to him who sat upon the cloud, 'Put in your sickle, and reap, for the hour to reap has come, for the harvest of the earth is fully ripe.' 16. So he who sat upon the cloud swung his sickle on the earth, and the earth was reaped.

17. And another angel came out of the temple in heaven, and he too had a sharp sickle. 18. Then another angel came out from the altar, the angel who has power over fire, and he called with a loud voice to him who had the sharp sickle, 'Put in your sickle, and gather the clusters of the vine of the earth, for its grapes are ripe.' 19. So the angel swung his sickle on the earth and gathered the vintage of the earth, and threw it into the great wine press of the wrath of God; 20. and the

wine press was trodden outside the city, and blood flowed from
the wine press, as high as a horse's bridle, for one thousand six
hundred stadia.

This vision of harvest and vintage is based on Jl 3 : 13—the
extermination of the pagan nations; John, in his customary manner, has developed each member of the original couplet. His
arrangement might seem to suggest that the Son of Man reaps
the harvest of the elect (Ap. 14 : 14-16), while an angel gathers
the vintage of the earth (14 : 17-20). Unhappily, this very attractive interpretation cannot really be sustained; the passage must
be read as a close parallel of 19 : 11-16.

14.   Cf. Dn. 7 : 13; Ap. 1 : 7, 13-16; 19 : 11-16. A 'white
cloud'; cf. Mt. 17 : 5—'a bright cloud'. The Son of Man wears a
conqueror's crown (cf. Ap. 4 : 4); the sharp sickle marks him as
judge. In Mk 13 : 26 the coming of the Son of Man on the
clouds is the beginning of judgment : 'And then they will see the
Son of Man coming in clouds with great power and glory'. It is
the fulfilment of Ap. 1 : 7.

15f.   The Son of Man waits for the word of the Father, who
alone knows the hour of judgment. Cf. Mk 13 : 32—'But of that
day or hour no one knows, not even the angels in heaven, nor the
Son, but only the Father'. But now 'the hour of his judgment has
come' (Ap. 14 : 7). The angel who issues from the temple comes
forth from the presence of God—a herald who carries to the
reaper the commission of the Lord. Cf. Jn 5 : 27—'[The Father]
has given him authority to execute judgment, because he is the
Son of Man'. For reaping as an image of judgment, cf. Is. 17 : 5;
27 : 12; Jer. 51 : 33; Jl 3 : 13; Mt. 3 : 12; 13 : 30, 39; Mk
4 : 29.

17f.   It is still the judgment of God : the angel comes from the
temple in heaven, from the divine presence. In the synoptics,
angels are ministers of the Son of Man at the judgment; cf. Mt.
13 : 39, 41f.—'the harvest is the close of the age, and the reapers
are angels. . . . The Son of Man will send his angels, and they
will gather out of his kingdom all causes of sin and all evildoers,
and throw them into the furnace of fire'. Cf. Mk 13 : 27ff. And

if, in our passage, it is an angel who reaps the grape harvest, in
Ap. 19 : 15 it is the Son of Man himself who treads the wine
press. For vintage as an image of judgment, cf. Is. 63 : 3-6; Jer.
25 : 30; Lam. 1 : 15; Jl 4 : 13. The 'angel who has power over
fire' comes forth from the 'altar'; the verse recalls Ap. 6 : 9f. and
8 : 3-5. In 8 : 5 an angel (called in 8 : 3 'another angel', cf. 14 :
18) cast down on the earth coals from the altar, coals which represented the prayers of the martyrs of 6 : 9f. Since, now, the earth
is 'fully ripe' (14 : 15), and its 'grapes are ripe' (14 : 18), the
number of the martyrs too is complete (6 : 11). Now is the judgment on their persecutors. The 'vine of the earth' stands in contrast to the vineyard planted and cultivated by God (Is. 5 : 1-7).
19f. Cf. Is. 63 : 3, 6. The whole passage of Is. 63 : 1-6 (cf. Ap.
19 : 11-16) suggests the great wine press of the wrath of God.
'Outside the city' the destruction of the pagan nations was expected to take place in the course of their final assault on the holy
city (cf. Jl 3 : 12; Zech. 14 : 2f., 12f.; Ezek. 38-39; Ap. 20 : 9).
'As high as a horse's bridle'—a link with the victorious horsemen
of Ap. 19 : 11, 14. The image of the river of blood, going back
ultimately to Is. 63 : 1-6, is more immediately suggested by the
apocalyptic tradition. Cf. 1 Enoch 100 : 1, 3—'In those days in
one place the fathers together with their sons shall be smitten . . .
till the streams flow with their blood. . . . And the horses shall
walk up to their breast in the blood of sinners, and the chariot
shall be submerged to its height'; 4 Ezra 15 : 35—'and there
shall be blood from the sword as high as a horse's belly'. 'One
thousand six hundred stadia' (about 200 miles): the harvest and
vintage had been 'of the earth', and in 19 : 19-21 it is all the
'inhabitants of the earth' who are slain by the rider on the white
horse. Thus, it may be that 1,600 (the square of 4 multiplied by
100) symbolizes the four 'corners' of the earth whence the pagan
nations were to be assembled for the great final battle (Boismard).

The passage 14 : 14-20 is a proleptic or anticipated vision of
the judgment on the world which will be described in greater
detail in 19 : 11-16 and 20 : 7-10. So, it becomes part of the
proclamation of the hour of judgment (14 : 6-13).

Preparatory vision of the seven last plagues (15)

> *Ex. 15: 1: Then Moses and the people of Israel sang this song to the Lord (cf. 15: 1-18).*
> *Jer. 10: 7: Who would not fear thee, O King of the nations?*
> *Ps. 86: 9: All the nations . . . shall come and bow down before thee, O Lord, and shall glorify thy name.*
> *Dn. 10: 5: Behold, a man [an angel] clothed in linen, whose loins were girded with gold of Uphaz.*
> *Ex. 40: 35: Moses was not able to enter the tent of meeting, because the cloud abode upon it, and the glory of the Lord filled the tabernacle.*
> *Is. 6: 4: And the house [the temple] was filled with smoke.*
> *Ezek. 10: 4: And the house [the temple] was filled with the cloud, and the court was full of the brightness of the glory of the Lord.*

1. Then I saw another portent in heaven, great and wonderful, seven angels with seven plagues, which are the last, for with them the wrath of God is ended.

2. And I saw what appeared to be a sea of glass mingled with fire, and those who had conquered the beast and its image and the number of its name, standing beside the sea of glass with harps of God in their hands. 3. And they sing the song of Moses, the servant of God, and the song of the Lamb, saying,

> 'Great and wonderful are thy deeds,
> O Lord God the Almighty!
> Just and true are thy ways,
> O King of the ages!

4.   Who shall not fear and glorify thy name, O Lord?
>   For thou alone art holy.
>   All nations shall come and worship thee,
>   For thy judgments have been revealed.'

5. After this I looked, and the temple of the tent of witness in heaven was opened, and out of the temple came the seven angels with the seven plagues, robed in pure bright linen, and their breasts girded with golden girdles. 7. And one of the four

living creatures gave the seven angels seven golden bowls full of the wrath of God who lives for ever and ever; 8. and the temple was filled with smoke from the glory of God and from his power, and no one could enter the temple until the seven plagues of the seven angels were ended.

The seven plagues which are the last (15 : 1)—and thus distinct from the plagues of seals and trumpets—are announced in ch. 15; the following chapter shows their execution. The vision which presents the angels of the bowls, while modelled on the presentation of the archangels of the trumpets (8 : 2-6), is also a development of it : first the seven appear, next there is a liturgical episode, and then the seven act.

15 : 1. 'Another portent' looks back to 12 : 1, 3. This opening verse, which depicts a scene cast on the screen of heaven, is rather like a heading to the chapter. In v. 6 we are told that the angels come out of the temple, thus really appearing for the first time. The seven plagues are explicitly called 'the last', thus marking them off from the previous two series; they are the last because 'with them the wrath of God is ended'. This is so even though the end is described in chapters 18-20; for the fact is that these chapters develop, in dramatic fashion, what is already present in the plagues of bowls. 'Seven plagues', cf. Lev. 26 : 21— 'If you walk contrary to me, and will not hearken to me, I will bring more plagues upon you, sevenfold as many as your sins'; cf. 26 : 24.

'The seven angels of the last seven plagues are mere angels, whereas the seven trumpeters were the seven angels of the presence, that is, the archangels. The apocalyptic drama steadily descends through the levels of the hierarchy. The seven unsealings are the work of Christ himself, the trumpet-blasts that of the archangels, the bowl-pourings of angels. We may compare the descent of revelation from God to Christ, from Christ to the angel, and from the angel to the Christian prophet (1 : 1). The descent is not to be seen as an anticlimax of power, but as a climax of immediacy. The higher agents themselves worked through inferior agents, whether spiritual or material—neither unsealing nor trumpeting was the direct cause of any plague, but a signal on which some lower force should act. The angels of the last plagues act directly, in pouring them on the earth. The parallel we have drawn between the descent of revelation and the descent of judgment is more than a parallel; St John actually draws the two themes together. When, in the descending scale of judgment, he reaches mere angels, he reaches a sort of beings who can step out of the frame of the visionary picture and act directly as the guides of his inspiration (17 : 1; 2 : 9)' (Farrer).

2. Again, John turns to the martyrs (cf. 7 : 9-17); he describes their bliss before he goes on to the terrors of the last plagues. The 'sea of glass' is that of 4 : 6—the seer is once more in heaven. But the calm sea of 4 : 6 is here 'mingled with fire', that is, it reflects the lightnings from God's throne, symbol of his judgment. Beside the sea stood the conquerors : the faithful ones 'who have not defiled themselves' (14 : 4) with the fornication of emperor-worship. They have conquered the beast—a dramatic reversal because the beast 'was allowed to make war on the saints and to conquer them' (13 : 7; cf. 13 : 15). They had won the victory in the same manner as the 'lamb who was slain' (cf. 3 : 21). 'This scene of the victors standing on the heavenly sea with harps in their hands and praising God recalls Israel's song of triumph over Egypt on the shore of the Red Sea' (Charles). 'Harps of God'—dedicated to the service of God, to accompany the songs of God (cf. 1 Chr. 16 : 42; 2 Chr. 7 : 6; Ap. 14 : 2).

3f. Cf. Ex. 15 : 1. However, unlike the song of Exodus, the marytrs' song is not one of triumph over their enemies—while it does praise God for their victory. As in Heb. 3 : 5, Moses is called God's servant and is set in contrast to the Son : 'Now Moses was faithful in all God's house as a servant . . . but Christ was faithful over God's house as a son'. The deliverance of the Israelites from Egypt was the type of the deliverance of the saints from the beast; thus the 'song of Moses' is also, and principally, the 'song of the Lamb' because the martyrs have won the victory by the blood of the Lamb (7 : 14; 12 : 11). The canticle itself is a mosaic of OT phrases. Cf. Ps. 111 : 2—'Great are the works of the Lord'; 139 : 14—'Wonderful are thy works'; Am. 4 : 13—'The Lord

God the Almighty (LXX)'; Ps. 145 : 17—'The Lord is just in all his ways'; Dt. 32 : 4—'The Rock, his work is perfect; for all his ways are justice; Jer. 10 : 7—'Who would not fear thee, O king of the nations?' (In Ap. 15 : 3, 'O King of the nations' (*ethnōn*—RSV*n*) is preferable to 'O king of the ages' (*aiōnōn*).) Ps. 86 : 9—'All the nations . . . shall come and bow down before thee, O Lord, and shall glorify thy name'; Mal. 1 : 11—'My name is great among the nations, says the Lord of hosts'; Ps. 98 : 2—'The Lord . . . has revealed his vindication in the sight of the nations'.

'Thy judgments' (*dikaiōmata*)—in the sense of 'righteous deeds'. The song holds out hope that the nations, in view of the righteous deeds of the Lord, will fear him and render him homage and worship. 'The song of the martyrs clearly states that God is *King of the nations* (and the idea is there even if we accept the variant reading, "King of the ages"), and will be recognized by the nations as their King; and it implies that this world-wide turning to God will be the outcome of the world-wide martyrdom. Since John cannot be supposed cynical enough to put into the mouths of the martyrs sentiments which he himself did not share, we must accept this opinion as an essential part of John's theology' (Caird).

5f.   The formula, 'After this I looked' (cf. 4 : 1; 7 : 1, 9; 18 : 1), serves to introduce a new vision of special importance. Cf. Ap. 11 : 19—'Then God's temple in heaven was opened'. Here 'the temple of the tent of witness in heaven' is a strange designation; but what John has in mind is the heavenly tabernacle, the archetype of the earthly tent of witness. Cf. Ex. 29 : 9—'According to all that I show you concerning the pattern of the tabernacle . . . so you shall make it'; Ac. 7 : 44; Heb. 8 : 5—'They [the levitical priests] serve a copy and shadow of the heavenly sanctuary'. Now John sees the heavenly sanctuary standing open and seven angels, bearers of the seven last plagues, in priestly robes (cf. Dn. 10 : 5), come forth in solemn procession; they come from the divine presence (cf. Ap. 14 : 15, 17f.). Swete suggests that 'they are "ministering spirits" (Heb. 1 : 14), and they are vested for their liturgy'. Cf. Ap. 1 : 13; 19 : 8, 14.

7.   In ch. 6 the four living creatures, each in turn, signalled the appearance of each of the four horsemen (the first four seals); here, one of the living creatures hands to the seven angels the bowls of God's wrath. In 5 : 8 the twenty-four elders held golden bowls full of the incense of the saints' prayers; but the golden bowls of our text are full of 'the wine of God's wrath' (14 : 10). 'Who lives for ever and ever' (cf. 4 : 9; 10 : 6). Cf. Heb. 10 : 31 —'It is a fearful thing to fall into the hands of the living God'.

8.   Cf. Ex. 40 : 35; Is. 6 : 4; Ezek. 10 : 4; 1 Kg. 8 : 10f. John has used the OT details of a theophany to emphasize the glory and majesty of God at this moment of imminent divine judgment. 'No one could enter the temple'—just as Moses (Ex. 40 : 35) and the priests (1 Kg. 8 : 11) could not enter tent or temple because of the cloud of the Lord's glory. Perhaps John means that the time for intercession is over : it is the hour of judgment.

The last plagues: The seven bowls (16)

The bowls (like the trumpets) are based on the plagues of Egypt, but this time the chastisement is universal and definitive : all the worshippers of the beast and the persecutors of Christians are stricken. Moreover, they are already gathered at Armageddon (16 : 14, 16) to await destruction (19 : 17-21).

The first four plagues of bowls (16: 1-9)

> *Ex. 9: 8: And the Lord said to Moses and Aaron, 'Take handfulls of ashes from the kiln, and let Moses throw them toward heaven in the sight of Pharaoh. And it shall become fine dust over all the land of Egypt, and become boils breaking out in sores on man and beast throughout all the land of Egypt.'*
>
> *Ex. 7: 20f.: He lifted up the rod and struck the water that was in the Nile, and all the water that was in the Nile turned to blood. And the fish in the Nile died; and the Nile became foul, so that the Egyptians could not drink water from the Nile; and there was blood throughout all the land of Egypt.*

1. Then I heard a loud voice from the temple telling the seven angels, 'Go and pour out on the earth the seven bowls of the wrath of God.'

2. So the first angel went and poured his bowl on the earth, and foul and evil sores came upon the men who bore the mark of the beast and worshipped its image.

3. The second angel poured his bowl into the sea, and it became like the blood of a dead man, and every living thing died that was in the sea.

4. The third angel poured his bowl into the rivers and the fountains of water, and they became blood. 5. And I heard the angel of water say,

> 'Just art thou in these thy judgments,
> thou who art and wast, O Holy One.

6. For men have shed the blood of saints and prophets,
> and thou hast given them blood to drink.
> It is their due!'

7. And I heard the altar cry,
> 'Yea, Lord God the Almighty,
> true and just are thy judgments!'

8. The fourth angel poured his bowl on the sun, and it was allowed to scorch men with fire; 9. men were scorched by the fierce heat, and they cursed the name of God who had power over these plagues, and they did not repent and give him glory.

16: 1. This time the 'loud voice', coming from a temple which 'no one could enter' (15 : 8), may be that of God (cf. v. 17); but it could well be the voice of one of the 'angels of the presence'. The bowls of God's wrath, 'poured out on the earth', are aimed at the 'inhabitants of the earth'.

2. Cf. Ex. 9 : 8f. (sixth plague). Cf. Dt. 28 : 35. While the Egyptian plague affected men and animals, here it is the followers of the beast, and only they, who are struck—the threat of Ap. 14 : 9-11 is being fulfilled.

3. Cf. Ex. 7 : 20f. (first plague). Cf. the second trumpet (Ap. 8 : 8f.). 'Like the blood of a dead man'—suggesting the picture of a murdered man sweltering in his blood (Swete). 'Every living

thing' (cf. Gen. 1 : 21) in the sea died, and not just a third of sea creatures (cf. Ap. 8 : 9).

4.   Cf. Ex. 7 : 20f. (first plague). Just as in the trumpets (8 : 8-11), John has made two plagues of the first Egyptian plague. Again, there is no restriction (cf. 8 : 10f.)—all fresh water became blood.

5f.   We meet again the idea of an angel in charge of the elements (cf. 7 : 1; 14 : 18; also 9 : 11). Cf. 1 Enoch 66 : 1f.—'He showed me the angels of punishment who are prepared to come and let loose all the powers of the waters which are beneath in the earth in order to bring judgment and destruction on all who dwell on the earth . . . for those angels were over the powers of the waters'. Swete comments that the words of the angel 'form a sort of anti-phon to the canticle of 15 : 3f.; they illustrate the divine righteousness and holiness proclaimed in the Song'. As in 11 : 17, God is addressed as 'thou who art and wast', no longer 'who wilt come' (cf. 1 : 4). The words of v. 6 emphasize the justice of God. The principle is that of Wis. 11 : 16—'that they might learn that one is punished by the very things by which he sins'. 'Saints and prophets', as in Ap. 11 : 18; 18 : 24. In 17 : 6 Babylon is 'drunk with the blood of the saints and the blood of the martyrs of Jesus'.

7.   'I heard the altar cry', that is, either the angel of the altar (14 : 18), or the altar of 6 : 9; 8 : 3f. personified. In either case, it is the voice of the martyrs of 6 : 9-11; their prayer has been answered. The words are an echo of 15 : 3; cf. 19 : 2.

8f.   The fourth trumpet (a plague of darkness) struck the sun (8 : 12); here, too, the sun is struck, but the effect is different : not darkness but excessive heat. The contrast with 7 : 16 is evi-dent : there those who have come out of the great tribulation are assured that 'the sun shall not strike them, nor any scorching heat'. Cf. Wis. 11 : 5—'For through the very things by which their enemies were punished, they themselves received benefit in their need'. v. 9 makes clear that not even these final plagues denied men the opportunity to repent; but the worshippers of the beast are obdurate. Like their master (13 : 1, 5f.; 17 : 3) they blasphemed God whom they blamed as the cause of their suffer-ings (cf. 11 : 10; 16 : 11, 21). For cursing (blaspheming) the name of God, cf. Rom. 2 : 24; 1 Tim. 6 : 1; Jas 2 : 7. They 'did not repent' (cf. Ap. 9 : 20f.; 16 : 11); contrast 11 : 13 where the Jews do repent. 'Give him glory', cf. 11 : 13; 14 : 7; 19 : 7. The solemn proclamation of 14 : 7 has gone unheeded.

The fifth bowl (16: 10f.)

Ex. 10: 21f.: Then the Lord said to Moses, 'Stretch out your hand toward heaven that there may be darkness over the land of Egypt, a darkness to be felt.' So Moses stretched out his hand toward heaven, and there was thick darkness in all the land of Egypt three days.

10. The fifth angel poured his bowl on the throne of the beast, and its kingdom was in darkness; men gnawed their tongues in anguish 11. and cursed the God of heaven for their pain and sores, and did not repent of their deeds.

10f.—Cf. Ex. 10 : 21f. (ninth plague). Cf. Ap. 8 : 12; 9 : 1-12. 'The throne of the beast'; cf. 13 : 2—'And to it [the beast] the dragon gave his power and his throne and great authority'. The throne of the beast is Rome; this plague assails the very seat of the world-power and covers the whole Empire ('its kingdom'). It is a grim prelude to definitive punishment. 'Men gnawed their tongues in anguish'—Wis. 17 has painted a vivid picture of the terrors of the plague of darkness. Besides, v. 11 shows that the effects of the earlier plagues continue. Again, as with Pharaoh, this plague only served to harden the hearts of the worshippers of the beast; they were driven to worse sin. They blasphemed 'the God of heaven' (cf. Dn. 2 : 44) and did not repent of their evil deeds (cf. 2 : 21; 9 : 20).

In 16 : 9, 11, 21 John's declaration that men blasphemed God points to those who had wholly taken on the character of the false god they served, the beast who is the great blasphemer (13 : 1, 5f.; 17 : 3). 'There can be no question about John's belief that in some men *the mark of the monster* might become indelible and earn for them final reprobation and annihilation (14 : 10f.; 20 : 15; 21 : 8; 22 : 15). But in this he is doing no more than faithfully representing the teaching of Jesus. It is a serious misrepresentation of his theology to magnify the passages in which he faces this possibility, and to neglect the many other passages in which he confidently speaks of the repentance and conversion of those who have been enemies of God and God's people (2 : 16, 21; 3 : 9; 11 : 13; 14 : 6f.; 15 : 3f.; 18 : 4)' (Caird).

The sixth bowl (16: 12-16)

> *Ex. 8: 5f.: And the Lord said to Moses, 'Say to Aaron, "Stretch out your hand with your rod over the rivers, over the canals, over the pools, and cause frogs to come upon the land of Egypt!"' So Aaron stretched out his hand over the waters of Egypt; and the frogs came up and covered the land of Egypt.*

12. The sixth angel poured his bowl over the great river Euphrates, and its water was dried up, to prepare the way for the kings from the east. 13. And I saw, issuing from the mouth of the dragon and from the mouth of the beast and from the mouth of the false prophet, three foul spirits like frogs; 14. for they are demonic spirits, performing signs, who go abroad to the kings of the whole world, to assemble them for battle on the great day of God the Almighty. 15. ('Lo, I am coming like a thief! Blessed is he who is awake, keeping his garments that he may not go naked and be seen exposed!') 16. And they assembled them at the place which is called in Hebrew Armageddon.

12. Cf. 9 : 14—'Release the four angels who are bound at the great river Euphrates'. Then the vision of the sixth trumpet went on to describe the invasion of a demonic army from beyond the river whose objective was the killing of 'a third of mankind' (9 : 15-19). Here the sixth bowl dries up the Euphrates to open the way for 'the kings from the east'. Cf. Ex. 14 : 21; Jos. 3 : 17; Jer. 51 : 36f.—'I will dry up her sea and make her fountain dry; and Babylon shall become a heap of ruins'; 50 : 38—'A drought upon her waters, that they may be dried up'; Is. 11 : 15. As in

Ap. 9 : 15-19 the Parthians are in mind—Rome's dreaded and mysterious enemies who typify all foreign invaders.

13f. Cf. Ex. 8 : 5f. (second plague). Quite like the locusts of the fifth trumpet (Ap. 9 : 1-11), these frogs are demonic beings. The 'false prophet' is the second beast of 13 : 11; cf. 19 : 20. Cf. Zech. 13 : 2—'On that day, says the Lord of hosts . . . I will remove from the land the prophets and the unclean spirit'. 'Demonic [unclean] spirits'; cf. Mk 1 : 23; Mt. 10 : 1, etc. These spirits, from the mouths of the satanic trinity, are lying spirits which deceive mankind (cf. Ap. 13 : 14) and lead men to their doom. Cf. Dt. 13 : 1f.; Mk 13 : 22; 2 Thess. 2 : 9-12. The 'kings from the east' are ready to move westward as soon as their way has been prepared. John may be thinking of the legend of *Nero redux* (or *redivivus*): the popular belief that the Emperor would return, at the head of a Parthian army, to destroy his enemies and regain his throne (cf. 13 : 3; 17 : 11). The demonic spirits summon the 'kings of the whole world' to join the eastern invaders. Yet, their concerted assault is not only on Rome (cf. 17 : 6f.); because they are deluded instruments of the beast, it is ultimately against the Lamb. Cf. Ps. 2 : 2—'The kings of the earth set themselves . . . against the Lord and his anointed'; Ap. 17 : 13f.; 19 : 19. 'The great day of God the Almighty'; cf. Jl 2 : 11—'For the day of the Lord is great and very terrible; who can endure it?' 2 : 30—'before the great and terrible day of the Lord comes'; cf. Ap. 6 : 17. The nations are marshalled for the eschatological battle; this is the breaking of the day of the Lord.

15. Obviously a parenthesis. Cf. 3 : 3f., 18. The voice is the voice of Jesus (cf. 14 : 13), again calling for watchfulness (Mt. 24 : 43; Lk. 12 : 39; cf. 1 Thess. 5 : 2). This is one of the seven beatitudes in Ap. (cf. 1 : 3; 14 : 13; 19 : 9; 20 : 6; 22 : 7, 14). The warning is not really out of place, though many commentators have judged it so. Jesus had warned his disciples that the end of Jerusalem would come unexpectedly, brooking no delay on the part of those who would escape: 'Let him who is on the housetop not go down, nor enter his house, to take anything away; and let him who is in the field not turn back to take his mantle' (Mk 13 :

15f.). Now he warns his followers to be prepared for the last days of Babylon; they must recognize his coming in that event. He comes 'like a thief' because both the hour of his coming and its manner in the events of history are hidden from them.

16.   The troops of the nations, assembled by the demonic spirits, were marshalled at Armageddon. The name means 'the mountain of Megiddo'. Megiddo lies at the foot of Mount Carmel, dominating the strategic pass from the coastal plain to the plain of Jezreel. Its position made it the scene of many battles; ever since the defeat and death of Josiah at Megiddo (2 Kg. 23 : 29f.) it had remained a symbol of disaster. John utilizes this symbolism : it spells the disaster of the assembled armies (cf. Ap. 19 : 11-21).

The seventh bowl (16: 17-21)

> *Dn. 12: 1: And there will be a time of trouble, such as never has been since there was a nation on the earth (Theo-dotion).*
> *Ex. 9: 23f.: Then Moses stretched forth his rod toward heaven; and the Lord sent thunder and hail, and fire ran down to the earth. And the Lord rained hail upon the land of Egypt; there was hail, and fire flashing continually in the midst of the hail, very heavy hail, such as had never been in all the land of Egypt since it became a nation.*

17. The seventh angel poured his bowl into the air, and a great voice came out of the temple, from the throne, saying, 'It is done!' 18. And there were flashes of lightning, loud noises, peals of thunder, and a great earthquake such as had never been since men were on the earth, so great was that earthquake. 19. The great city was split into three parts, and the cities of the nations fell, and God remembered great Babylon, to make her drain the cup of the fury of his wrath. 20. And every island fled away, and no mountains were to be found; 21. and great hailstones, heavy as a hundredweight, dropped on men from heaven, till men cursed God for the plague of the hail, so fearful was that plague.

17.   This final plague is of cosmic range; so the seventh angel poured his bowl 'into the air'. The same voice which had sent the angels on their mission (16 : 1) now declares that their work is accomplished (cf. 21 : 6): these plagues are indeed 'the last' (15 : 1).

18.   Cf. 8 : 5; 11 : 19. These are the traditional accompaniments of a great visitation. Cf. Dn. 12 : 1; Ex. 9 : 24; Mk 13 : 19— 'For in those days there will be such tribulation as has not been from the beginning of the creation which God created until now'. Fittingly, at the close of the last plague of all, the earthquake is of unprecedented violence.

19.   The 'great city', 'great Babylon', is Rome (14 : 8). In 11 : 13 a tenth of Jerusalem fell; but now Rome is 'split into three parts' by the violent earthquake which also destroys the cities of the heathen—the destruction is world-wide. God had seemed to overlook the wickedness of Rome as she went her proud way, mistress of the world. But his justice could not be flouted and the hour of her retribution has come. She 'who made all the nations drink the wine of her impure passion' (14 : 8) must now, herself, drink the wine of God's wrath (cf. 14 : 10).

20f.   These verses describe the further effects of the outpouring of the seventh bowl. The disappearance of mountains is one of the signs of the end of the world (cf. 6 : 14). Cf. *Assumption of Moses* 10 : 4—'And the high mountains shall be made low, and the hills shall be shaken and fall'. v. 21—cf. Ex. 9 : 23f. (seventh plague). Traits of the seventh Egyptian plague already appeared in v. 18, but the central scourge of hail is emphasized here. John, with his hailstones 'heavy as a hundredweight', merely makes more concrete the 'very heavy hail' of Exodus. As in Ap. 16 : 9, 11 the effect of this plague too is to harden the hearts of the heathen. 'So ends this last series of plagues which are to descend upon mankind through the instrumentality of angels. We have now to turn in detail to the final struggle' (Turner).

THE CHASTISEMENT OF BABYLON (ROME) (17: 1—19: 10)

Although the fall of Rome is proclaimed in 14: 8, and is briefly described in 16: 19, the end of that city, the great persecuting power, cannot be treated so casually. The whole of chapter 17 is given over to a description of Babylon—the goddess Rome— seated on the satanic beast; the fall of Rome is solemnly acclaimed in 19: 1-8. Then follow a satirical lament (19: 9-24) and a triumphal liturgy in heaven (19: 1-10).

The great harlot (17: 1-6)

> *Jer. 51: 6-9, 12f.: Flee from the midst of Babylon, let every man save his life! Be not cut off in her punishment, for this is the time of the Lord's vengeance, the requital he is rendering her. Babylon was a golden cup in the Lord's hand, making all the earth drunken; the nations drank of her wine, therefore the nations went mad. Suddenly Babylon has fallen and been broken; wail for her! Take balm for her pain; perhaps she may be healed. We would have healed Babylon but she was not healed. Forsake her, and let us go each to his own country; for her judgment has reached up to heaven and has been lifted up even to the skies. . . . Set up a standard against the walls of Babylon; make the watch strong; set up watchmen; prepare the ambushes; for the Lord has both planned and done what he spoke concerning the inhabitants of Babylon. O you who dwell by many waters, rich in treasures, your end has come, the thread of your life is cut.*

1. Then one of the seven angels who had the seven bowls came and said to me, 'Come, I will show you the judgment of the great harlot who is seated upon many waters, 2. with whom the kings of the earth have committed fornication, and with the wine of whose fornication the dwellers on earth have become drunk.' 3. And he carried me away in the Spirit into a wilder-

ness, and I saw a woman sitting on a scarlet beast which was
full of blasphemous names, and it had seven heads and ten
horns. 4. The woman was arrayed in purple and scarlet, and
bedecked with gold and jewels and pearls, holding in her hand
a golden cup full of abominations and the impurities of her
fornication; 5. and on her forehead was written a name of
mystery : 'Babylon the great, mother of harlots and of earth's
abominations.' 6. And I saw the woman, drunk with the blood
of the saints and the blood of the martyrs of Jesus.

17 : 1f.   The plagues of bowls were the last; what follows fills
out the details of these plagues. That is why one of the seven
angels of the bowls now serves as John's guide. The judgment of
Rome, which has been twice proclaimed (14 : 8; 16 : 19), is to be
described at length. 'Harlot'—in the prophetic literature idolatry
is termed 'fornication' and a city given to idolatry is termed a
'harlot'. Thus in Ezek. 16 Jerusalem is a harlot and in Ezek. 23
Samaria and Jerusalem, sisters, are a pair of harlots. Pagan
cities, too, were so designated. Cf. Is. 23 : 15-17—'At the end of
seventy years, it will happen to Tyre as in the song of the harlot :
"Take a harp, go about the city, O forgotten harlot! . . ." At the
end of seventy years the Lord will visit Tyre, and she will return
to her hire, and will play the harlot with all the kingdoms of the
world upon the face of the earth'; Nah. 3 : 4 (of Nineveh)—'And
all for the countless harlotries of the harlot, graceful and of deadly
charms, who betrays nations with her harlotries, and people with
her charms'. 'Seated upon many waters'—cf. Jer. 51 : 12f. The
description does not, literally, fit Rome; John has simply taken
it from Jeremiah and has applied it to his 'Babylon'. For v. 2
cf. Jer. 51 : 7; Ap. 14 : 8; 18 : 3. Babylon appears as the great
harlot because of her idolatrous emperor-worship propagated
throughout the Empire. With idolatry went vice of all kinds; and
Paul has painted a lurid picture of the vices of paganism (Rom.
1 : 24-32). The 'kings of the earth' are the rulers who have pur-
chased the favour of Rome; the 'dwellers on earth' are the
enemies of God and the infatuated worshippers of the beast.
3.   John, fallen into a trance (cf. 1 : 10; 4 : 2), was transported

by his angel guide into a desert. The desert is a bivalent symbol : in chapter 12 it is the place of God's protection where the woman rests secure, but here it is the abode of evil. In this desert, too, John sees a woman, the very antithesis of her of chapter 12. The beast is the one of chapter 13; but now he appears arrayed in splendid scarlet, and he bears blasphemous names all over, not only on his seven heads (13 : 1). The beast is the Empire, and the Empire reeked with the blasphemous worship of the emperors (Swete). The woman is the goddess Rome, born aloft by the great Empire.

4f.   The woman was proudly decked in imperial purple and scarlet and made a display of costly finery. Yet, all her magnificence pales before the shining splendour of the woman of 12 : 1 and before the simple beauty of the bride of the Lamb (19 : 7f.). The harlot holds a golden cup full of 'the wine of her impure passion' (14 : 8) which the nations have drunk (18 : 3). Like the prostitutes of Rome who displayed their names on their brows, she, too, wore her name on her forehead. It is a name of mystery, that is, a name known only to the initiated (cf. 1 : 20). 'The Woman on the Beast represents, is the symbol of, Babylon the Great, while Babylon itself is a mystical name for the city which is now the mistress of the world. Her gaily attired, jewelled, gilded person, and her cup of abominations, proclaim her to be the Mother-Harlot of the earth. All the harlots of all the subject races are her children; all the vices and the superstitions of the provinces were suckled at her breasts. The metropolis of the Empire is the source and fountain-head of its impurities, the mother of harlots, even as the Church is the mother of Christ and his saints (12 : 5, 17)' (Swete). 'Abominations' (*bdelygma*) is the same expression as the abomination of Dn. 9 : 27; 11 : 31; 12 : 11 (cf. Mk 13 : 14), the altar of Zeus set up in the profaned temple by Antiochus IV; therefore, it means idolatry.

6.   John saw that the woman was drunk, but drunk with blood (cf. 18 : 24). We may see here an allusion to the bloody persecution of Nero (cf. 17 : 10). Rome is guilty of the double crime of idolatry (v. 4) and of murder (v. 6); Ezekiel had accused Jerusalem of these same crimes (cf. Ezek. 16 : 36-38; 23 : 37, 45). The slain 'saints' are evidently martyrs; the repetition may serve to enhance the guilt of Rome. The marvelling of the seer in face of a vision is a feature of apocalyptic (cf. Dn. 7 : 15). Despite himself, John is impressed by the grandeur of Rome. Besides, he had been invited to see God's judgment on Babylon, yet no ruined city had met his gaze; he had seen a bejewelled woman on a scarlet beast. He needs an interpreter.

The interpretation of the vision of Babylon and the beast (17: 7-18)

> *Dn. 7: 24: As for the ten horns, out of this kingdom ten kings shall arise.*
> *Dt. 10: 17: For the Lord your God is God of gods and Lord of lords.*
> *Ps. 136: 3: O give thanks to the Lord of lords.*
> *Dn. 2: 47: Truly, your God is God of gods and Lord of kings.*
> *Ezek. 16: 39-41: And I will give you into the hand of your lovers . . . and they shall strip you of your clothes and take your fair jewels, and leave you naked and bare . . . and they shall burn your houses.*
> *Ezek. 23: 25-29: Your survivors shall be devoured by fire. They shall also strip you of your clothes . . . and they shall deal with you in hatred . . . and leave you naked and bare.*

7. When I saw her I marvelled greatly. But the angel said to me, 'Why marvel? I will tell you the mystery of the woman, and of the beast with seven heads and ten horns that carries her. 8. The beast that you saw was, and is not, and is to ascend from the bottomless pit and go to perdition; and the dwellers on earth whose names have not been written in the book of life from the foundation of the world, will marvel to behold the beast, because it was and is not and is to come. 9. This calls for a mind with wisdom : the seven heads are seven hills on which the woman is seated; 10. they are also seven kings, five of whom have fallen, one is, the other has not yet come, and when he comes he must remain only a little while.

11. As for the beast that was and is not, it is an eighth but it belongs to the seven, and it goes to perdition. 12. And the ten horns that you saw are ten kings who have not yet received royal power, but they are to receive authority as kings for one hour, together with the beast. 13. These are of one mind and give over their power and authority to the beast; 14. they will make war on the Lamb, and the Lamb will conquer them, for he is Lord of lords and King of kings, and those with him are called and chosen and faithful.'

15. And he said to me, 'The waters that you saw, where the harlot is seated, are peoples and multitudes and nations and tongues. 16. And the ten horns that you saw, they and the beast will hate the harlot; and they will make her desolate and naked, and devour her flesh and burn her up with fire, 17. for God has put it into their hearts to carry out his purpose by being of one mind and giving over their royal power to the beast, until the words of God shall be fulfilled. 18. And the woman that you saw is the great city which has dominion over the kings of the earth.'

7. In apocalyptic, angels commonly fill the role of interpreter (cf. Dn. 7: 15-28; 8: 15-26). The angel lists the significant details of the vision: the woman, the beast, his seven heads, and his ten horns. But, in his explanation, he takes the beast first (17: 8-17) and briefly mentions the harlot last of all (v. 18).

8. Cf. chapter 13 where the beast is said to have recovered from a deadly wound (13: 3, 12, 14). Again, John turns the legend of *Nero redivivus* to his purpose. Here the beast is said to have died of his wound ('is not') and gone to the abyss (cf. 11: 7), and has returned again but only to go to final doom (cf. 19: 20). As in 13: 3, men will stand in awe of the beast, amazed at its vitality. But now 'the whole world' of 13: 3 is made more specific: only the 'dwellers on the earth', whose names are not found in the Lamb's book of life (13: 8; 20: 12, 15), will marvel at him. 'It was and is not and is to come' is a parody on the divine title, 'who is and who was and who is to come' (1: 4).

9f. 'This calls for a mind with wisdom'—what follows is enigmatic, like the number of the beast (13 : 8). The angel offers a two-fold explanation of the seven heads. In the first place, the heads stand for seven hills; and Rome was widely known, even in antiquity, as the city on the seven hills. But the heads have a further significance: they are 'kings'—without doubt, seven Roman emperors. We are told that 'five have fallen' and that 'one is'—the sixth, in whose reign the book is thus set. Since the list most probably begins with Augustus and leaves aside the three imperial competitors of AD 69 (following the death of Nero)—Galba, Otho and Vitellius—it would read as follows: Augustus, Tiberius, Caligula, Claudius, Nero, Vespasian, Titus. It turns out that the sixth emperor is Vespasian (AD 69-79). The one still to come and who 'must remain only a little while' is, appropriately, Titus, whose reign was short (79-81). The number seven is, of course, symbolic and implies totality; John is not concerned with the exact number of emperors who reigned after Nero.

11. The author plays on the number seven. Titus was followed by Domitian (AD 81-96); by means of the Nero legend, John can make the eighth emperor one of the seven. And he can do so plausibly because Domitian, like Nero, is a persecutor of Christians: he is Nero all over again. With his appearance the beast ascends from the abyss—but only to go to his destruction (v. 8).

12. Cf. Dn. 7: 24; Ap. 13 : 1. These ten kings belong to the future; they will receive authority for one hour with the beast, that is, at his appearing. 'For one hour', cf. 18 : 10, 17, 19; this, probably, refers to the destruction of Rome by the beast and the ten kings (17 : 16f.).

13f. The kings are unanimous in their wholehearted support of the beast. When they have, with him, brought about the downfall of Rome (17 : 12, 16f.), they follow him in war against the Lamb. But the beast has arisen only 'to go to perdition' (17 : 8, 11): he and his followers will be conquered by the Lamb; the battle will be described in 19 : 11-21 (cf. 16 : 13-16). Cf. Dt. 10 : 17; Ps. 136 : 3; Dn. 2 : 47; 2 Mac. 13 : 4; 1 Tim. 6 : 15. The faithful followers of the Lamb will share his victory. These are the martyrs 'who have conquered him [Satan] by the blood of the Lamb and by the word of their testimony' (12 : 11); they are the conquerors who have been given 'power over the nations' (2 : 26f.). 'Called and chosen and faithful', cf. Mt. 22 : 14.— 'For many are called, but few are chosen'. These are not only called and chosen, but have sealed their call and election by their fidelity; they are those 'who follow the Lamb wherever he goes' (Ap. 14 : 4).

15. The 'many waters' of 17 : 1, a feature borrowed from Jeremiah's description of Babylon (Jer. 51 : 13), are now said to represent the teeming and mixed peoples of the Empire. John is going on to develop the theme of the destruction of Rome which was suggested in v. 12; it now appears that the great coalition of peoples, which forms the strength of the Empire, will prove the undoing of Rome (v. 16).

16f. The ten horns grow from the heads of the beast (v. 3) who uses them to destroy the harlot. Cf. Ezek. 16 : 39, 41; 23 : 25-29. 'The savaging of the whore by the monster and its horns is John's most vivid symbol for the self-destroying power of evil' (Caird). Yet, after all, these kings, and the beast itself, are instruments of God's purpose (cf. Is. 7 : 18; 45 : 1). The words of God which must be fulfilled are his decree against Rome (Ap. 14 : 8; 16 : 19; 18 : 8).

It would seem that John has in mind, but has freely adapted after his manner, the legend of Nero *redux* and *redivivus*. According to popular belief, attested by Tacitus and Suetonius, Nero had not really died in AD 68 but had found refuge among the Parthians. It was believed that he would return, at the head of a Parthian army, to regain his throne. And in fact, three pretenders appeared between AD 69 and 88, under Nero's name, as claimants of the imperial throne. Cf. Tacitus, *The Histories,* II, 8—'About this time Achaia and Asia Minor were terrified by a false report that Nero was at hand. Various rumours were current about his death, and so there were many who pretended and believed that he was still alive.' This tradition of *Nero-redux* (the return of Nero) passed into Jewish apocalyptic : Nero's return to destroy Rome was seen as God's punishment on the devastators of Jerusalem (*Sibylline Oracles,* IV, 119-22, 137-9; V, 143-8, 361-4). Towards the close of the first century, the legend had taken the form of the return to life of the Emperor (*Nero-redivivus*) who had become an instrument or incarnation of Satan (*Sibyl. Or.,* V, 28-34, 214-27). Since the beast, in 17 : 11, is Nero *redivivus*, John can depict him leading an assault on Rome and also (because he is a satanic being) as making war on the Lamb. The same legend, taken in general, and used very freely, lies behind Ap. 16 : 12-16.

18. Though v. 9 is already sufficiently clear, John takes care to spell out the identity of the harlot. Allo remarks that the verse is bitingly sarcastic : this city believes herself to be absolute mistress of the kings of the earth—the very kings who are destined to destroy her.

Proclamation of the fall of Babylon (18: 1-8)

Ezek. 43: 2: The glory of the God of Israel came from the east . . . and the earth shone with his glory.

Jer. 51: 8: Suddenly Babylon has fallen and been broken.

Is. 21: 9: Fallen, fallen is Babylon; and all the images of her gods he has shattered to the ground.

Is. 13: 19-22: And Babylon, the glory of kingdoms . . . will be like Sodom and Gomorrah when God overthrew them. . . . Wild beasts will lie down there, and its houses will be full of howling creatures . . . and there satyrs will dance.

Jer. 50: 39: Therefore wild beasts and jackals shall dwell in Babylon, and ostriches shall dwell in her; she shall be peopled no more for ever, not inhabited for all generations.

Jer. 51: 6, 45: Flee from the midst of Babylon, let every man save his life. . . . Go out of the midst of her, my people! Let every man save his life from the fierce anger of the Lord!

Jer. 50: 15, 29: For this is the vengeance of the Lord: take vengeance on her, do to her as she has done. . . . Requite her according to her deeds, do to her according to all that she has done.

Is. 40: 2: She has received from the Lord's hand double for all her sins.

1. After this I saw another angel coming down from heaven, having great authority; and the earth was made bright with his splendour. 2. And he called out with a mighty voice,

> 'Fallen, fallen, is Babylon the great!
> It has become a dwelling place of demons,
> a haunt of every foul spirit,
> a haunt of every foul and hateful bird;

3.   for all nations have drunk the wine of her impure passion,
> and the kings of the earth have committed fornication with her,
> and the merchants of the earth have grown rich with the wealth of her wantonness.'

4.   Then I heard another voice from heaven saying,
> 'Come out of her, my people,
> lest you take part in her sins,
> lest you share in her plagues;

5.   for her sins are heaped high as heaven,
> and God has remembered her iniquities.

6.   Render to her as she herself has rendered,
> and repay her double for her deeds;
> mix a double draught for her in the cup she mixed.

7.   As she glorified herself and played the wanton,
> so give her a like measure of torment and mourning.
> Since in her heart she says, "A queen I sit,
> I am no widow, mourning I shall never see,"

8.   so shall her plagues come in a single day,
> pestilence and mourning and famine,
> and she shall be burned with fire;
> for mighty is the Lord God who judges her.'

In the proleptic vision of 14 : 8 the fall of Babylon had been proclaimed and the seventh bowl had brought its destruction. John now develops the oracle of doom against the great city which he has described in chapter 17.

18 : 1. John sees an angel of great authority—not his guide of ch. 17—come down from heaven. He has come forth from the

presence of God and reflects the divine splendour. Cf. Ezek.
43 : 2.

2f. The fall of Babylon is presented as an event of the past
because it has been accomplished by the final plague (16 : 17-19;
cf. 14 : 8; Jer. 51 : 8; Is. 21 : 9). The terms of John's desolate
description of the ruined city were readily available to him in the
OT prophets: Is. 13 : 19-22; Jer. 50 : 39; Is. 34 : 11-15; Zeph.
2 : 13f. v. 3 gives the reason for her punishment : in the first place,
her idolatry (Ap. 14 : 8; 17 : 2). But there is also the great luxury
of the city; the traders of the Empire grew rich by pandering to
the extravagant tastes of the capital. The lament of the 'kings of
the earth' is given in 18 : 9f. and that of the merchants in 18 :
11-16.

4f. Again, a voice from heaven (cf. 10 : 4, 8; 11 : 12; 14 : 2,
13); it cannot be the voice of God, for he is named in the third
person in vv. 5 and 8. It is, perhaps, the voice of the Lamb. The
invitation is an echo of Jer. 51 : 6, 45; cf. Is. 48 : 20; 52; 11.
Compare the admonitions to flight given in the synoptic apocalypse (Mk 13 : 14-18; Mt. 24 : 16-20). The texts of Jeremiah
and Isaiah urge the chosen people to leave Babylon before that
city reaps its punishment. Now Christians are bidden to flee Rome
lest they become involved in her sin and chastisement. It may
well be that here speaks John the pastor, as in the letters to the
churches and in 13 : 9f. and 16 : 15, with a message for his
Christians of Asia. However, Caird makes an interesting observa-
tion : 'The only inhabitants now left in the great city are those
who, through all the premonitory plagues, have obdurately
refused to repent (10 : 20; 16 : 9, 11). Yet even at this late hour
it is still possible for men to prove themselves God's *people* and to
escape their share in Babylon's *plagues* by dissociating themselves
from *her sins*. To the bitter end the miracle of grace remains open,
and God never ceases to say "My people", to those who before
were not his people (Hos. 2 : 23; Rom. 9 : 25f.; 1 Pet. 2 : 10).'
John goes on to declare that the sins of Rome are piled high as
heaven (cf. Jer. 51 : 9) and that God's justice has taken stock of
her crimes.

6. Cf. Jer. 50 : 15, 29; Ps. 137 : 8. The command is addressed

H

to the ministers of divine justice; the angels of the plagues and
also the unsuspecting instruments of Ap. 17 : 16f. Vengeance is
the prerogative of God alone (Dt. 32 : 35; Rom. 12 : 19; Heb.
10 : 30). 'Repay her double', cf. Is. 40 : 2; Jer. 16 : 18; 17 : 18.
'A double draught'—allusion to the special mixtures of different
wines calculated to achieve more surely the desired effect in
orgies (Boismard). 'The cup she mixed' (cf. Ap. 14 : 8, 10; 17 : 4;
18 : 3).

7f.   These verses develop the idea of proportionate retribution :
let her share of misery match her arrogance. 'Pestilence and
mourning and famine' (cf. 6 : 5-8), and burning with fire (cf.
ch. 18)—because the city will be destroyed in war by an invading
army (17 : 16). The words of the mighty God must be fulfilled
(17 : 17).

Dirges over Babylon (18: 9-19)

The fall of Rome finds dramatic expression in the three dirges
chanted over her conflagration by the kings (18 : 9f.), the merchants (vv. 11-16), and the shipowners and sailors (vv. 17-19) of
the world. The whole passage is manifestly inspired by Ezekiel's
dirge over Tyre (Ezek. 27-28).

a) The kings' lament (18: 9f.)

> *Ezek. 26: 16f.: Then all the princes of the sea will step
> down from their thrones, and remove their robes, and strip
> off their embroidered garments; they will clothe themselves
> with trembling; they will sit upon the ground and tremble
> every moment, and be appalled at you. 17. And they will
> raise a lamentation over you, and say to you, 'How you
> have vanished from the seas, O city renowned, that was
> mighty on the sea, you and your inhabitants, who imposed
> your terror on all the mainland!'*

9. And the kings of the earth, who committed fornication
and were wanton with her, will weep and wail over her when

they see the smoke of her burning; 10. they will stand far off,
in fear of her torment, and say,

> 'Alas! alas! thou great city,
> thou mighty city, Babylon!
> In one hour has thy judgment come.'

9f. Cf. Ezek. 26 : 16f. The 'kings of the earth': cf. Ap. 17 : 2;
18 : 3. The vassal kings deplore the fate of the city whose luxury
as well as idolatry they had shared. 'With a touch of grim
humour John paints them as standing at a safe distance from the
conflagration, and contenting themselves with idle lamentations'
(Swete). 'In one hour' (vv. 17, 19); cf. 17 : 12—the ten kings,
with the beast, receive authority 'for one hour', in order to destroy
Rome (17 : 16).

b) The merchants' lament (18: 11-17a)

> *Ezek. 27: 2f., 12f., 22: Now you, son of man, raise a lamen-
> tation over Tyre, and say to Tyre, who dwells on the
> entrance to the sea, merchant of the peoples on many coast-
> lands, thus says the Lord God: 'O Tyre, you have said, "I
> am perfect in beauty". . . .' Tarshish trafficked with you
> because of your great wealth of every kind; silver, iron, tin,
> and lead they exchanged for your wares. Javan, Tubal, and
> Meshech traded with you; they exchanged the persons of
> men and vessels of bronze for your merchandise. . . . The
> traders of Sheba and Raamah traded with you; they ex-
> changed for your wares the best of all kinds of spices, and
> all precious stones, and gold.*

11. And the merchants of the earth weep and mourn for
her, since no one buys their cargo any more, 12. cargo of gold,
silver, jewels and pearls, fine linen, purple, silk and scarlet, all
kinds of scented wood, all articles of ivory, all articles of costly
wood, bronze, iron and marble, 13. cinnamon, spice, incense,
myrrh, frankincense, wine, oil, fine flour and wheat, cattle and
sheep, horses and chariots, and slaves, that is, human souls.

14. 'The fruit for which thy soul longed has gone from thee,
and all thy dainties and thy splendour are lost to thee,
never to be found again!'

15. The merchants of these wares, who gained wealth from
her, will stand far off, in fear of her torment, weeping and
mourning aloud,

16. 'Alas, alas, for the great city
that was clothed in fine linen, in purple and scarlet,
bedecked with gold, with jewels, and with pearls!

17. In one hour all this wealth has been laid waste.'

11-13. Cf. Ezek. 27 : 2f., 12f., 22; Is. 23 : 1-12. The self-
interest of the merchants is pronounced—they mourn for their
vanished trade and not for Babylon. We know that Rome's com-
merce was vast at the time; the long list of imports vividly
depicts its extent and predominantly exotic nature. The list,
which ranges through precious metals and stones, costly textiles,
rare fabrics, cosmetics, foodstuffs, and live stock, reaches its
climax with the traffic in slaves. v. 13, 'Slaves, that is, human
souls'—better : 'slaves and human live stock' (cf. Ezek. 27 : 13);
the last category would refer to slaves destined for the amphi-
theatre or for prostitution.

14.   Many commentators feel that this verse is out of place here
and would fit better in the context of 18 : 22f. However, it is not
too unlike 18 : 16, 19. The desired ripe autumn fruit will never
be gathered : Rome will not reap the harvest which her labours
have promised. Her luxury and her splendour have vanished for
ever.

15f.   The merchants, like the kings, stand well clear of the
stricken city; their dirge opens with the words of the previous
lament (v. 10). But while the kings address the 'mighty city', the
merchants turn to her wealth and splendour, which they describe
in terms reminiscent of 17 : 4—the description of the harlot.
Doom has fallen upon her 'in one hour' (vv. 10, 19); but the
merchants' prime concern is the loss of so much wealth.

c) The seafarers' lament (18: 17b-19)

Ezek. 27: 28-36: At the sound of the cry of your pilots the countryside shakes, and down from their ships come all that handle the oar. The mariners and all the pilots of the sea stand on the shore and wail aloud over you, and cry bitterly. They cast dust on their heads and wallow in ashes; they make themselves bald for you, and gird themselves with sackcloth, and they weep over you in bitterness of soul, with bitter mourning. In their wailing they raise a lamentation for you, and lament over you: 'Who was ever destroyed like Tyre in the midst of the sea? When your wares came from the seas, you satisfied many peoples; with your abundant wealth and merchandise you enriched the kings of the earth. Now you are wrecked by the seas, in the depths of the waters; your merchandise and all your crew have sunk with you. All the inhabitants of the coastlands are appalled at you; and their kings are horribly afraid, their faces convulsed. The merchants among the peoples hiss at you; you have come to a dreadful end and shall be no more for ever.'

17b. And all shipmasters and seafaring men, sailors and all whose trade is on the sea, stood far off 18. and cried out as they saw the smoke of her burning, 'What city was like the great city?' 19. And they threw dust on their heads, as they wept and mourned, crying out,

'Alas, alas, for the great city
where all who had ships at sea grew rich by her wealth!
In one hour she has been laid waste.'

17-19. Cf. Ezek. 27 : 28-36. Like the merchants, the shipowners and sailors find that their interests, too, have suffered a dire blow. In Ezek. 27 the downfall of the island city of Tyre is, with dramatic appropriateness, portrayed as a shipwreck; and though Rome was not, like Tyre, a seaport, the capital of the Empire was the focus of world trade. The attitude and words of these mourners are similar to those of the others (cf. vv. 10, 15f.). Again, 'in one hour' she has been laid waste (vv. 10, 16).

The heavenly dirge (18: 20-24)

Jer. 51: 63f.: When you finish reading this book, bind a stone to it, and cast it into the midst of the Euphrates, and say, 'Thus shall Babylon sink, to rise no more, because of the evil that I am bringing upon her.'
Jer. 25: 10: I will banish from them the voice of mirth and the voice of gladness, the voice of the bridegroom and the voice of the bride, the grinding of the millstones and the light of the lamp (cf. 7: 34).
Ezek. 26: 13: I will stop the music of your songs, and the sound of your lyres shall be heard no more.
Is. 24: 8: The mirth of the timbrels is stilled, the noise of the jubilant has ceased, the mirth of the lyre is stilled.
Is. 23: 8: Who has purposed this against Tyre . . . whose merchants were princes, whose traders were the honoured of the earth?

20. 'Rejoice over her, O heaven,
   O saints and apostles and prophets,
   for God has given judgment for you against her!'
21. Then a mighty angel took up a stone like a great millstone and threw it into the sea, saying,
   'So shall Babylon the great city be thrown down with violence,
   and shall be found no more;
22. and the sound of harpers and minstrels, of flute players and trumpeters, shall be heard in thee no more;
   and a craftsman of any craft
   shall be found in thee no more;
   and the sound of the millstone
   shall be heard in thee no more;
23. and the light of a lamp
   shall shine in thee no more;
   and the voice of bridegroom and bride
   shall be heard in thee no more;

for thy merchants were the great men of the earth,
and all nations were deceived by thy sorcery.
24. And in her was found the blood of prophets and of
saints;
and of all who have been slain on earth.'

20. This verse, which anticipates the canticle of 19 : 1-8, introduces the symbolic judgment and the heavenly lament. The first
part of the verse is an echo of 12 : 12a—'Rejoice then, O heaven
and you that dwell therein !'; and 12 : 12b goes on to warn of the
devil's wrath now vented on the earth. In our verse the 'saints
and apostles and prophets', the martyrs who have come triumphantly through the great tribulation engineered by the devil
(cf. 16 : 6), now join in the heavenly rejoicing. *krima* ('judgment') here has the meaning of lawsuit or court case : God has
given judgment for the church against Babylon; the 'accuser of
our brethren', who had been cast out of heaven (12 : 10), fails,
too, in his action against the children of the woman (12 :12, 17).
21. 'A mighty angel' (cf. 5 : 2; 10 : 1). The symbolic action of
the angel, and his words, are reminiscent of Jer. 51 : 63f.; the
gesture symbolizes the complete submergence, the final disappearance, of imperial Rome; it rounds off the proclamation of
18 : 1-3. 'And shall be found no more', cf. Ezek. 26 : 21.
22f. Cf. Jer. 25 : 10; Ezek. 26 : 13; Is. 24 : 8; 23 : 8. The
solemn repetition of the phrase 'shall be found no more' gives an
air of pathetic finality to the fate of Rome. All the arts of civilized
life have come to an end. The bright festive lights will shine out
no more and the sounds of joy are stilled for ever. The ruined
city has become the abode of wild beasts and of demons (18 : 2).
'Thy merchants' (cf. 18 : 11-16), proud and self-sufficient in their
wealth, were effective propagandists of the sorcery of Rome.
pharmakia is 'magic', 'sorcery' (cf. 9 : 21)—'but the word is probably used by St John in the wider sense of the witchery of
gay and luxurious vice and its attendant idolatries, by which the
world was fascinated and led astray' (Swete).
24. This is the chief reason for Rome's destruction. She is guilty
of 'the blood of prophets and of saints' (cf. 16 : 6; 17 : 6; 18 :

20), not only those slain in Rome but also those who have
suffered throughout the Empire. Cf. Jer. 51 : 49—'Babylon must
fall for the slain of Israel, as for Babylon have fallen the slain of
all the earth'; Lk. 11 : 50—'that the blood of all the prophets,
shed from the foundation of the world, may be required of this
generation'; Mt. 23 : 35.

Triumph in heaven (19: 1-10)

> *Is. 34: 10: Night and day it shall not be quenched; its*
> *smoke shall go up for ever.*
> *Ps. 115: 13: He will bless those who fear the Lord, both*
> *small and great.*
> *Dn. 8: 17: When he [the angel] came near, I was frightened*
> *and fell upon my face.*

1. After this I heard what seemed to be the mighty voice of
a great multitude in heaven, crying,
Hallelujah! Salvation and glory and power belong to our
God,
2. for his judgments are true and just;
he has judged the great harlot who corrupted the earth
with her fornication,
and he has avenged on her the blood of his servants.'
3. Once more they cried,
'Hallelujah! The smoke from her goes up for ever and
ever.'
4 And the twenty-four elders and the four living creatures
fell down and worshipped God who is seated on the
throne, saying, 'Amen. Hallelujah!'
5. And from the throne came a voice crying,
'Praise our God, all you his servants,
you who fear him, small and great.'
6. Then I heard what seemed to be the voice of a great
multitude, like the sound of many waters and like the sound
of mighty thunderpeals, crying,
'Hallelujah! For the Lord our God the Almighty reigns.

7. Let us rejoice and exult and give him the glory,
    for the marriage of the Lamb has come,
    and his Bride has made herself ready;

8. it was granted her to be clothed with fine linen, bright
    and pure'—
    for the fine linen is the righteous deeds of the saints.

9. And the angel said to me, 'Write this: Blessed are those
who are invited to the marriage supper of the Lamb.' And he
said to me, 'These are true words of God.' 10. Then I fell down
at his feet to worship him, but he said to me, 'You must not
do that! I am a fellow servant with you and your brethren who
hold the testimony of Jesus. Worship God.' For the testimony
of Jesus is the spirit of prophecy.

19: 1-3. This is the response to the appeal of the seer in 18:
20—'Rejoice over her, O heaven'. The 'mighty voice of the great
multitude' is that of the angel host of 5: 11. 'Hallelujah' is a
transliteration of a Hebrew word which means 'Praise Yahweh'
and which is found in many of the Psalms. It was used in synagogue worship and it figured early in the Christian liturgy. In
the NT it occurs only in Ap. 'Salvation and glory and power
belong to our God' (cf. 4: 11; 5: 12; 7: 10, 12; 12: 10). The
occasion for this psalm of praise is given: the execution of
judgment on Babylon with her crimes of idolatry and blood-
guilt. The great harlot, who had seduced the whole earth and who
had become drunk with the blood of martyrs (17: 1-6), has
met her just deserts. She has 'corrupted', brought moral ruin
upon, the earth—the time has come 'for destroying the destroyers
of the earth' (11: 18). Cf. 2 Kg. 9: 7—'That I may avenge on
Jezebel the blood of my servants the prophets, and the blood of
all the servants of the Lord'. 'The smoke from her goes up for
ever and ever' (cf. Is. 34: 10; Ap. 14: 11)—the destruction is
definitive, Babylon 'shall be found no more' (18: 21).
4. The elders and the living creatures (last mentioned in 14: 3)
add their 'Amen' to the canticle of the angels (cf. 5: 14). 'Amen.
Hallelujah', cf. Ps. 106: 48. The passage 19: 4-6 shows a close
correspondence with the seventh trumpet (11: 15-19); both pas-

sages describe the end. Thus, we find the declarations of divine sovereignty (11 : 15f.; 19 : 4, 6), the 'servants who fear him . . . both small and great' (11 : 18; 19 : 5), and the thunderpeals (11 : 19; 19 : 6).

5.   Cf. Ps. 115 : 13; Ac. 26 : 22. The voice from the throne is, perhaps, that of one of the heavenly creatures; the expression 'our God' indicates that it is not the voice of Christ. 'Praise our God', cf. Ps. 113 : 1; 134 : 1; 135 : 20. 'His servants' are the martyrs (19 : 2).

6.   The 'great multitude' of v. 1 was the angelic host; here it would appear to be the host of martyrs (cf. 7 : 9). The great hymn of praise sounded like the roar of waters (1 : 15; 14 : 2) or like mighty thunderpeals (6 : 1; 10 : 3f.). The theme of their prayer is no longer the fall of Babylon; they rejoice that their often repeated prayer—'Thy kingdom come'—has been answered : the Lord reigns! (cf. 11 : 15). This is the perspective so evident in Daniel : when the enemy of God has been overthrown, then, God's kingdom will appear.

7f.   'Let us rejoice and exult'; cf. Mt. 5 : 12—'Rejoice and be glad [exult], for your reward is great in heaven'. 'Give him the glory', cf. Ap. 11 : 13; 14 : 7; 16 : 9. The saints rejoice because the marriage of the Lamb has come : his bride is ready. Israel as the bride of Yahweh is a prophetic theme (Hos. 2 : 16; Is. 54 : 6; Ezek. 16 : 7f.); Paul has transferred the imagery to Christ and his church (2 Cor. 11 : 2; Eph. 5 : 25, 32). In Eph. 5 : 25 Paul declares that 'Christ loved the church and gave himself up for her'; and, in Ap., those who form the bride of Christ have been redeemed 'by the blood of the Lamb' (5 : 9; 7 : 14; 14 : 3f.). Jesus, too, had spoken of himself as a bridegroom (Mk 2 : 19f.; Mt. 22 : 1). It is quite in John's style to introduce the bride of the Lamb abruptly (cf. Ap. 11 : 7; 14 : 8); the image will be explained in a later scene (21 : 9-14). The bride has made herself ready : she has put on her wedding-dress. In Eph. 5 : 26f. Christ has prepared his bride by washing her in the bath of baptism and by making her immaculate. Here the situation is quite the same— 'it was granted her to be clothed' : her wedding-dress is a gift. In Eph. 5 : 26 Christ 'sanctified' his bride; here she 'is given' the white bridal dress of holiness. Always, her sanctity is his achievement. Her dress is made of *byssus*, the fine, costly linen of Egypt; 'bright and pure', cf. 15 : 6. John explains that this fine linen is the sanctity of God's people (cf. 14 : 13). ' "The righteous deeds of the saints" are the sum of the saintly acts of the members of Christ, wrought in them by his Spirit, which are regarded as making up the clothing of his mystical Body. As each guest at the wedding feast has a "wedding garment" (Mt 22 : 11), as the Saints are individually clad in robes made white in the Blood of the Lamb (Ap. 7 : 9, 14); so corporately the whole Church is seen to be attired in the dazzling whiteness of their collective purity' (Swete).

We need to be conscious of the fluidity of John's images. Thus it appears that, while the bride is the church, the wedding guests are the members of the church, and their deeds are her bridal dress. Similarly, in chapter 12, the woman is the church (12: 1-6), and yet Christians can be described as 'her children' (12: 17); and in 7 : 17 the Lamb is also a shepherd. In all cases the symbolism is clear; John simply manages his image with complete freedom. Only three female figures appear in the visions of Ap. : the 'woman clothed with the sun' of ch. 12, the 'woman arrayed in purple and scarlet' of ch. 17, and the 'woman clothed with fine linen' of ch. 19. The first and third represent the church, while the other is her great adversary.

9. 'And an angel said to me'—literally, 'and he said to me'; the RSV correctly interprets this 'he' as an angel (cf. 22 : 8f.), probably the angel guide of 17 : 1. Cf. Lk. 14 : 15—'Blessed is he who shall eat bread in the kingdom of God'. 'Marriage supper': a common figure for the kingdom (cf. Mt. 7 : 11; 22 : 1-14; 25: 1-13; 26 : 29; Lk. 14). Those who are invited (called) are the 'called and chosen and faithful' of Ap. 17 : 14; the martyrs are privileged guests. The beatitude of 14 : 13 ('Blessed are the dead who die in the Lord . . . that they may have rest from their labours') is carried a step further: the 'rest' has turned into the joy of the Lamb's marriage festival. 'These are the true words of God' (cf. 21 : 5; 22 : 6). If the speaker is the angel of 17 : 1, then the meaning would appear to be that the seal of divine

truth is set on the series of revelations, 17 : 1-19 : 9. John has his Christian readers in view and would assure them yet again that the apparent triumph of the enemies of God is, indeed, illusory. The final, desperate assault of evil can only serve to mark the victory of God, of the Lamb, and of the faithful.

10.   Cf. Dn. 8 : 17; 10 : 9f., 15. John was overwhelmed by a vision confirmed by the solemn words of God and, spontaneously, fell at the feet of the angel. The verb *proskynein* can mean 'to worship' (cf. v. 10b), but it also has a wider sense. Cf. the promise to the Christians of Philadelphia that Christ would make the Jews 'come and bown down (*proskynēsousin*) before your feet' (3 : 9). However, here (and in 22 : 8f.) the angel chooses to inter- pret John's gesture as a form of worship; and worship is due to God alone (cf. Mt. 4 : 10; Lk. 4 : 8). The angel's admonition : 'You must not do that!', repeated in 22 : 9, may perhaps be meant as a warning against angel worship, a practice not un- known in Asia Minor. Cf. Col. 2 : 18—'Let no one disqualify you, insisting on self-abasement and worship of angels'. 'Fellow servant'—from Ap. 22 : 9 ('I am a fellow servant with you and your brethren the prophets'), it follows that John is a prophet, a spokesman for God. Thus the angel plays a similar role; and this is also the reason for the reference to prophecy at the end of our verse. In Heb. 1 : 14 the angels are 'ministering spirits sent forth to serve'. 'Who hold the testimony of Jesus', cf. Ap. 1 : 2, 9; 6 : 9; 12 : 17; 20 : 4; in the parallel passage, 22 : 9, the prophets 'keep the words of this book'. 'For the testimony of Jesus is the spirit of prophecy'—'of Jesus' is the subjective genitive (as in 1 : 2, 9; 12 : 17) : the message put in the mouth of a Christian prophet is the word of God attested by Jesus. Caird translates : 'For the testimony of Jesus is the spirit that inspires prophets'.

IV.   THE END (19 : 11—20 : 15)

Victory over the beasts (19: 11-21)

> *Ezek. 1: 1: The heavens were opened, and I saw visions of God.*
> *Is. 11: 3-5: He shall not judge by what his eyes see, or*

*decide by what his ears hear; but with righteousness he
shall judge the poor, and decide with equity for the meek of
the earth; and he shall smite the earth with the rod of his
mouth, and with the breath of his lips he will slay the
wicked. Righteousness shall be the girdle of his waist, and
faithfulness the girdle of his loins.*

*Is. 63: 1-3: Who is this that comes from Edom, in crim-
soned garments from Bozrah, he that is glorious in his
apparel, marching in the greatness of his strength? 'It is I,
announcing vindication, mighty to save.' Why is thy apparel
red, and thy garments like his that treads in the wine press?
'I have trodden the wine press alone, and from the peoples
no one was with me; I trod them in my anger and trampled
them in my wrath; their lifeblood is sprinkled upon my
garments, and I have stained all my raiment.'*

*Wis. 18: 14-16: For while gentle silence enveloped all things,
and night in its swift course was now half gone, thy all-
powerful word leaped down from heaven, from the royal
throne, into the midst of the land that was doomed, a stern
warrior carrying the sharp sword of thy authentic command, and stood and filled all things with death, and touched
heaven while standing on the earth.*

*Ps. 2: 9: You shall break them with a rod of iron, and dash
them in pieces like a potter's vessel.*

*Ezek. 39: 17-20: Thus says the Lord God: Speak to the birds
of every sort and to all beasts of the field, 'Assemble and
come, gather from all sides to the sacrificial feast which I am
preparing for you, a great sacrificial feast upon the mountains of Israel, and you shall eat flesh and drink blood. You
shall eat the flesh of the mighty, and drink the blood of the
princes of the earth. . . . And you shall be filled at my table
with horses and riders, with mighty men and all kinds of
warriors,' says the Lord God.*

11. Then I saw heaven opened, and behold, a white horse!
He who sat upon it is called Faithful and True, and in
righteousness he judges and makes war. 12. His eyes are like a

flame of fire, and on his head are many diadems; and he has a name inscribed which no one knows but himself. 13. He is clad in a robe dipped in blood, and the name by which he is called is The Word of God. 14. And the armies of heaven, arrayed in fine linen, white and pure, followed him on white horses. 15. From his mouth issues a sharp sword with which to smite the nations, and he will rule them with a rod of iron; he will tread the wine press of the fury of the wrath of God the Almighty. 16. On his robe and on his thigh he has a name inscribed, King of kings and Lord of lords.

17. Then I saw an angel standing in the sun, and with a loud voice he called to all the birds that fly in midheaven, 'Come, gather for the great supper of God, 18. to eat the flesh of kings, the flesh of captains, the flesh of mighty men, the flesh of horses and their riders, and the flesh of all men, both free and slave, both small and great.' 19. And I saw the beast and the kings of the earth with their armies gathered to make war against him who sits upon the horse and against his army. 20. And the beast was captured, and with it the false prophet who in its presence had worked the signs by which he deceived those who had received the mark of the beast and those who worshipped its image. These two were thrown alive into the lake of fire that burns with brimstone. 21. And the rest were slain by the sword of him who sits upon the horse, the sword that issues from his mouth; and all the birds were gorged with their flesh.

This passage deals with the victory of Christ and his followers over the beast, the false prophet, and the kings of the earth, an episode already described proleptically in 14 : 14-20; 16 : 12-16; 17 : 12-14.

11. In 4 : 1 John saw an open door in heaven, and in 11 : 19 the temple in heaven was opened (cf. 15 : 5); now heaven itself is opened for the parousia. Cf. Ezek. 1 : 1. The words, 'behold, a white horse, and he who sat upon it', are repeated from Ap. 6 : 2. In both cases the 'white horse' is the symbol of victory—but there the resemblance ends. The rider here is not the personification of

victorious warfare of 6 : 2; he is the Word of God (19 : 13). He 'is called', that is, 'he is known as' (cf. Lk. 6 : 15; 8 : 2; Ac. 8 : 10). 'Faithful and true', cf. the 'faithful and true witness', 3 : 14; cf. 1 : 5; 3 : 7. Cf. Is. 11 : 3-5; Ps. 96 : 13; Ps. Sol. 17 : 23-31. 'He judges' (*krinei*) in the sense of handing down a condemnatory sentence; his judgments are righteous (cf. Is. 11 : 4; Ap. 15 : 3; 16 : 5, 7; 19 : 2). 'He judges and makes war'—he carries out God's righteous judgment on the intransigent enemies of God. Cf. 1 Cor. 15 : 24f.—'Then comes the end, when he [Christ] delivers the kingdom to God the Father after destroying every rule and every authority and power. For he must reign until he has put all his enemies under his feet.'

12. 'His eyes are like a flame of fire', cf. 1 : 14; 2 : 18. Like the 'faithful and true' of the previous verse, this offers a cross-reference to the letters. The dragon wears seven diadems (12 : 3) and the beast ten (13 : 1); the 'many diadems' of the rider represent a royalty beyond any earthly sovereignty—he is King of kings and Lord of lords (v. 16). 'A name . . . which no one knows' : in Semitic thought the 'name' stands for the person. No one can 'know', that is, fully understand, who the rider is, except himself (cf. 2 : 17). Cf. Lk. 10 : 22—'No one knows who the Son is except the Father, or who the Father is except the Son'. 'Notwithstanding the dogmatic helps which the Church offers, the mind fails to grasp the inmost significance of the person of Christ, which eludes all efforts to bring it within the terms of human knowledge. Only the Son of God can understand the mystery of his own Being' (Swete).

13. Cf. Is. 63 : 1-3; Wis. 18 : 14-16. The robe dipped in (rather than sprinkled with'—a variant reading) blood surely echoes Is. 63 : 3. Some commentators have suggested that this is the rider's own blood, the blood of the passion, and urge in support of this view the fact that the garment is already soaked in blood before the battle begins (v. 19). Thus, accordingly, it is the blood of the Lamb that was slain, the blood which he shed for the salvation of the world. However, the obvious attractiveness of this interpretation should not blind us to the evident background and context of the verse. The influence of Is. 63 : 1-3 and Wis. 18 :

14-16 is unmistakable (cf. v. 15): it is a context of judgment. Already in Ap. 14: 14-16 John has cast the Son of Man in the role of judge. And if the rider wears a robe dipped in blood as he rides out to join battle, that is because John chooses to describe him in the language of Isaiah. Swete, who maintains that the Isaian meaning is certainly present to John's mind, feels that the other idea may not be absent: 'In applying the figure to Christ, he could hardly have failed to think also of the "Blood of the Lamb" (1 : 5; 5 : 9; 7 : 14; 12 : 11) which was shed in the act of treading the enemy under foot. . . . But this view, if admitted, must be kept subordinate to the other. In this vision Christ is not presented as the Redeemer, but as the Judge and Warrior.' Fittingly, the rider is called 'The Word of God': the 'stern warrior' of Wis. 18 : 15, God's Word come down from heaven to destroy the first-born of the Egyptians. Yet, the title 'Word of God', in a Johannine writing, is distinctive; cf. Jn 1 : 1, 14; 1 Jn 1 : 1.

14.   Though at first sight it might appear that 'the armies of heaven' are the angelic hosts (cf. Mt. 26 : 53), it is far more likely that they are the army of martyrs. Cf. the parallel text of Ap. 17 : 14 where those who accompany the conquering Lamb are 'called and chosen and faithful', a description which does not apply to angels. Already in 2 : 27 the conqueror is promised that he will 'rule the nations with a rod of iron', the very words which in 19 : 15 are used of Christ himself. These are the 144,000 'who follow the Lamb wherever he goes' (14 : 14). They are clad in pure, white linen (like the bride of the Lamb, 19 : 8) because they 'have washed their robes and made them white in the blood of the Lamb' (7 : 14; cf. 6 : 11); and, like their leader, they ride on white horses, symbol of victory.

15.   The sharp sword issuing from the mouth of the rider (cf. 1 : 16; 2 : 12) is here the destroying sword of judgment and sentence (cf. Is. 11 : 4; Wis. 18 : 16; Hos. 6 : 5; 2 Thess. 2 : 8) on the nations. Cf. Ps. 2 : 9; Ap. 2 : 27; 12 : 5. The combination of the messianic texts Is. 11 : 4 and Ps. 2; 9 is found in the *Psalms of Solomon*: 'He [the Messiah] shall destroy the pride of the sinner as a potter's vessel : With a rod of iron he shall break in

pieces all their substance, he shall destroy the godless nations with the word of his mouth' (17 : 26f.). The picture of a warrior Messiah is found in the *Fragmentary Palestinian Targum* on Gen. 49 : 11f.—'He girds his loins and goes out to wage war on those who hate him, and slays kings with their rulers, making the mountains red with the blood of their slain and making the hills white with the fat of their warriors and his vestments are soaked in blood. He is like a presser of grapes.' v. 15b, literally, reads : 'he will tread the wine press of the wine of the fury of the wrath of God the Almighty'. It combines the figures of the wine press (14 : 19) and of the cup of wrath (14 : 10) : from the wine press trodden by the Messiah flows the wine of divine wrath which his enemies are to be made to drink. If this suggests that the wine is, in fact, their own blood, there is the excellent supporting text of Is. 49 : 26—'I will make your oppressors eat their own flesh, and they shall be drunk with their own blood as with wine'. Already suggested in v. 13, it now becomes clear by whom the wine press is trodden. We understand, too, that the vintage of 14 : 17-20 (like the reaping, 14 : 14-16) is, ultimately, the work of the Son of Man.

16. 'On his robe and on his thigh' probably means 'on the cloak and on that most exposed part of it which covers the thigh' (Swete). At any rate, it is a title prominently displayed, one which cannot be overlooked or ignored. 'King of kings and Lord of lords', cf. 17 : 14. The name is obviously not that secret name of v. 12; by presenting him as the invincible conqueror, terrible to his enemies, it presages his victory. The portrait of the divine warrior appearing in sovereign power is meant to encourage John's readers, to assure them that their Lord *has* overcome the world (Jn 16 : 33; cf. 1 Cor. 8 : 6).

17f. Cf. Ezek. 39 : 17-20. 'In the sun' (cf. 'in midheaven', 8 : 13; 14 : 6)—it is a proclamation of universal import : this is the final battle. Ezekiel's text is concerned with the destruction of the forces of Gog and Magog (cf. Ap. 20 : 8), a slaughter which is regarded as a sacrifice : God immolates his enemies. Here, too, it is a sacrificial meal; but John goes beyond Ezekiel in offering to the birds of prey the bodies of all the slain, and not only of the great. Cf. Mt. 24 : 28—'Wherever the body is, there the vultures will be gathered together'; Lk. 17 : 37. Victory is taken for granted: the solemn invitation to the birds is issued before battle is joined.

19.   The 'kings of the earth' are those of 17 : 12-14 who blindly follow the beast. When, at his instigation (but, in the last resort, as God's instruments), they have destroyed Rome (17 : 12, 16f.), he leads them against the Lamb (17 : 14). This is the assembly of Armageddon (16 : 16); it is the decisive encounter between Christ and the forces of Antichrist; it is the climax of the conspiracy of 'the kings of the earth . . . against the Lord and his anointed' (Ps. 2 : 2).

20.   Victory is not only total; it is immediate (cf. 17 : 14)—there is no battle. Cf. 2 Thess. 2 : 8—'Then the lawless one will be revealed, and the Lord Jesus will slay him with the breath of his mouth and destroy him by his appearing and his coming'. The captured leaders of the assault, the beast and the false prophet (cf. 13 : 11-17), are not cast into the bottomless pit, a place of safe custody (9 : 1f.; 20 : 1-3), but into the lake of fire—the place of final punishment (cf. 14 : 10; 20 : 10). Cf. Dn. 7 : 11—'As I looked, the beast was slain, and its body destroyed and given over to be burned with fire'.

21.   The followers of the two leaders, slain by the sharp sword of the rider on the white horse (v. 15), await, in Sheol, the final judgment (20 : 12f.)—then they too will be thrown into the lake of fire (20 : 15). The 'lake of fire' (a term proper to Ap. in the NT) is the same as the Gehenna of the synoptics and the Fourth Gospel. Gehenna is described as a place of 'the unquenchable fire' (Mk 9 : 43), and as the 'furnace of fire' (Mt. 13 : 42, 50). At the last judgment the wicked will be condemned to 'the eternal fire prepared for the devil and his angels' (Mt. 25 : 41).

Blessedness of the martyrs: The reign of a thousand years (20: 1-6)

Dn. 7: 9, 21f., 26: As I looked, thrones were placed and one that was ancient of days took his seat; his raiment was white as snow, and the hair of his head like pure wool; his throne

was fiery flames, its wheels were burning fire.... As I looked,
this horn made war with the saints, and prevailed over them,
until the Ancient of Days came, and judgment was given
for the saints of the Most High, and the time came when
the saints received the kingdom. . . . But the court shall sit
in judgment, and his dominion shall be taken away, to be
consumed and destroyed to the end.

1. Then I saw an angel coming down from heaven, holding
in his hand the key of the bottomless pit and a great chain. 2.
And he seized the dragon, that ancient serpent, who is the
Devil and Satan, and bound him for a thousand years, 3. and
threw him into the pit, and shut it and sealed it over him, that
he should deceive the nations no more, till the thousand
years were ended. After that he must be loosed for a
little while.

4. Then I saw thrones, and seated on them were those to
whom judgment was committed. Also I saw the souls of those
who had been beheaded for their testimony to Jesus and for
the word of God, and who had not worshipped the beast or
its image and had not received its mark on their foreheads or
their heads. They came to life, and reigned with Christ a
thousand years. 5. The rest of the dead did not come to life
until the thousand years were ended. This is the first resurrection. 6. Blessed and holy is he who shares in the first resurrection! Over such the second death has no power, but they
shall be priests of God and of Christ, and they shall reign
with him a thousand years.

This passage, together with its sequel dealing with victory over
the dragon (20 : 7-10), is perhaps the most difficult section in the
book. We think it well to give an exegesis of both passages before
presenting an interpretation of the whole.
20. 1.   'Then I saw' (and not 'After this, I saw', cf. 18 :1; 19 :
1)—a number of visions are thus loosely linked (cf. 19 : 11, 17,
19; 20 : 4, 11, 12; 21 : 1). 'It must not, therefore, be assumed
that the events now to be described chronologically follow the
destruction of the beast and the false prophet and their army'

(Swete). As in 18 : 1, an angel comes down from heaven, charged with a special mission. He holds the key to the abyss (cf. 9 : 1)—the prison of demonic spirits before their final relegation to the lake of fire. The 'great chain' is designed to fetter no ordinary prisoner.

2f. The dragon, identified as in 12 : 9, is made a prisoner for 'a thousand years'—we shall see that the number is symbolic and has no time value. Making assurance double sure, the angel casts the shackled Satan into the abyss and seals the shaft of the abyss (cf. 9 : 1f.). This temporary imprisonment of the dragon, preceding his definitive fate (20 : 10), coincides with his banishment from heaven described in 12 : 7-12. Because of the parallelism, the expression 'that he should deceive the nations no more' echoes that of 12 : 9, 'the deceiver of the whole world'. It is a description of the dragon, pointing to his distinctive characteristic; it has the same value as 'the accuser of our brethren' (12 : 10; cf. Jn 8 : 44). Everything depends on the meaning of the 'thousand years'. In our view, it has no chronological value but serves to symbolize the blessedness of the martyrs and the helplessness of Satan in their regard. The key to the expression is to be sought in the *reign* of a thousand years of 20 : 4-6; the thousand years' imprisonment of Satan is dictated by this. 'After this he must be loosed for a little while'—the phrase has quite the same meaning as '. . . his time is short' (12 : 12). The difficulty in our passage is due to the fact that the 'thousand years', though it is a symbol without time value, has to be treated in a seemingly chronological manner : it invites, indeed demands, chronological phraseology. Hence the phrases, 'till the thousand years were ended' (20 : 3, 5, 7), 'after that' (20 : 3).

4. Cf. Dn. 7 : 9, 21f., 26. From v. 7 it follows that this vision is simultaneous with Satan's captivity. Literally, v. 4 reads : 'And I saw thrones, and they sat on them, and judgment was given to them, and the souls. . . .' Obviously, it is difficult (if not impossible) to determine what John really means; but at least we may say that we should not be going contrary to the trend of the book if we assume that the occupants of the thrones are 'those who had been beheaded'. Cf. the promise of 3 : 21—'He who con-

quers, I will grant him to sit with me on my throne' (cf. 2 : 26f.).
'For their testimony to Jesus and for the word of God', cf. 1 : 9;
6 : 9; 12 : 17; 19 : 10. 'Who had not worshipped the beast. . .',
cf. 13 : 15; 14 : 9; 16 : 2; 19 : 20. 'They came to life again, and
reigned with Christ a thousand years'—the martrys came to life
again, like the Lamb (2 : 8); they alone share in this first resurrection' (v. 5f.). Throughout the book John has insisted on the
triumph and happiness of the martyrs from the moment of death
(cf. 6 : 9-11; 7 : 9-17; 12 : 7-11; 14 : 1-5, 13; 15 : 2-4; 19 : 9);
in 20 : 4-6 he makes the same point, in terms of the 'first resurrection' and the reign of a thousand years with Christ. *'ho
Christos* occurs in the Apocalypse only in 11 : 15; 12 : 10; 20 :
4, 6 and is probably in each instance a reminiscence of Ps. 2 : 2.
The Lord's Anointed, against whom the kings of the earth con-
spired, has triumphed over his enemies, and his victory ensures
that of those who have fought on his side' (Swete).

The origin of the notion of millennium is to be found in Jewish
speculation on the messianic reign. In the OT this reign is presented as final and permanent (cf. Dn. 2 : 44; 7 : 14, 27); but
later, extra-biblical speculation, from about 100 BC to AD 100,
looked for a temporary triumph of righteousness before the consummation of all things. To this golden age various periods were
assigned : 100, 600, 1,000, 7,000 years. Since it was commonly
held that the age of the world would correspond to the time taken
for its creation, and each day of creation was said to be a
thousand years (cf. Ps. 90 : 4; 2 Pet. 3 : 8), the seventh day, the
equivalent of the sabbath rest, would be the reign of the Messiah.
Thus, a thousand years is a particularly satisfactory length for
the duration of the Messiah's reign on earth. Without doubt,
John was familiar with these conceptions; but just as he freely
adapts OT imagery, so also he takes this idea too and bends it to
his own purpose. Merely because the original Jewish idea envisaged a temporary messianic reign on earth, it does not necessarily follow that John is thinking along the same lines in Ap.
The symbol must be seen not in its original setting, but according to the significance that John attaches to it.

5.   Since he has used the image of resurrection to describe the

bliss of the martyrs, John is careful to distinguish his image from the general resurrection (cf. v. 12f.), so he calls it the 'first resurrection'.

6.   The fifth of the seven beatitudes of Ap. (cf. 1 : 3; 14 : 13; 16 : 15; 19 : 9; 22 : 7, 14); but here the one who receives the blessing is not only happy but holy as well. The martyrs, to whom the beatitude is addressed, have two reasons for rejoicing : in the first place, the second death (cf. 2 : 11), the 'lake of fire' (20 : 14; 21 : 8), has no claim on them. Jer. 51 : 39, 57 warn that the inhabitants of Babylon, objects of divine chastisement, 'shall sleep a perpetual sleep and not wake'. In each case the *Targum* renders the phrase : 'they shall die the second death and shall not live in the world to come' (which means exclusion from the resurrection —they will remain in the grave). It could be that in our verse the 'second death' may mean exclusion from the resurrection; but it is more likely that it is to be understood, like the other Ap. texts, in terms of final punishment. In the second place, the martrys will be priests and kings (cf. 1 : 6; 5 : 9f.); the first-fruits of the redeemed (14 : 4), they partake, in a privileged manner, in the royal priesthood of Christians (cf. 1 Pet. 2 : 9).

Victory over the dragon (20: 7-10)

> *Ezek. 38: 2, 14-16: Son of man, set your face toward Gog, of the land of Magog . . . and prophesy against him. . . . Thus says the Lord God: On that day when my people Israel are dwelling securely, you will bestir yourself and come from your place out of the uttermost parts of the north, you and many peoples with you, all of them riding on horses, a great host, a mighty army; you will come up against my people Israel, like a cloud covering the land.*
> *Ezek. 38: 18, 21f.: On that day, when Gog shall come up against the land of Israel, says the Lord God, my wrath will be roused. . . . I will summon every kind of terror against Gog, says the Lord God . . . and I will rain upon him and his hordes and the many peoples that are with him, torrential rain and hailstones, fire and brimstone.*

*Hab. 1: 6: I am rousing the Chaldeans . . . who march
through the breadth of the earth.*

7. And when the thousand years are ended, Satan will be
loosed from his prison 8. and will come out to deceive the
nations which are at the four corners of the earth, that is, Gog
and Magog, to gather them for battle; their number is like the
sand of the sea. 9. And they marched up over the broad earth
and surrounded the camp of the saints and the beloved city;
but fire came down from heaven and consumed them, 10. and
the devil who had deceived them was thrown into the lake of
fire and brimstone where the beast and the false prophet
were, and they will be tormented day and night for ever
and ever.

7f. If we see the 'thousand years' as a symbol, without chronological value, then the phrase 'when the thousand years are ended'
does not at all mean that the 'loosing' of Satan comes after his
imprisonment. His 'binding' is strictly in relation to those who
reign with Christ; the situation is exactly that of 12 : 10f., where,
cast out of heaven, he is powerless to exercise his role of 'accuser
of the brethren' in regard to the martyrs in heaven. The 'loosing'
of Satan is required by the literary construction of the passage :
the author, who has already described the eschatological battle
(19 : 11-21), with the defeat and capture of the beast and the
false prophet and the destruction of their forces, now describes the
same battle over again. However, this time, he concentrates on
the dragon who is the real villain of the piece. With his defeat we
have really come to the end, and the judgment can follow (20 :
11-15). There is nothing very surprising in this repetition; John
makes reference to the eschatological battle not twice only but
four times (cf. 16 : 12-16; 17 : 14; 19 : 11-21; 20 : 7-10). Compare his several references to the destruction of Rome (14 : 8;
16 : 19; 17 : 16f.; 18 : 21), and his two descriptions of the judgment (14 : 14-20; 20 : 11-15). 'The nations which are at the four
corners of the earth'—Satan gathers his forces from the most
remote regions of the world (cf. 16 : 12-16). In 7 : 1 the harmful
winds which will hurt the earth blow from the four angles or

corners of the earth; perhaps John sees the destructive hosts pro-
ceeding from the same sources. Cf. Ezek. 7 : 2—'An end! The
end has come upon the corners of the land'.

In 19 : 17-19 John has been inspired by Ezek. 39; now he
turns to Ezek. 38. In Ezek. 38-39 the prophet warns of the
emergence of Gog, king of Magog, the foe whose invasion from
the north has been heralded by Jeremiah (4-6) and by Zephaniah
(1 : 7). Cf. Ezek. 38 : 2, 14-16. Gog figures as the type of victorious barbarbian who, in an unspecified distant future, will
launch the final attack on Israel, only to be utterly destroyed by
Yahweh. Whereas in Ezekiel Gog is king of Magog, in Ap. Gog
and Magog symbolize all the pagan nations leagued against the
church at the end of time. Here John follows current tradition
because, in apocalyptic and rabbinical writings, Gog and Magog,
as nations, represent Israel's enemies. Cf. *Sib. Or.,* III, 319, 512.
'To gather them for battle', cf. Ap. 16 : 14. Their number is like
the sand of the sea'; cf. Jos. 11 : 4—'They came out, with all their
troops, a great host, in number like the sand that is upon the
seashore'; Gen. 22 : 17; Jg. 7 : 12; 1 Sam. 13 : 5; 2 Sam. 17 :
11; Jdt. 2 : 20; 1 Mac. 11 : 1.

9.   Cf. Ezek. 38 : 18, 21f.; Hab. 1 : 6; 2 Kg. 1 : 12. Cf. 1 Enoch
51 : 6f.—'And they shall go up and tread under foot the land of
his elect ones. . . . But the city of my righteous shall be a hindrance
to their horses.' The two terms, 'camp of the saints' (Palestine)
and the 'holy city' (Jerusalem), together stand for the people of
God, the church. It is the dragon's final, desperate assault on the
woman (cf. 12 : 13-16). As in 17 : 14; 19 : 20f., the hosts of evil
are immediately and utterly destroyed by the Lamb. The destruction of Gog by fire from heaven, with the resurrection following immediately after (cf. Ap. 20 : 9, 11-15), is paralleled in the
Targum of Pseudo-Jonathan on Num. 11 : 26—'And they [Gog
and his forces] wage war in the land of Israel against the sons of
the captivity. The Lord, however, is near them [the Israelites] in
the hour of affliction and kills all of them by a burning breath, by
a flame of fire, that goes out from beneath the throne of glory. . . .
And after this all the dead of Israel shall come to life . . . and
shall receive the reward of their deeds'.

10. Like the beast and the false prophet (19 : 20), this 'deceiver of the whole world' (12 : 9) is not slain with his forces but is cast into the place of definitive punishment, the 'lake of fire' (cf. 19 : 20; 20 : 14f.). The three ringleaders are at length involved in the same hopeless ruin; they are immersed in a fiery flood which tortures them unceasingly. 'It is not certain that these terrible words can be pressed into the service of the doctrine of the last things; since two of the three subjects of the *basanismos* (torment) represent systems and not persons, it is safer to regard them as belonging to the scenery of the vision rather than to its eschatological teaching. But beyond a doubt St John intends at least to teach that the forces, personal and impersonal, which have inspired mankind with false views of life and antagonism to God and to Christ will in the end be completely subjugated, and, if not annihilated, will at least be prevented from causing further trouble. From the Lake of Fire there is no release, unless evil itself should be ultimately consumed; and over that possibility there lies a veil which our writer does not help us to lift or pierce' (Swete).

The reign of a thousand years

Many Christian writers of the early centuries (such as Papias, Justin, Irenaeus, Tertullian, and Hippolytus) had taken the millennium literally: Christ would reign for a thousand years in Jerusalem before the final judgment. St Augustine at first accepted this view, but eventually came to oppose it; his later explanation became the classic and accepted one in the church. He saw in the captivity of Satan nothing else than the binding of the strong man by the one stronger than he—as the Lord had foretold (Mt. 12 : 29; Mk. 3 : 27; Lk. 11 : 22). He took the thousand years to mean the whole interval from the resurrection of Christ to the last conflict, that is, the whole duration of the Church; and he saw in the 'first resurrection' baptism (cf. Rom. 6 : 1-10).

Others have thought it more satisfactory to regard the resurrection of the martyrs as symbolizing the renewal of the church after the persecution of Rome: the 'millennium', therefore, corresponds to the earthly phase of the kingdom of Christ, from the end of persecution (the fall of Rome) to the eschatological combat (Ap. 20 : 7-10). The key seems to be provided by Ezek. 37-39 : in ch. 37 (the vision of the dry bones) the metaphorical resurrection of the people of God immediately precedes the attack on the holy land by Gog, king of Magog (chapters 38-39; cf. Ap. 20 : 8).[39]

We have preferred a different approach.[40] If we consider the whole passage Ap. 20 : 1-10, we find that two events are juxtaposed : on the one hand, there is the overthrow of Satan in two phases; on the other hand, there is the reign of a thousand years. Chapter 7 of Daniel furnishes the background of the vision. The first condemnation of the dragon coincides with the moment of judgment when dominion is given to the Son of Man (Dn. 7 : 9-14); henceforth, the dragon's power is taken from the beast and belongs to the Son of Man and the saints. Thus, in Ap., while Christ and his faithful reign, the devil will remain powerless in their regard, imprisoned in the abyss, his 'place'. The binding of Satan for a thousand years also coincides with his downfall described in the parallel passage, Ap. 12 : 7-12—Satan, the 'accuser of our brethren', is cast out of heaven by the victory of Christ; he can no longer accuse or harm the faithful ones who are in heaven with Christ.

The reign of the saints and the imprisonment of Satan last *a thousand years*. John has in mind the Jewish idea of a temporal messianic reign; but, for him, the thousand years is a symbol. In fact, his preoccupation with the martyrs comes once again to the fore; and this is the reason, or a reason, why the passage 20 : 7-10 is a doublet of the eschatological battle passage 19 : 17-21. These are still the same troops and the battle is that of Armageddon (16 : 12-16). The final assault of the dragon was made through the intermediary of the beasts and their followers, and all suffer disastrous defeat. But, because of his concern over the

[39] See M.-E. Boismard, *L'Apocalypse (BJ)*, 81 ; A. Feuillet, *The Apocalypse, op. cit.*, 121.

[40] See Cerfaux-Cambier, *L'Apocalypse de Saint Jean lue aux Chrétiens, op. cit.*, 172-8; A. Wikenhauser, *Offenbarung des Johannes* (Regensburg, Pustet, 1949), 127-31.

martyrs—his desire to stress yet again that Satan has no power over them—he has to describe, separately, the fall of Satan. In this, too, Daniel serves him well. The heavenly judgment scene (Dn. 7 : 9-14) depicts the condemnation of the beasts and the conferring of dominion on the Son of Man. Then, in the earthly repercussions of these heavenly events (7 : 19-27), the pagan empires are destroyed and the saints of the Most High receive the kingdom. John follows a similar pattern.

Only the martyrs reign with Christ for a thousand years; only they had risen from the dead—it is the 'first resurrection'. The same point of interest recurs throughout the book : it must be shown that the martyrs are happy before the parousia and the general resurrection (cf. 14 : 13). Here, the effect is achieved by reference to Dn. 7 : a judgment anticipates the general judgment (thrones were placed and the judges took their seats); the martyrs are assured of specific happiness ('over them the second death has no power'), thanks to a resurrection which anticipates the general resurrection. For a Semite like John, happiness, a true concrete happiness, must involve the whole person; hence there must be a 'resurrection' if the martyrs are to be fully and eternally happy.

In reality, the thousand years begin when a Christian has shed his blood for Christ. The reign of a thousand years coincides with the Feast of Tabernacles which the martyrs celebrate in heaven (7 : 9-17); it is the time of joy in a heaven free of Satan (12 : 9-12), it is the reign of the companions of the Lamb (14 : 1-5). It gives concrete expression to the solemn affirmation of 14 : 13— 'Blessed are the dead who die in the Lord ! Henceforth, says the Spirit, they can rest for ever from their labours.' It is a joyous liturgy by the heavenly Red Sea in celebration of a new deliverance (15 : 2-4). It is the time of the marriage supper of the Lamb, at which the martyrs are privileged guests (19 : 9). The reign of a thousand years, and the time of the Church ('a time, two times, and half a time'), are not consecutive but simultaneous.

In short, John has made use of the Jewish tradition of a temporary messianic reign to symbolize the truth that the martyrs

already reign with Christ. The thousand years, then, is a symbol
—it has no time value. It must be interpreted as a symbol, and the
reality which it typifies must be sought out. The reign of a thousand years signifies the reign of the martyrs with Christ, who has
won the final victory for them. Satan is bound for a thousand
years : he cannot touch the martyrs, those who have 'conquered
him by the blood of the Lamb' (12 : 11). If he is represented as
being set loose at the end of a thousand years, this is due to the
literary construction of the passage and to the image employed;
and he is loosed not to take effective action against the elect, but
to hasten the doom of his followers, and his own doom, in the
final cataclysm.

The last judgment (20: 11-15)

> *Dn. 7: 9f.: As I looked, thrones were placed and one that
> was ancient of days tooks his seat; his raiment was white as
> snow, and the hair of his head like pure wool. . . . The court
> sat in judgment, and the books were opened.*
> *Dn. 12: 1: At that time your people shall be delivered, every
> one whose name shall be found written in the book.*

11. Then I saw a great white throne and him who sat upon
it; from his presence earth and sky fled away, and no place was
found for them. 12. And I saw the dead, great and small,
standing before the throne, and books were opened. Also
another book was opened, which is the book of life. And the
dead were judged by what was written in the books, by what
they had done. 13. And the sea gave up the dead in it, Death
and Hades gave up the dead in them, and all were judged by
what they had done. 14. Then Death and Hades were thrown
into the lake of fire. This is the second death, the lake of fire;
15. and if any one's name was not found written in the book
of life, he was thrown into the lake of fire.

The conquest of all the powers hostile to God is followed by the
general resurrection of the dead and the last judgment. With the

conquest of Satan, 'the prince of this world' (Jn 12 : 31), the present world order has come to an end.

11.   In the earliest of his heavenly visions, the first thing that John saw was a throne (4 : 2); now, again, he sees, 'a great white throne', white like the raiment of the Ancient of Days (Dn. 7 : 9). 'He who sat upon it' is the Almighty Father (cf. Ap. 4 : 2f., 9; 5 : 1, 7, 13; 6 : 16; 7 : 10, 15; 19 : 4; 21 : 5)—he is the supreme judge at the last judgment (cf. Mt. 18 : 35; Rom. 14 : 10). In other NT texts Christ appears as judge (Mt. 16 : 27; 25 : 31-46; Jn 5 : 24; Ac. 17 : 31; 2 Cor. 5. 10; 2 Tim. 4 : 1). But it is the Father who has given the Son all his authority (Jn 5 : 24; Ac. 17 : 31). Earth and sky flee from the face of the judge; material creation itself has been contaminated by the sin of mankind (cf. Gen. 3 : 17; Rom. 8 : 19-22). 'No place was found for them', may equally well be rendered, 'leaving not a trace to be found'. Cf. Dn. 2 : 35—'. . . so that not a trace of them could be found'; Ap. 12 : 8. The vanished sky and earth will be replaced by a new heaven and a new earth (21 : 1). Elsewhere the NT speaks of a renewal or rebirth of creation (Mt. 19 : 28), or the setting free of creation (Rom. 8 : 21). One way or another, the old creation must be transformed in the new age. Cf. Mk. 13 : 31— 'Heaven and earth will pass away'. For the vanishing of earth and sky immediately before the judgment, cf. Enoch 65 : 6— 'When all creation visible and invisible, as the Lord created it, shall end, then every man goes to the great judgment.'

12.   'Great and small' (cf. 13 : 16; 19 : 18), that is, all without exception; it is the general resurrection of all the dead (cf. Mt. 25 : 32; Jn 5 : 28; 2 Cor. 5 : 10). 'Books were opened', cf. Dn. 7 : 10, the books which contain a record of the deeds of every human being now come for judgment. Cf. 4 Ezra 6 : 20—'When the seal is placed upon the age which is about to pass away, then I will show these signs: the books shall be opened before the firmament, and all shall see it together'; 1 Enoch 90 : 20—'And I saw till a throne was erected in the pleasant land, and the Lord of the sheep sat himself thereon, and the other took the sealed books and opened those books before the Lord of the sheep'; 2 Baruch 24 : 1—'For behold! the days come and the books shall be

opened in which are written the sins of all those who have sinned'. The 'book of life' (3 : 5; 13 : 8; 17 : 8; 20 : 15; 21 : 27). Cf. Dn. 12 : 1; Ex. 32 : 32f.; Ps. 69 : 29; Mal. 3 : 16; Lk. 10 : 20; Phil. 4 : 3; Heb. 12 : 23. Cf. 1 Enoch 47 : 3—'The books of the living were opened before him'. The book of life is the register of the citizens of the heavenly Jerusalem; it is the 'book of life of the Lamb that was slain', and the names in it were there 'before the foundation of the world' (Ap. 13 : 8). 'Thus into the scale in men's favour are set the gracious, predestining purpose of God and the redemptive love of him who died to ransom men for God' (Caird). We are face to face with the mystery of salvation : men are judged by their deeds—and yet salvation is a free gift (v. 15). God's choice is not arbitrary; and John has warned that a name may be cancelled from the book (3 : 5).

13. The resurrection of the dead, implied in v. 12, is now described. It was widely believed that those who had been lost at sea had no access to Hades; in specifically naming the sea, John emphasizes that he is describing the *general* resurrection. Death and Hades (cf. 1 : 18; 6 : 8) are personified : 'Here they appear as two voracious and insatiable monsters who have swallowed all past generations, but are now forced to disgorge their prey' (Swete). 'All were judged . . .', literally 'they were judged, each by his own deeds' : personal responsibility is underlined.

14. Death and Hades have served their purpose; they no longer have any *raison d'être*. 'The immersion of this symbolical pair in the lake of fire is parallel to that of the Beast and the False Prophet (19 : 20); it can only mean the annihilation of the forces indicated' (Swete). Cf. 1 Cor. 15 : 26—'The last enemy to be destroyed is death'. The 'second death' (Ap. 2 : 11; 20 : 6) is identified here, and again in 21 : 8, with the 'lake of fire'. Cf. *Targum* Is. 65 : 5f.—'Their punishment shall be in Gehenna where the fire burns all the day. Behold, it is written before me : ". . . I will deliver their body to the second death".' Clearly, 'Gehenna' and 'the second death' are one and the same.

15. Here, for the first and only time, the 'lake of fire' is associated with the fate of human beings. Cf. 1 Enoch 90 : 26— 'And I saw at that time how a like abyss was opened in the midst

of the earth, full of fire, and they brought those blinded sheep, and they were all judged and found guilty and cast into the fiery abyss, and they burned'. John manifestly echoes apocalyptic imagery and language. His judgment scene certainly depicts a sifting, a separation of good and wicked. But from his words we learn nothing precise about the fate of the wicked; the details of the afterlife are clothed in imagery.

THE CHRIST OF PART II

At one moment in time, a man cries out from a cross just outside the 'beloved city' of Jerusalem the scarcely-breathed, 'It is finished'; and, at the end of time, a new song of triumph is heard in heaven by those who behold 'great Babylon', Rome, destroyed by an earthquake—the exultant 'It is done!' The Christ of this section of the Apocalypse is he who relates these two events, uniting them as one. The Christians of the first century have been assured earlier in John's work that Jesus loves them; that he promises them his sheltering protection and an era of blessedness when, a shepherd amidst his sheep, he will lead them to fountains of living water and kiss the tears from their eyes. But these are Christians facing imminent persecution and martyrdom: now they need their Lord's word that by their very death, by their response to and unconditional acceptance of 'a call for the endurance and faith of the saints', they do share their Lord's victory, they do share his resurrection and its triumphant joy from the moments of their deaths. Each needs the immediate hope, received from Christ alone and his own victory on the cross, that though he be 'beheaded for testimony to Jesus', and though he be assaulted by all the evils of the Roman Empire symbolized by the dragon and his two beasts, still he will not have given his life in vain: 'the Lamb *will* conquer' the forces of evil, 'for he is Lord of lords and King of kings, and those with him are called and chosen and faithful'.

Thus, John centres this part of the Apocalypse around martyrdom in order to assure his readers that Jesus himself knows not only their 'trials and patient endurance', but also the more speci-

fic and violent assaults of Satan himself on 'those who keep the
commandments of God and bear testimony to Jesus'. Here is the
Christ who has led them in 'loving not their own lives unto death';
here is the Lamb by whose very blood the martyrs know that the
'second death' will have no power over them and that they share
in his priesthood at the moment of their own sacrifice. Indeed,
they are 'blessed and holy', 'happy', by dying in their Lord; they
have the certainty that they will be judged according to their
lives and works, that their patient acceptance of even death itself
is their greatest 'deed'—one united with the Love which has
attained their salvation. For ultimately, the downfall of Satan is
the manifestation of the 'eternal gospel', the 'good news' that God
wills redemption for all.

The Christians were face to face with the very experience
which transformed the cry of an end to the song of a new beginning for creation, the 'sound of harpers playing on their harps':
they understood why the 'sea of glass' was 'mingled with fire' and
why the wilderness was both a refuge and an evil abode. The
'woman clothed with the sun' still had to pass through the darkness of travail—the people of God suffering to bring forth the
Messiah, the young church partaking in the birth on Calvary, and
(if John's discernment reached so far) even Mary herself in pain
because her Son was to be a sign of contradiction and the 'rest of
her offspring' spiritually upon earth would still be vulnerable to
Satan's grasp. And the 'stern warrior' of Wis. 18 'leaped down'
while 'gentle silence enveloped all things': the birth of the Word
of God, both at Bethlehem and on the cross of Jerusalem, was
silent and hidden in the midst of the night—the same dark
unknown confronting the martyrs at the hour of death when
Satan's assault seemed most invincible.

But the author of the Apocalypse wishes to tell them that this
hour marks the very defeat of Satan—that Christ lifted up on the
cross was at that moment their triumphant Lord elevated and
glorified in heaven, and that help and protection for them was
as swift and strong as the eagle's wings which bore the woman
beyond the reach of the dragon. Moreover, the very crisis of the
era demanded that he not only *tell* them, but *show* them as

vividly as possible the victory of their Messiah, 'one who is to rule the nations with a rod of iron'. They need to know that the manna with which God nourishes his church is real! Thus, John has portrayed the Son of Man wearing a conqueror's crown, carrying the sickle of a judge, and treading the wine press of his Father's wrath, all images which heighten the certainty that Christ *has* overcome.

The harlot sits upon the apparently powerful, secure and beneficent beast only to be destroyed by him. The Christians do not sit comfortably, but 'follow the Lamb wherever he goes' and with constant vigilance wait upon his apparently meek and humble word, his coming at a time they least expect; but they are become an army robed in white following their leader, the conquering rider who is 'called Faithful and True'. The harlot has said, 'A queen I sit, I am no widow, mourning I shall never see'—only to find that 'the fruit for which thy soul longed has gone from thee, and all thy dainties and splendour are lost to thee'; evil soon deprives itself of its false music and superficial light, its selfish 'voice of bridegroom and bride'. On the other hand, the 'saints and prophets' whose blood has been shed are bidden, 'Come, gather for the great supper of God', for 'the marriage of the Lamb has come, and his bride has made herself ready'. Finally, the harlot is robed in the gaudy, ephemeral robes of her own accomplishments; whereas the bride is clothed with the pure, eternal linen of the saints' deeds, accomplished by leaning on Christ alone.

In this section of the Apocalypse, Christ is the triumphant Messiah who ensures, through all the images he places at John's command, final disaster for all the assembled armies, the demonic representatives of the dragon, gathered at Armageddon. To his faithful followers, persecuted by an Empire riddled with luxury, with 'pearls, linen, scented wood', with traffic in slaves, he promises that the dirge over the 'great city' will become a song of exultation for those who have found the pearl of great price: 'Rejoice over her, O heaven, for *God has* given judgment for you against her!' Christians are not his slaves or servants, but his friends! Thus, he is also the Jesus who has gained his triumph

only through the cross on Mount Zion; here, in heaven, he
assembles the chosen remnant, his own people made spotless by
the blood he himself once shed there through his love—a love
which still calls out to those of us still left in the Babylon of a
hardened heart,

'Come out of her, my people!'

PART III. THE NEW JERUSALEM (21: 1—22: 5)

The new Jerusalem (21: 1-8)

Is. 65: 17-19: For, behold, I create new heavens and a new earth; and the former things shall not be remembered or come into mind. But be glad and rejoice for ever in that which I create; for behold, I create Jerusalem a rejoicing, and her people a joy. I will rejoice in Jerusalem, and be glad in my people; no more shall be heard in it the sound of weeping and the cry of distress.

Ezek. 37: 27: My dwelling place shall be with them; and I will be their God, and they shall be my people.

Zech. 8: 8: I will bring them to dwell in the midst of Jerusalem; and they shall be my people and I will be their God, in faithfulness and in righteousness.

Is. 43: 18f.: Remember not the former things, nor consider the things of old. Behold, I am doing a new thing; now it springs forth, do you not perceive it?

Is. 55: 1: Every one who thirsts, come to the waters; and he who has no money, come, buy and eat! Come, buy wine and milk without money and without price.

1. Then I saw a new heaven and a new earth; for the first heaven and the first earth had passed away, and the sea was no more. 2. And I saw the holy city, new Jerusalem, coming down out of heaven from God, prepared as a bride adorned for her husband; 3. and I heard a great voice from the throne saying, 'Behold, the dwelling of God is with men. He will dwell with them, and they shall be his people, and God himself will be with them; 4. he will wipe away every tear from their eyes, and death shall be no more, neither shall there be

mourning nor crying nor pain any more, for the former things have passed away.'

5. And he who sat upon the throne said, 'Behold, I make all things new.' Also he said, 'Write this, for these words are trustworthy and true.' 6. And he said to me, 'It is done! I am the alpha and the omega, the beginning and the end. To the thirsty I will give water without price from the fountain of the water of life. 7. He who conquers shall have this heritage, and I will be his God and he shall be my son. 8. But as for the cowardly, the faithless, the polluted, as for murderers, fornicators, sorcerers, idolaters, and all liars, their lot shall be in the lake that burns with fire and brimstone, which is the second death.'

The final part of Ap. opens with the vision of a new heaven and a new earth, the setting of the new Jerusalem. The apocalyptic drama nears its close. The former creation has passed away (20 : 11) and all evil has been destroyed; now is the final phase of God's plan.

21 : 1. 'A new heaven and a new earth', cf. Is. 65 : 17; 66 : 22. John means a new creation, not the transformation of the old (cf. Rom. 8 : 19-22). Cf. 1 Enoch 91 : 16—'And the first heaven shall depart and pass away, and a new heaven shall appear'. The text of 2 Pet. 3 : 10-13 offers a close parallel; for, even though there is no suggestion in Ap. that this world will disappear in a conflagration (2 Pet. 3 : 10, 12), yet the other author, like John, is sure that the end of this world of ours will mark the emergence of the 'new heavens and a new earth in which righteousness dwells' (3 : 13). But it will still be a heaven and an earth—a dwelling place for men. 'And the sea was no more'—the sea, traditionally the habitat of beings hostile to God (cf. Ap. 13 : 1), has no place in the new creation. Cf. *Assumption of Moses* 10 : 6—'And the sea shall retire into the abyss, and the fountains of water shall fail, and the rivers shall dry up'.

2. The structure of Ap. 21 : 1 is modelled on Is. 65 : 17-19— the appearance of a new world, the disappearance of the former things, and the manifestation of a new Jerusalem. In John's

accustomed manner, the new Jerusalem is briefly introduced here
(21 : 2-8); it will be described more fully in vv. 9-27. Cf. Is. 52 :
1—'Awake, awake, put on your strength, O Zion; put on your
beautiful garment, O Jerusalem, the holy city'. 'Coming down out
of heaven from God' (cf. Ap. 3 : 12); it is a city of heavenly
origin, a city 'whose builder and maker is God' (Heb. 11 : 10).
Cf. Gal. 4 : 26—'the Jerusalem above is free, and she is our
mother'; Phil. 3 : 20—'but our commonwealth is in heaven';
Heb. 12 : 22—'But you have come to Mount Zion and to the
city of the living God, the heavenly Jerusalem'; 13 : 14—'For
here we have no lasting city, but we seek the city which is to
come'. Jerusalem was an accepted figure of the people of Israel,
of the people of God; it was a tangible sign of the covenant, the
focus of Jewish faith and hope. To present a new Jerusalem was,
in the concrete language of imagery, to proclaim the election of
a new people and the sealing of a new covenant.[41] 'Prepared as a
bride adorned for her husband', cf. Ap. 19 : 7; 21 : 8-14. Cf.
Is. 49 : 18—'You [Zion] shall put them on as an ornament, you
shall bind them on as a bride does'; Is. 61 : 10—'He has clothed
me with the garments of salvation . . . as a bride adorns herself
with her jewels'; 52 : 1. The double image of 'city' and of 'bride'
is traditional. The image of the *city* comes from an apocalyptic
strand going back to Ezek. 40; the metaphor of *bride* is common
in OT and NT (cf. Hos. 2 : 16, 19; Is. 54 : 6; Ezek. 16; 2 Cor.
11 : 2; Eph. 5 : 25). In this chapter John combines the images,
slipping abruptly from one to the other.

3f.   As in 19 : 5, the great voice is not easily identified; it may
be that of one of the living creatures, or of an 'angel of the presence'. It explains the significance of the vision. Cf. Ezek. 37 :
27; Zech. 8 : 8; Lev. 26 : 11f.; Jer. 31 : 33. 'Dwelling' (*skēnē* :
cf. Ap. 13 : 6; 15 : 5) may recall the *shekinah* (Aramaic *shekin-
ta*): the presence of God among his people. God's dwelling, then,
is the *shekinah*; already manifested in a special way by the incarnation ('the Word became flesh and dwelt—*eskēnōsen*—
among us', Jn 1 : 14), it is now consummated. 'His people',

---

[41] See J. Comblin, 'La Liturgie de la Nouvelle Jérusalem', *Ephemerides
Theologicae Lovanienses*, 29 (1953), 11f.

variant: 'his peoples'; the plural is to be preferred. 'One important and doubtless deliberate change has been made in the terms
of these prophecies; our writer has substituted "peoples" for
"people"—the many peoples of redeemed humanity for the elect
nation, the world for Israel' (Swete). 'He will wipe away every
tear . . .', cf. Is. 25 : 8; Ap. 7 : 17. 'Death shall be no more' (cf.
Is. 25 : 8) renews the assurance of Ap. 20 : 14. If in Babylon
the sounds of joy have ceased for ever (18 : 22), in the new Jerusalem sorrow and pain will have no place. The 'former things'
are the things belonging to the first heaven and the first earth
(v. 1). In Ap. the enemies of God are the 'inhabitants of the
earth' (cf. 6 : 10; 8 : 13; 11 : 10; 13 : 8; 14 : 6; 17 : 2, 8; 20 :
8) and their leaders are the 'kings of the earth' (cf. 6 : 15; 17 : 2,
18; 18 : 3, 9, 23; 19 : 19); but the positive defeat of the satanic
forces has brought to an end all that made up a world of sin:
God has 'made all things new' (Cerfaux-Chambier). Cf. 4 Ezra
8 : 53—'And Death is hidden, Hades fled away; corruption forgotten, sorrows passed away; and in the end the treasures of
immortality are made manifest'; 2 Enoch 65 : 10—'for all corruptible things shall pass away, and there will be eternal life'.

5. Now, and for the first time unmistakably, God speaks: he
speaks the creative word which calls the new world into being.
Cf. Is. 43 : 18f. The vision of Ap. 21 : 1-4 has become a reality.
'Also he said': *kai legei*, coming between *kai eipen* ('and he said')
in v. 5 and in v. 6, might appear to indicate a change of speaker;
but it seems simpler, and raises no difficulty, to suppose that God
is the speaker throughout. An order to write has been given
before; by an angel (1 : 10f.), by Christ (1 : 19), by 'a voice from
heaven' (14 : 13), and by another angel (19 : 9). 'These words
are trustworthy and true', repeated in 22 : 6; cf. 3 : 14; 19 : 9,
11. God himself bears witness to the reality of this great promise;
the hope of John's readers is firmly grounded on the divine assurance.

6. 'It is done!' (cf. 16 : 17)—not only are the visions true, but
all has already come to pass. John has seen the new heaven and
the new earth, he has looked upon the new Jerusalem (21 : 1-4);
in 21 : 9-22 : 5 the details of his vision are described. The solemn

gegonan ('it is done') is final. God is the alpha and the omega (cf. 1 : 8), the beginning and the end. He is at the origin of all and at the end of all; all things have tended towards God, and now all things are found in him. The same title is given to Christ in 22 : 13. 'When he calls God *alpha and omega*, John is no deist, placing God at the beginning and the end of a cosmic process which is allowed to run mechanically without intervention. God is the living God; and whenever men find themselves in the presence of the living God, there they confront *the beginning and the end*, the ground and the goal of their being. All that man has and is, but above all man's salvation, is from start to finish the work of God. He requires nothing of man but an emptiness ready to be filled, a thirst to be slaked from *the spring of the water of life*' (Caird). 'To the thirsty . . .', cf. Is. 55 : 1; Ap. 7 : 16f.; 22 : 17. In the OT water is a symbol of life, and as such is to be a feature of the messianic age (cf. Is. 12 : 3; 41 : 17f.; 44 : 3f.; Ezek. 47; Zech. 13 : 1; 14 : 8). In the NT it is a symbol of the Spirit, source of divine life for men. Cf. Jn 4 : 14—'Whoever drinks of the water that I shall give him will never thirst; the water that I shall give him will become in him a spring of water welling up to eternal life'; 7 : 37f. These words of Jesus were spoken at the Feast of Tabernacles (Jn 7 : 2, 14, 37) and recall the rite of the libation of water on the altar during this feast; the liturgy of Tabernacles may be present to the thought of our author. 'Without price' (*dōrean*—gratuitously)—the gift is utterly free. Cf. Rom. 3 : 24—'They are justified by his grace as a gift (*dōrean*)'—the same idea of the gratuitousness of God's gifts underlies Paul's doctrine of justification by faith alone.

7. 'He who conquers' carries the reader back to the seven promises of chapters 2-3; 'shall have this heritage' is an eighth promise that completes and embraces the rest. 'Heritage', cf. Mt. 25 : 34—'Come, O blessed of my Father, inherit the kingdom prepared for you from the foundation of the world'; Rom. 8 : 17—'if children, then heirs, heirs of God and fellow heirs with Christ, provided we suffer with him in order that we may also be glorified by him' (such, indeed, is the lot of the conquerors); Gal. 4 : 7. 'I will be his God', cf. 2 Sam. 7 : 14—'I will be his father,

and he shall be my son'; Ps. 98 : 27. Heb. 1 : 5; 5 : 5 have shown that Nathan's prophecy is perfectly realized in Christ; John extends it to embrace all the elect of God who have been faithful witnesses of Christ. Their sonship is here regarded as belonging to the future, when they will enter into their full inheritance. Cf. Rom. 8 : 23—'We ourselves, who have the first fruits of the Spirit, groan inwardly as we wait for adoption as sons, the redemption of our bodies'.

8.   In vv. 7f. John is the pastor, just as he was in the letters to the churches; so we have a promise to the conquerors and warnings for others. The heritage is a free gift of God, but it is granted only to those who are worthy to receive it. John lists those who are unworthy. The 'cowardly' are Christians who lack the courage, in a time of trial and persecution, to stand for Christ; they are in sharp contrast to the conquerors. The 'faithless' are the disloyal, Christians who deny their faith. The others seem to be pagans, worshippers of the beast and polluted by the fornication of idolatry (cf. 16 : 6; 17 : 294; 18 : 3, 23). Yet, since the warning is addressed to Christians, John may well be choosing to deck sin in lurid colours; cf. 9 : 20f. 'All liars' (cf. 22 : 15) are all who are opposed to Christ, the faithful and true (3 : 14; 19 : 11), and have been seduced by the dragon, 'the deceiver of the whole world' (12 : 9). Such as these do not share the inheritance of the saints. They will not drink of the water of life (v. 6), for their lot is in the lake of fire (20 : 15)—both images are equally symbolic.

The glory of the new Jerusalem (21: 9-27)

Ezek. 40: 1-3, 5: The hand of the Lord was upon me, and brought me in the visions of God into the land of Israel, and set me down upon a very high mountain, on which was a structure like a city opposite me. When he brought me there, behold, there was a man, whose appearance was like bronze, with a line of flax and a measuring reed in his hand; and he was standing in the gateway. . . . And behold, there was a wall all around the outside of the temple area, and the

*length of the measuring reed in the man's hand was six long
cubits, each being a cubit and a handbreadth in length; so
he measured the thickness of the wall, one reed; and the
height, one reed.*

*Ezek. 48: 30-35: These shall be the exits of the city: On the
north side, which is to be four thousand five hundred cubits
by measure, three gates, the gate of Reuben, the gate of
Judah, and the gate of Levi, the gates of the city being
named after the tribes of Israel. On the east side, which is
to be four thousand five hundred cubits, three gates, the gate
of Joseph, the gate of Benjamin, and the gate of Dan. On the
south side, which is to be four thousand five hundred cubits
by measure, three gates, the gate of Simeon, the gate of
Issachar, and the gate of Zebulun. On the west side, which
is to be four thousand five hundred cubits, three gates, the
gate of Gad, the gate of Asher, and the gate of Naphtali. The
circumference of the city shall be eighteen thousand cubits.
And the name of the city henceforth shall be, The Lord is
there.*

*Ezek. 48: 16: And these shall be its dimensions: the north
side four thousand five hundred cubits, the south side four
thousand five hundred, the east side four thousand five hundred, and the west side, four thousand five hundred.*

*Is. 54: 11f.: O afflicted one, storm-tossed and not com-
forted, behold, I will set your stones in antimony, and lay
your foundations with sapphires. I will make your pinnacles
of agate, your gates of carbuncles, and all your wall of
precious stones.*

*Tob. 13: 16f.: For Jerusalem will be rebuilt with sapphires
and emeralds, her walls with precious stones, and her towers
and battlements with pure gold. The streets of Jerusalem
will be paved with beryl and ruby and stones of Ophir.*

*Is. 60: 1-5, 11, 19f.: Arise, shine, for your light has come,
and the glory of the Lord has risen upon you. For behold,
darkness shall cover the earth, and thick darkness the
peoples; but the Lord will arise upon you, and his glory
will be seen upon you. And nations shall come to your light,*

and kings to the brightness of your rising. Lift up your eyes round about, and see; they all gather together, they come to you; your sons shall come from far, and your daughters shall be carried in the arms. Then you shall see and be radiant, your heart shall thrill and rejoice; because the abundance of the sea shall be turned to you, the wealth of the nations shall come to you. . . . Your gates shall be open continually; day and night they shall not be shut; that men may bring to you the wealth of the nations, with their kings led in procession. . . . The sun shall be no more your light by day, nor for brightness shall the moon give light to you by night; but the Lord will be your everlasting light, and your God will be your glory. Your sun shall no more go down, nor your moon withdraw itself; for the Lord will be your everlasting light, and your days of mourning shall be ended.

Is. 52: 1: Awake, awake, put on your strength, O Zion; put on your beautiful garments, O Jerusalem, the holy city; for there shall no more come into you the uncircumcised and the unclean.

9. Then came one of the seven angels who had the seven bowls full of the seven last plagues, and spoke to me, saying, 'Come, I will show you the Bride, the wife of the Lamb.' 10. And in the Spirit he carried me away to a great, high mountain, and showed me the holy city Jerusalem coming down out of heaven from God, 11. having the glory of God, its radiance like a most rare jewel, like a jasper, clear as crystal. 12. It had a great, high wall, with twelve gates, and at the gates twelve angels, and on the gates the names of the twelve tribes of the sons of Israel were inscribed; 13. on the east three gates, on the north three gates, on the south three gates, and on the west three gates. 14. And the wall of the city had twelve foundations, and on them the twelve names of the twelve apostles of the Lamb.

15. And he who talked to me had a measuring rod of gold to measure the city and its gates and walls. 16. The city lies

foursquare, its length the same as its breadth; and he measured the city with his rod, twelve thousand stadia; its length and breadth and height are equal. 17. He also measured its wall, a hundred and forty-four cubits by a man's measure, that is, an angel's. 18. The wall was built of jasper, while the city was pure gold, clear as glass. 19. The foundations of the wall of the city were adorned with every jewel; the first was jasper, the second sapphire, the third agate, the fourth emerald, 20. the fifth onyx, the sixth carnelian, the seventh chrysolite, the eighth beryl, the ninth topaz, the tenth chrysoprase, the eleventh jacinth, the twelfth amethyst. 21. And the twelve gates were twelve pearls, each of the gates made of a single pearl, and the street of the city was pure gold, transparent as glass.

22. And I saw no temple in the city, for its temple is the Lord God the Almighty and the Lamb. 23. And the city has no need of sun or moon to shine upon it, for the glory of God is its light, and its lamp is the Lamb. 24. By its light shall the nations walk; and the kings of the earth shall bring their glory into it, 25. and its gates shall never be shut by day—and there shall be no night there; 26. they shall bring into it the glory and the honour of the nations. 27. But nothing unclean shall enter it, nor any one who practises abomination or falsehood, but only those who are written in the Lamb's book of life.

The book closes with a majestic view of the new Jerusalem, the heavenly church of the future, the veritable kingdom of God.
9.   One of the seven angels of the bowls had shown John the great harlot (17 : 1); one of the seven now steps forward to show him the bride. The contrast between harlot and bride is thus deliberately emphasized, a contrast that is all the more marked because they are images of rival cities: Babylon and new Jerusalem. 'The bride, the wife of the Lamb', cf. 19 : 7; 21 : 2; Eph. 5 : 25. The bride-image, however, is not developed but yields to that of the holy city. We find a parallel in 4 Ezra. In the fourth vision of that book, the seer talks with a woman who is in mourning for her children; he does not realize that the woman is Zion. But, 'while I was talking to her, her face suddenly shone exceed-

ingly, and her countenance flashed like lightning. . . . And I looked, and behold, the woman was no longer visible to me, but there was an established city, and a place of huge foundations showed itself' (10 : 25-27).

10f.   Cf. Ezek. 40: 1-3, 5. John's model for his presentation of the new Jerusalem is Ezekiel's vision of the messianic kingdom (Ezek. 40-48). That prophet was carried, in vision, from Babylon to Israel and was set upon a very high mountain; there he found, opposite him, 'a structure like a city': the temple of the future. He was guided throughout this city by an angel carrying a measuring rod (40: 3—43 : 12). His guide also showed him a spring in the temple and a great stream flowing from it (47 : 1-12). An epilogue describes the gates of the city (48 : 30-35). 'In the Spirit', the seer falls into a trance (cf. Ap. 1 : 10; 4 : 2). A 'great, high mountain', cf. Ezek. 40: 2; Mt. 4 : 8—'the devil took him to a very high mountain'; it is a lofty vantage point. For v. 10b, cf. v. 2. 'Having the glory of God'—because of its heavenly origin, it reflects the divine glory. For that matter, it is filled with the presence of God (v. 22f.). Cf. Is. 60: 1f.; Ezek. 43 : 2. In Ap. 4 : 3 the one seated on the throne appeared 'like jasper'; here the heavenly city reflects that divine radiance.

12f.   Cf. Ezek. 48 : 30-35. In antiquity, a wall was an essential feature of a city (cf. Is. 26 : 1); these walls are 144 cubits in height (v. 17). In his description of the gates John follows Ezekiel closely; in v. 13 the repetition, as in Ezekiel, conveys an impression of stability. The heavenly city has heavenly gatekeepers (cf. Is. 62: 6—'Upon your walls, O Jerusalem, I have set watchmen'); and the gates of the new Jerusalem bear the names of the tribes of Israel. 'If the gates bear the names of the Twelve Tribes, the names of the Twelve Apostles (v. 14) are engraved on the foundations. Thereby the seer maintains the continuity of the OT and the Christian Church' (Charles). In vv. 24-26 it is declared that the gates remain always open, inviting the entry of the nations; this factor, together with the disposition of the gates according to the four cardinal points, recalls Lk. 13 : 29—'And men will come from east and west, and from north and south, and sit at table in the kingdom of God'.

14. Since there are twelve gates, the wall surrounding the city is divided into twelve sections, with each section resting upon a single foundation stone. These foundation stones are the precious stones listed in vv. 19f. Like the gates, the foundation stones, too, are inscribed; they bear the names of the twelve apostles. But it is precisely as *apostles of the Lamb* that the twelve are foundation stones in the new Jerusalem. Cf. Mt. 19 : 28—'In the new world, when the Son of Man shall sit on his glorious throne, you who have followed me will also sit on twelve thrones, judging the twelve tribes of Israel'. However. Matthew's text simply gives the juxtaposition of apostles and tribes; of greater relevance is Eph. 2 : 20—'built upon the foundation of the apostles and prophets, Christ Jesus himself being the chief cornerstone' (cf. Ac. 4 : 11; 1 Pet. 2 : 6). Cf. Heb. 11 : 10—'For he [Abraham] looked forward to the city which has foundations, whose builder and maker is God'. 'A city which is built on the foundation of the apostles (cf. Eph. 2 : 20) is built on the apostolic tradition, the revelation of God of which the apostles were eye-witnesses and guarantors' (Caird).

15-17. Cf. Ezek. 40 : 3, 5. In Ap. 11 : 1 the seer had measured the 'temple of God'; but the heavenly temple is measured by a heavenly being (John's angel guide) and with a measuring rod of gold. Yet the measurements taken by the angel are those in common use among mankind (v. 17c). The measuring here (unlike that of 11 : 1f.) would seem to serve the purpose of filling out the vision by giving the architectural specifications of the heavenly city. Like the city of Ezekiel's vision (Ezek. 45 : 2; 48 : 16) this city 'lies foursquare'; but John goes beyond the former prophet in contemplating a city that was a perfect cube. In Solomon's temple the holy of holies was a cube (cf. 1 Kg. 6 : 20); the cube is a symbol of perfection. 'Twelve thousand stadia', about fifteen hundred miles (cf. Ap. 14 : 20). This obviously symbolic figure ($12 \times 1,000$) carries within it a reference to the number of the tribes of Israel and to the twelve apostles (vv. 12, 14). The wall of 144 cubits (= 216 feet in height) is ridiculously out of proportion to the gigantic size of the city—if we are dealing with actual figures and measurements! 'A hundred and forty-four'

(12 × 12) is a fitting symbolic description of a wall that associates the twelve tribes of Israel and the twelve apostles of the Lamb (vv. 12-14).

18. The fabric of the wall is jasper, the gem which symbolizes the radiance of the divine splendour, 4 : 3; cf. 21 : 11. Cf. Is. 54 : 11f.; Zech. 2 : 5—'For I will be to her [Jerusalem] a wall of fire round about, says the Lord, and I will be the glory within her'. 'Pure gold *clear as glass*', like the heavenly 'sea of glass' (4 : 6). The city itself was built of transparent gold (v. 21).

19f. In his description John develops Is. 54 : 11f.; cf. Tob. 13 : 16f. Though at first it might seem that he is saying that the twelve foundation stones of the wall (v. 14) were decked with precious stones, it appears rather that each stone is one vast gem. For the most part, these jewels correspond to those set on the high priest's breastplate, each one bearing the name of one of the twelve tribes (Ex. 28 : 17-20; 39 : 10, 13; Cf. Ezek. 28 : 13, LXX).

21. Cf. Is. 54 : 12—'your gates of carbuncles'—but, for John, the gates are pearls. Cf. a Talmudic tradition, attributed to Rabbi Jonathan (early third century AD), which may be of much earlier origin : 'One day will the Holy One (blessed be he) bring precious stones and pearls thirty cubits long by thirty cubits broad and excavate openings in them of ten cubits in breadth and twenty cubits in height, and they shall stand in the gates of Jerusalem' (*Baba bathra*, 75a). 'The street'—perhaps *hē plateia* should be taken generically as 'the streets'. Cf. v. 18.

22. We might expect the glowing description of the city to be followed by a particularly striking description of its temple (the temple was the glory of the earthly Jerusalem). Instead—a brilliant touch—we learn that there is no temple, nor any need of one : God himself dwells there with the Lamb. Now, indeed, 'the dwelling of God is with men' (v. 5) and the glory of his presence pervades the whole city (vv. 11, 18), making the new Jerusalem one vast temple. It is reminiscent of 7 : 15 where God himself is the tent in the heavenly Feast of Tabernacles; for the liturgy of that feast appears to be present to the seer throughout this passage. In the light of our verse, we may read the assurance of 3 : 2

('I will make him a pillar in the temple of my God') as a promise of permanent citizenship in the Holy City. Cf. Jn 4 : 21—
'The hour is coming when neither on this mountain nor in Jerusalem will you worship the Father'. For the Lamb as temple, cf.
Jn 2 : 21—'but he spoke of the temple of his body'. God and
Lamb are again associated in v. 23 and in 22 : 1, 3.

23.   Cf. Is. 60 : 19; 60 : 1; Ezek. 43 : 4f. The glory of the divine
presence renders all created light superfluous (cf. 22 : 5). 'No
words could more clearly demonstrate the purely spiritual character of St John's conception of the new Jerusalem' (Swete). 'Its
lamp is the Lamb' : a nightly ceremony with bright lights and
rejoicing was a feature of the Feast of Tabernacles; in the new
city, God will replace the sun and the Lamb will give light by
night.

24-26.   Cf. Is. 60 : 1-5, 11. These verses (with v. 27), which
seem rather to refer to the historical stage of the church (and
not to the heavenly Jerusalem), may be explained, in their present
context, by the fact that the author is echoing traditional OT
concepts and language. Already we have seen that Ap., more than
once, pictures a final assault on the people of God (16 : 12-16;
17 : 14; 19 : 17-21; 20 : 7-9). These passages reflect a feature of
post-exilic prophecies of the new Jerusalem in which the
announcement of the failure of a hostile attack on Zion is presented in a wide range of concepts. 'Another cycle of concepts
which is attached to the eschatological city of God, and is also
frequently taken up and transformed in a variety of ways by the
prophets, is that of a pilgrimage of the nations to the city on
Mount Zion. This concept differs from the other in that it describes a peaceful event : its subject is the salvation of the nations,
and not their judgment. . . . The fullest development of this
traditional material is to be found in Is. 60, and this makes the
chapter very important for the correct evaluation of others which
are related to it. Like Is. 2 : 2-4 it speaks of a transfiguration of the
city of God, the "coming of a light", as a result of which Jerusalem emerges from her previous insignificance and thus sets in
train the pilgrimage of the nations. . . . This belief in a future
pilgrimage of the nations to Zion is seen to be a very fluid tradi-

tion, which the prophets could actualize in quite different ways.'[42] John is manifestly inspired by Is. 60 and his language is still couched in symbols. He is indeed describing the heavenly Jerusalem : its inhabitants have come from all directions, thus accomplishing the universalist prophecies of the OT. He chooses to express this truth in traditional terms (Cerfaux-Cambier). John simply applies to the heavenly city the image which Isaiah had referred to the messianic age—the image of pilgrims flocking to Jerusalem. This means, in fact, that John understands the imagery in a manner different from Isaiah; for, on the new earth there are no longer pagan nations, but only those of mankind whose names stand in the book of life (Ap. 20 : 15; 21 : 8). John's viewpoint is this : when the kingdom of God comes on the new earth, there will no longer be any enemies of God who can rise up in battle against Christ and his Church. Then all men who dwell on earth will serve the true God and joyfully offer him their treasures (Wikenhauser). They will celebrate an everlasting Feast of Tabernacles, walking in the light of God by day and of the Lamb by night (cf. 7 : 9, 15-17).

27. Cf. Is. 52 : 1; 35 : 8; Ezek. 44 : 9. This verse is to be read as a pastoral warning to the readers of the book. 'Unclean' (*koinos*); Mk. 7 : 20-23 tells us what uncleanness or defilement is : 'What comes out of a man is what defiles (*koinoō*) a man. For from within, out of the heart of man, come evil thoughts, fornication, theft, murder, adultery, coveting, wickedness, deceit, envy, slander, pride, foolishness. All these evil things come from within, and they defile a man.' The kingdom of God is not for such. 'Who practises abomination or falsehood'; cf. 17 : 2-4; 18 : 3; 21 : 8. Only those have place in the new Jerusalem whose names have been written 'before the foundation of the world in the book of life of the Lamb that was slain' (13 : 8; cf. 3 : 5; 17 : 8; 20 : 12, 15).

[42] G. von Rad, *Old Testament Theology* II, Edinburgh, Oliver & Boyd, 1965, 294-6.

Within the new Jerusalem (22: 1-5)

> *Gen. 2: 9f.: And out of the ground the Lord made to grow every tree that is pleasant to the sight and good for food, and the tree of life also in the midst of the garden. . . . A river flowed out of Eden to water the garden.*
>
> *Ezek. 47: 1: 6b-7, 12: Then he brought me back to the door of the temple; and behold, water was issuing from below the threshold of the temple toward the east (for the temple faced east); and the water was flowing down from below the south end of the threshold of the temple, south of the altar. . . . Then he led me back along the bank of the river. As I went back, I saw upon the bank of the river very many trees on the one side and on the other. . . . And on the banks, on both sides of the river, there will grow all kinds of trees for food. Their leaves will not wither nor their fruit fail, but they will bear fresh fruit every month, because the water for them flows from the sanctuary. Their fruit will be for food, and their leaves for healing.*
>
> *Zech. 14: 7: And there shall be continuous day (it is known to the Lord), not day and not night, but at evening time there shall be light.*

1. Then he showed me the river of the water of life, bright as crystal, flowing from the throne of God and of the Lamb 2. through the middle of the street of the city; also, on either side of the river, the tree of life with its twelve kinds of fruit, yielding its fruit each month; and the leaves of the tree were for the healing of the nations. 3. There shall no more be anything accursed, but the throne of God and of the Lamb shall be in it, and his servants shall worship him; 4. they shall see his face, and his name shall be on their foreheads. 5. And night shall be no more; they need no light of lamp or sun, for the Lord God will be their light, and they shall reign for ever and ever.

22: 1f. Cf. Gen. 2 : 9f.; Ezek. 47 : 1, 6b-7, 12; Jl 3 : 18; Zech. 14 : 8. In Ezekiel's vision, a life-giving torrent of water issued from beneath the threshold of the east gate of the sanctuary. It

flowed into the Dead Sea, turning its waters fresh and making
them swarm with fish. Along the banks of the river grew trees
which bore a crop of fruit each month and had curative proper-
ties in their leaves. John has combined Ezekiel's vision with Gen.
2 : 9f.

The seer at last sees the very spring of the waters of life, the
waters promised to the thirsty (Ap. 7 : 17; 21 : 6; 22 : 17). 'Bright
as crystal', cf. 4 : 6. The new Jerusalem has no temple—'for its
temple is the Lord God the Almighty and the Lamb' (21 : 22);
consistently, the waters which in Ezek. 47 flow from the sanctuary, here flow from 'the throne of God and of the Lamb'. In
3 : 21 the conquering Christ has 'sat down with his Father on his
throne'; cf. 1 Enoch 51 : 3—'And the Elect One shall in those
days sit on my throne'; 62 : 3, 5. But with his phrase, 'the throne
of God and of the Lamb', John intends, unmistakably, to assimilate the Lamb to God. The water of life flowing from the throne
of the Lamb has a parallel in Jn 7 : 38f.—'If any one thirst let
him come to me, and let him who believes in me drink. As the
scripture has said, "Out of his heart shall flow rivers of living
water". Now this he said of the Spirit, which those who believed
in him were to receive.' In the Fourth Gospel, as in Ap., there is
a communication of divine life. Thus, in Ap. 22 : 1 we find an
allusion to the Trinity, since the river of water (21 : 6) is a symbol of the Spirit (Boismard). The river of the water of life flows
through the middle of the city street. And 'the tree of life' may
be understood as a generic singular, meaning 'trees' as in Ezekiel;
thus the trees grow along the banks of the river. However, one
may put a full stop after v. 1 and render v. 2 as follows : 'Down
the middle of the city street and on either side of the river, were
the trees of life. . . .' Either way, the significance of the text is
sufficiently clear. 'The tree [trees] of life' (cf. Gen. 2 : 9; 3 : 22;
Ezek. 47 : 12)—this is the fruit promised to the conqueror, the
fruit of the tree 'which is in the paradise of God' (Ap. 2 : 7). The
true tree of life grows in the new paradise. 'The leaves of the
trees were for the healing of the nations' (cf. Ezek. 47 : 12)—the
nations are those of Ap. 21 : 24-26.

3f.   Cf. Zech. 14 : 11—'And it shall be inhabited, for there shall be no more curse; Jerusalem shall dwell in security.' This is to say, Jerusalem is securely inhabited because the divine curse (the divine 'ban' or 'anathema'), which sentenced a city to destruction, is no more. John, in his turn, declares that no accursed person, object of God's displeasure, will find place in the new city (cf. Ap. 21 : 27). 'The throne of God and of the Lamb', cf. v. 1. When the throne of God was first revealed to John, he glimpsed it through a door opened in heaven (4 : 1); now he sees it in the heavenly Jerusalem come down to earth, and on it sits not only the Father, but also the incarnate and glorified Son. 'And his servants shall worship him'—'To the final revelation of God there corresponds a perfected service; where the Throne is always in sight the service must be perpetual' (Swete). It is the fulfilment of 7 : 15. The Israelites had gone in pilgrimage to the temple to adore, and to 'behold the face of God' (Ps. 17 : 15; 42 : 2); they had beheld him only in wish because one cannot see God (Ex. 33 : 20, 23). But now, in the new age, that desire is satisfied (cf. Mt. 5 : 8; 1 Cor. 13 : 12; Heb. 12 : 14; 1 Jn 3 : 2—'Beloved, we are God's children now; it does not yet appear what we shall be, but we know that when he appears we shall be like him, for we shall see him as he is'). 'His name shall be on their foreheads', cf. Ap. 3 : 12; 7 : 3f.; 14 : 1. Throughout our verses the pronoun (shall worship *him*, *his* face, *his* name) refers to God and Lamb together. The association of God and Lamb, noted elsewhere, is here expressed most forcefully; 'the face of God or the face of the Lamb, the name of God or the name of the Lamb—it comes to the same thing; it is the mystery of the equality and oneness of Father and Lamb' (Cerfaux-Cambier).

5. Cf. Zech. 14 : 7; Ap. 21 : 23, 25. Night and darkness have no place in the new city. Worshipping him, looking upon his face, basking in the light of his glory, the servants of God 'shall reign for ever and ever'. Christ has made of his own 'a kingdom of priests to his God and Father' (1 : 6; cf. 5 : 10; 20 : 6); now at last, in the heavenly Jerusalem, worshipping before the throne of God and Lamb (22 : 3), these royal priests shall reign without end.

Is. 40: 10: Behold, the Lord God comes with might . . . behold, his reward is with him, and his recompense before him.

Is. 55: 1: Ho, every one who thirsts, come to the waters; and he who has no money, come, buy and eat!

Dt. 4: 2: You shall not add to the word which I command you, nor take from it.

Dt. 12: 32: Everything that I command you, you shall be careful to do; you shall not add to it or take from it.

6. And he said to me, 'These words are trustworthy and true. And the Lord, the God of the spirits of the prophets, has sent his angel to show his servants what must soon take place. 7. And behold, I am coming soon.'

Blessed is he who keeps the words of the prophecy of this book.

8. I John am he who heard and saw these things. And when I heard and saw them, I fell down to worship at the feet of the angel who showed them to me; 9. but he said to me, 'You must not do that! I am a fellow servant with you and your brethren the prophets, and with those who keep the words of this book. Worship God.'

10. And he said to me, 'Do not seal up the words of the prophecy of this book, for the time is near. 11. Let the evil-doer still do evil, and the filthy still be filthy, and the righteous still do right, and the holy still be holy.'

12. 'Behold, I am coming soon, bringing my recompense, to repay every one for what he has done. 13. I am the alpha and the omega, the first and the last, the beginning and the end.'

14. Blessed are those who wash their robes, that they may have the right to the tree of life and that they may enter the city by the gates. 15. Outside are the dogs and sorcerers and forni-cators and murderers and idolaters, and every one who loves and practises falsehood.

16. 'I Jesus have sent my angel to you with this testimony

for the churches. I am the root and the offspring of David, the bright morning star.'

17. The Spirit and the Bride say, 'Come.' And let him who hears say, 'Come.' And let him who is thirsty come, let him who desires take the water of life without price.

18. I warn every one who hears the words of the prophecy of this book : if any one adds to them, God will add to him the plagues described in this book, 19. and if any one takes away from the words of the book of this prophecy, God will take away his share in the tree of life and in the holy city, which are described in this book.

20. He who testifies to these things says, 'Surely I am coming soon.' Amen. Come, Lord Jesus!

21. The grace of the Lord Jesus be with all the saints. Amen.

Like the Fourth Gospel and 1 John, this book also closes with an appendix or epilogue, which gives the last words of the angel, the seer, and the Lord.

6f.   The speaker may be the angel guide (21 : 9, 15; 22 : 1), or, better, he is Christ's angel of the prologue (1 : 1). The 'trust-worthy and true words' (cf. 21 : 5) are the teachings of the whole book : Christ, through his angel, authenticates the words of the prophecy of this book. 'The God of the spirits of the pro-phets'—the God from whom the charism of prophecy proceeds. Cf. Num. 27 : 16—'The Lord, the God of the spirits of all flesh'; 1 Cor. 14 : 32—'and the spirits of prophets are subject to pro-phets'. v. 6b echoes 1 : 1—'The revelation of Jesus Christ, which God gave him to show to his servants what must soon take place; and he made it known by sending his angel to his servant John'. 'His servants', cf. 1 : 1; 10 : 7; 11 : 18; 22 : 16—here they are the Christian prophets. 'I am coming soon', cf. 3 : 11; 16 : 15; 22 : 12, 20. 'The Voice of Christ is heard behind, or speaking through, the voice of his angel' (Swete). The beatitude (the sixth of the book) is a shorter form of 1 : 3. Blessings were often appended to an exhortation or to a legal text (cf. Ex. 23 : 20-33; Lev. 26 : 3-13; Dt. 28 : 1-4); they were designed to encourage the practical implementation of the prophetic message or the observance of the Law (Cerfaux-Cambier).

8f. Just as he did at the beginning of the book (1 : 1, 9), the author gives his name. He acknowledges himself to be the seer of all these visions : 'these things' which he had heard and seen comprise the revelation of this entire book. They are 'all that he saw' (1 : 1f.) in the 'revelation of Jesus Christ' made known to John by an angel. vv. 8b-9 are, seemingly, a doublet of 19 : 9f. The 'brethren' of 19 : 10 are here explicitly identified as the prophets; and 'those who hold the testimony of Jesus' (19 : 10; cf. 1 : 2, 9; 6 : 9; 12 : 17; 20 : 4) are here those who 'keep the words of this book'.

10.   'And he said to me'; although the apparent speaker is the angel of v. 6, yet since vv. 12f. give the words of Christ, he is surely the speaker here too (cf. v. 7). The instruction is the exact reverse of that given to Daniel (Dn. 8 : 26; 12 : 4, 9; cf. Ap. 10 : 4). Dn. 8 : 26—'But seal up the vision, for it pertains to many days hence'; 12 : 4—'But you, Daniel, shut up the words and seal the book, until the time of the end'. Usually (as in Daniel) eschatological prophecies were sealed, set aside for the future. But for John the moment of fulfilment is here : the coming of Christ in glory (22 : 12, 20).

The author of Ap. does not seek to attenuate that feeling of the nearness of the end which earlier Christians had felt (cf. 1 : 3, 7; 3 : 11; 22 : 12, 20). His prologue assures his readers—those who hear the words of the prophecy, the revelation of Jesus Christ—that 'the time is near'; his epilogue echoes the assurance. In this phrase, two worlds are contrasted; this world of time and the heavenly world beyond—the world which, to the Hebrew imagination, already exists in heaven like the new Jerusalem (21 : 10) and the ark of the covenant (Heb. 8 : 5; 9 : 12). With the coming of Christ, this other world has drawn close to us, time has lost its value; the end is near. These two worlds have drawn close together; the heavenly realities have penetrated the temporal order and have diminished the significance of time. Quantitatively, it remains the same, it may have a long course to run; and yet it is short because it is of little importance in comparison with the timeless realities that are now manifest (Cerfaux-Cambier).

11.   Cf. Dn. 12 : 10—'Many shall purify themselves, and make

themselves white, and be refined; but the wicked shall do wickedly; and none of the wicked shall understand; but those who are wise shall understand.' Here evil is characterized by the 'evildoers' and 'filthy' (the immoral), and good by 'the righteous' and 'the holy'. In each case there is action ('do evil', 'do right') and a state ('be filthy', 'be holy')—the twofold attitude of human decision and of submission to a supernatural power, whether diabolical or divine. Cf. Mt. 13 : 30, 39—'Let both grow together until the harvest . . . the harvest is the close of the age'. Perhaps our verse is a warning; cf. Ap. 16 : 15—'Lo, I am coming like a thief! Blessed is he who is awake.' Or it may mean that, despite human conduct, God's plan is always accomplished. 'The self that stands in the judgment will be the self developed in life. And the judgment is fundamentally that the kind of self a man has elected to be is the kind of self that he must be. . . . In this there is nothing arbitrary. It is but the corollary of the love that endowed man with moral freedom to choose for himself the kind of self he would be.'[43]

12f. Cf. Is. 40 : 10. The time has come 'for rewarding thy servants, the prophets and saints, and those who fear thy name, both small and great' (Ap. 11 : 18). It is certainly Christ who speaks. He comes, exercising a diving prerogative; he comes, 'bringing his reward with him'—for *he* is the reward. 'For what he has done'; cf. 2 : 23—'I will give to each of you as your works deserve'; cf. 20 : 12f. Cf. Ps. 62 : 12—'For thou dost requite a man according to his work'; Mt. 16 : 27—'For the Son of Man is to come with his angels in the glory of his Father, and then he will repay every man for what he has done'; Rom. 2 : 6—'For he will render to every man according to his works'. But, all the while, salvation is an utterly free gift (cf. Ap. 20 : 12, 15). v. 13—the titles of the Father (1 : 8; 21 : 6) are now claimed by Jesus. 'It is the crowning instance in this book of the attribution of divine prerogatives to the Incarnate Son; only "who is and who was" seems to be withheld from the Son, perhaps because it represents the underived Source of the Divine Life' (Swete).

[43] H. H. Rowley, *The Relevance of Apocalyptic,* New York, Association Press, London, Lutterworth Press, 1964[3], 176.

14.   The seventh and last beatitude of Ap. (cf. 1 : 3; 14 : 13; 16 : 15; 19 : 9; 20 : 6; 22 : 7). 'Who wash their robes', that is, 'in the blood of the Lamb' (7 : 14). Here, not only martyrs, but all Christians are envisaged. The verse links up with 1 : 5—he 'has freed us from our sins by his blood'; in and through Christ alone can they win salvation and gain their reward. The 'tree of life', cf. 2 ː 7; 22 : 2. For the gates of the heavenly city, cf. 21 : 12f., 21, 25, 27. The tree of life is within the city, so they must pass through the gates to reach it. The beatitude makes eternal life accessible to all, but only through the cross of Christ.

15.   This is practically the same list as in 21 : 8; they are those whose lot is 'the second death', those who worship the beast and bear its mark (14 : 9-11). 'Dogs' is a traditional Jewish description of the heathen gentiles. In Phil. 3 : 2 Paul applied the name to some of his fellow-countrymen, so turning back on them their own insulting estimate of gentiles. The 'all liars' of 21 : 8 become here the much more forceful 'every one who loves and practises falsehood'. Cf. Jn 3 : 20—'Every one who does evil hates the light, and does not come to the light'. One who *loves* falsehood is one to whom it has become second nature, one who shows an affinity with Satan, 'for he is a liar and the father of lies' (Jn 8 : 44). 'These are precisely the people whose lot is the lake of fire (21 : 8). When the new heaven and earth finally comes, there will be no *outside* for them to occupy; they will have disappeared into oblivion. It makes sense, then, to say that they are *outside* only if the city is considered to be a present reality at such time as they still exist. In the midst of the daily life of Smyrna and Pergamum, Babylon and Jerusalem exist side by side. Their citizens rub shoulders in the streets of Sardis and Philadelphia. The Conqueror in Ephesus may see an open gate in heaven giving him *the right to the tree of life* (2 : 7)' (Caird).

16.   The whole of the Apocalypse is 'the revelation of Jesus Christ', his 'testimony', made known, through an angel, to John (1 : 1); it is a message 'to the seven churches that are in Asia'— and for the whole church (1 : 4). At the close, Jesus sets the seal of approval on the fidelity of his prophet. 'The root and offspring of David'; cf. Is. 11 : 1; Ap. 5 : 5. Jesus is both root and branch,

he combines all the messianic claims of the Davidic family, he is the 'begining and the end' (v. 13) of the whole messianic economy. 'The bright morning star' (2 : 28). Cf. Num. 24 : 17—'A star shall come forth out of Jacob, and a sceptre shall rise out of Israel'. The context is messianic. Christ, the incarnate Son, proclaims the Father as the morning star announces the sun. The star is a symbol of resurrection and triumphant glory. Christ reigns as the morning star and appears radiant in his new life because he rose from the dead. Cf. Ac. 2 : 36; Rom. 1 : 4; Ap. 1 : 5 (Boismard).

17. 'The last verses have an unmistakable liturgical ring about them, beginning as they do with an invitation to communion and ending with the prayer of the expectant Church' (Caird). 'The Spirit' is the Spirit of Jesus that inspires the prophets (2 : 7; 14 : 13; cf. 19 : 10), 'the Bride' is the church (21 : 2, 9). 'Come' is addressed to Christ; it is the *marana tha* ('Our Lord, come!'; cf. 1 Cor. 16 : 22) of the liturgy. The Spirit inspires the church (the earthly church) to respond with eager joy to the Lord's announcement of his coming. It is, somehow, reminiscent of Paul : 'We do not know how to pray as we ought, but the Spirit himself intercedes for us with sighs too deep for words' (Rom. 8 : 26). 'Let him who hears'—the prayer is to be taken up by every hearer of the book (cf. 1 : 3); the Lord looks for the response of the individual Christian. For the church is no vague personification; it is a living organism, made up of living men and women. While the hearer welcomes the coming of Christ, 'he who is thirsty' (cf. Is. 55 : 1; Ap. 7 : 16; 21 : 6) is invited to come to Christ. Cf. Jn 6 : 35—'he who comes to me shall not hunger, and he who believes in me shall never thirst'; 7 : 37f.—'If any one thirst let him come to me, and let him who believes in me drink'. In Ap. 3 : 20 we observed a eucharistic flavour in the promise of a meal shared by Christ with the Christian; it would seem that the eucharistic interest is present here too in this offer of the water of life. Ultimately, it is the water of life of the new Jerusalem (21 : 6; 22 : 1).

18f. Cf. Dt. 4 : 2; 12 : 32. It was a fairly common practice for writers to append a warning of this kind to their books; cf.

Letter of Aristeas (a writing which gives a legendary account of the translation of the Pentateuch into Greek—the LXX), 311; 1 Enoch 104 : 10f.; 2 Enoch 48 : 74f.; John finds a biblical precedent of this practice in Deuteronomy. Swete has pointed up the significance of the adjuration here : 'Consciously to rob this Book of any part of its essential teaching is to rob oneself of the bliss which it promises; to add to it⌐ teaching is to incur the visitations which it threatens. For either act, if deliberate, proclaims a will which is out of harmony with the will of God and with his ordering of the world; and the rebellious will, while it continues such, cannot receive the things of the Spirit of God here or hereafter. The warning is addressed to Christians who by their attitude towards this Book show themselves to be unworthy of their inheritance.'

20.   For the third time (cf. chapters 7, 12), Christ, who gives his own solemn testimony to the contents of the book, assures his church that he is coming soon. It is a response to the earnest prayer of the church (v. 16) and a link with the promise at the beginning of the book : 'Behold, he is coming with the clouds' (1 : 7). But this time the promise stands in the liturgical setting of the eucharist. 'Come, Lord Jesus' is a rendering of the Aramaic *marana tha*. 'The invocation must have had its place in the celebration of the Eucharist (cf. *Didache*, 10 : 6). The "coming" for which it prays may be either the eschatological coming or the coming in the celebration of the eucharist. Most probably the two comings should not be too sharply distinguished. The eucharist was a messianic banquet and was a perpetual symbol and assurance of the Parousia (1 Cor. 11 : 26).'[44] 'Lord Jesus' (cf. I Cor. 12 : 3) is found in Ap. here only and in the following verse; it is the favourite title of Christian faith and prayer.

21.   The book, which opens with an epistolary formula (1 : 4), also closes with a type of final greeting customary in letters. The formula is like those of the Pauline epistles, but it finds no exact parallel there. Variant readings are : 'with all' and 'with the saints'. It was not usual for apocalypses to end in this way; but,

[44] J. L. McKenzie, *Dictionary of the Bible,* Milwaukee, Bruce, London, Geoffrey Chapman, 1965, 541.

John's work is presented as a letter to the churches, one intended to be read in the church services. 'The saints' designate the faithful ones 'who keep the commandments of God and the faith of Jesus' (14 : 12; cf. 8 : 3f.; 11 : 18; 13 : 7, 19; 16 : 6; 17 : 6; 18 : 20, 24; 19 : 8; 20 : 9). But, it is the grace of the Lord Jesus alone which makes them such. And in this 'letter to the churches', that grace is offered to all Christians.

THE CHRIST OF PART III

The Christ of the last chapters of the Apocalypse is the giver of joy and peace. All the reasons for rejoicing which John has given to the faithful throughout his book seem combined to create the new Jerusalem, and this joy in turn seems to subside into and be sustained by the quiet peace which prevails in the epilogue because of the promise, 'I am coming soon'. It is as if the joy of the angelic host which heralded the birth of Jesus had here embraced the joy of the whole church following his rebirth for her on Calvary and his glorification—as if the shepherds then had joined hands with the men and women of the Christian community here to share the 'peace on earth' they had all received through the coming of the Saviour, who was to make them 'God's friends'. 'He who conquers shall have this heritage' : this is John's final assurance to those who must walk by faith alone amidst trials whose outcome they cannot see. He portrays Jesus as the person whose presence transforms the grounds of their hope into living reality, who rewards their believing with the blessedness of entering his own city and partaking in the tree of life. For, in the words of Paul, Jesus himself is the 'God of hope'; and to eat the fruit of this tree is to be filled with 'all joy and peace in believing' (Rom. 15 : 13).

And there is every reason for rejoicing ! For, if God the creator has spoken the words, 'Behold, I make all things new', surely the greatest and most renewing act of his creative love was the sending of his Son upon earth as the Word made flesh to walk the human way and to offer newness of life to all. 'Behold, the dwelling of God is with men. He will dwell with them, and they shall be his people.' It is Jesus who, as a man amidst men, will 'give water without price' to the thirsty and 'wipe away every tear'. It is the Lamb who ensures that 'death shall be no more' because he himself has opened up eternal life to all who are willing to follow him to the cross at Jerusalem and then to welcome that city as his new bride, 'the new heaven and the new earth', making their own robes washed white in his blood part of her pure raiment. And it is Christ who, as the triumphant Messiah, provides for the city the light by which 'the nations shall walk' and tends the leaves which are 'for the healing of the nations'. Indeed, the entire Christian community could rejoice simply because of their certainty that their Lord's words are authentic, 'trustworthy and true' : 'I Jesus have sent my angel to you with this testimony for the churches'.

But perhaps even more meaningful to the 'faithful witnesses' was the joy each could experience in his own heart through personal friendship with Jesus—a joy whose fruit is not only 'peace on earth', but also that quiet, inner peace which springs from perfect trust and confidence in God. Each had to pass through the trials and rewards of ordinary daily living to learn that, through Christ, there would neither be 'mourning nor crying nor pain any more'. Only a person's encounter with, and struggle against, the dragons of 'former things' could open him to the peace prevailing when they 'have passed away'—to grasp the joy and freedom of a new life, a new dwelling, which was not merely an abstract promise or an ideal to strive for, but the actual experience of living side-by-side with God and the Lamb : 'they shall see his face, and his name shall be on their foreheads'. Each individual mattered to Jesus and would be included in the new city, for he could lean upon the regal strength of its 'chief corner stone' and share in the priestly authority of its 'foundations'. And each Christian knew through his own eyes which had scanned dark skies waiting for dawn, through his own heart and its vision, what it meant to him personally to receive Christ himself as 'the bright morning star'.

'The city has no need of sun or moon to shine upon it, for the glory of God is its light, and its lamp is the Lamb' : yes, the early Christian community had every reason to rejoice, to let their hearts and lives be filled with peace, because all their needs have been met by Christ's love. They lack nothing because, right then and there, he provided for them with the food and drink of his own body and blood, with the grace to help them stand steadfast and faithful where they would be sure to fall on their own. 'These things I have spoken to you, that my joy may be in you, and that your joy may be full' (Jn 15 : 11): it is out of the fullness of their joy that the faithful greet his promise to come soon with their eager longing, 'Come, Lord Jesus!' For he shall appear once again in their midst as the Jesus of the gospels whose care leaves no room for their hearts to be troubled or afraid—who can be taken at his word because he is 'the beginning and the end'. He is *the* Word, fulfiling what was prophesied of him and promised by him—the very greeting of one Christian to another— 'Peace I leave with you, my peace I give to you; not as the world gives do I give to you' (Jn 14 : 27). And, in the end, he is simply Jesus, whose love makes all things new, joyous, and at peace.

Select Bibliography

The bibliography lists books and articles which have been especially helpful in the preparation of this commentary.

(1) Commentaries

Allo, E.-B., *Saint Jean: L'Apocalypse,* Paris, Gabalda, 1921.[2]

Barclay, W., *The Revelation of John,* Edinburgh, The St Andrew Press, 1960.[2]

Boismard, M.-E., *L'Apocalypse (BJ),* Paris, Cerf, 1959.[3]

Brutsch, C., *La Clarté de l'Apocalypse,* Geneva, Éditions Labor et Fides, 1966.[5]

Caird, G. B., *The Revelation of St John the Divine,* New York, Harper & Row, 1966, London, A. and C. Black, 1966.

Cerfaux, L. and Cambier, J., *L'Apocalypse de Saint Jean lue aux Chrétiens,* Paris, Cerf, 1955.

Charles, R. H., *The Revelation of St John* (ICC), Edinburgh, Clark, 1920, 2 vols.

Farrer, A., *The Revelation of St John the Divine,* O.U.P., 1964.

Gelin, A., 'Apocalypse', in Pirot-Clamer, *La Sainte Bible* XII, Paris, Letouzey, 1951.[3]

Martindale, C. C., 'The Apocalypse' in *A Catholic Commentary on Holy Scripture,* London, Nelson, 1953.

Richards, H., *What the Spirit Says to the Churches,* London, Geoffrey Chapman, 1967.

Swete, H. B., *The Apocalypse of St John,* London, Macmillan, 1922.[3]

Turner, N., 'Revelation' in *Peake's Commentary on the Bible,* London, Nelson, 1962.[3]

Wikenhauser, A., *Offenbarung des Johannes,* Regensburg, Pustet, 1949.

(2) Other Literature

Boismard, M.-E., 'L'Apocalypse' in Robert-Feuillet, *Introduction à la Bible* II, Paris, Desclée, 1959.

— 'L'apocalypse ou les apocalypses de Saint Jean', *Revue Biblique* 56 (1949), 507-41.

— 'Notes sur l'Apocalypse', *Revue Biblique* 69 (1952), 161-72.

Charles, R. H., *The Apocrypha and Pseudepigrapha of the Old Testament,* II, Oxford, Clarendon Press, 1913.

Comblin, J., 'La Liturgie de la Nouvelle Jérusalem', *Ephemerides Theologicae Lovanienses* 29 (1953), 5-40.

Feret, H. M., *The Apocalypse of St John,* London, Blackfriars, 1958.

Feuillet, A., *The Apocalypse,* New York, Alba House, 1965.

— *Johannine Studies,* New York, Alba House, 1964.

Harrington, W. J., *Record of the Fulfillment: The New Testament,* Chicago, The Priory Press, 1966, London, Geoffrey Chapman, 1967.

McKenzie, J. L., *Dictionary of the Bible,* Milwaukee, Bruce, London, Geoffrey Chapman, 1965.

McNamara, M., *The New Testament and the Palestinian Targum to the Pentateuch,* Rome, Pontifical Biblical Institute, 1966.

Ramsay, W. M., *The Letters to the Seven Churches of Asia,* Grand Rapids, Mich, Baker Book House, 1963.

Rowley, H. H., *The Relevance of Apocalyptic,* New York, Association Press, London, Lutterworth Press, 1964.[3]

— 'Apocalyptic Literature' in *Peake's Commentary on the Bible,* Nelson, London, 1962,[2] 418-21.